BERLIT

D0320736

# CHINESE
## for travellers

By the staff of Berlitz Guides

# How best to use this phrase book

● We suggest that you start with the **Guide to pronunciation** (pp. 8-10), then go on to **Some basic expressions** (pp. 11-16). This gives you not only a minimum vocabulary, but also helps you get used to pronouncing the language.

● Consult the **Contents** pages (3-5) for the section you need. In each chapter you'll find travel facts, hints and useful information. Simple phrases are followed by a list of words applicable to the situation.

● Separate, detailed contents lists are included at the beginning of the extensive **Eating out** and **Shopping guide** sections (Menus, p. 40, Shops and services, p. 97).

● If you want to find out how to say something in Chinese, your fastest look-up is via the **Dictionary** section (pp. 166-190). This not only gives you the word, but is also cross-referenced to its use in a phrase on a specific page.

● If you want to learn more about constructing sentences, check the **Basic grammar** (pp. 160-163).

● Note the **colour margins** are indexed in Chinese and English to help both listener and speaker. And, in addition, there is also an **index in Chinese** for the use of your listener.

● Throughout the book, this symbol ☞ suggests phrases your listener might use to answer you. If you still can't understand, hand the phrase book to the Chinese-speaker to encourage pointing to an appropriate answer.

Revised edition – 1st printing                     Printed in Switzerland

# Contents

4

Acknowledgments
We are particularly grateful to Hu Xiaoming, Sun Daqing and
Paddy Jackson for their help in the preparation of this book.

### Chinese characters

Several thousand years ago, while still in the Stone Age, China had already developed good pictorial techniques. Though the designs used in this era in a certain way constituted the dawn of writing, they were virtually limited to representation of men, animals and objects; feelings and other abstract ideas could not as yet be expressed in this manner.

The ancient hunting and gathering societies gradually gave way to more sophisticated agricultural ways of life, with a settled, rather than a nomadic mode of existence. Little by little, clans and tribes coalesced into something more like small states. Human relations were expanded and languages merged. By this stage, it would have been quite clear to those in the know that the human figure in the drawing shown below was meant to represent "man" in general. Art was put to the service of language, giving rise to an ideographic system of writing in which drawings were progressively reduced to their basic elements.

| | | | |
|---|---|---|---|
| | (Stag and hunter) | | |
| | stag | bow* | man |
| 2100 B.C. | | | |
| 221 B.C. | | | |
| today | | | |

* and action by hand

In 1890, bones and tortoise shells bearing engraved characters dating back to the *Shāng* dynasty (around 1600-1066 B.C.) were discovered in Henan Province. Altogether, around 3,500 ideograms from this period have been identified, though only 1,500 of them are in a sufficient state of preservation to be accurately interpreted.

The *Zhōu* (1066-256 B.C.) replaced the *Shāng*, taking over their culture, technology and writing. During the period of ascendancy of the Eastern *Zhōu*, the country split into a number of political units with various writing systems. In 221 B.C., the *Qín* dynasty united the country, at the same time standardizing the system of writing in the *zhuàn* style.

Since their primitive beginnings, Chinese characters have changed considerably, principally in the first half of their history. Though their strictly representational nature has largely disappeared, the original underlying structure remains. Today, about 50,000 ideograms exist, of which 5,000 or so are in common use.

The various dialects of Chinese, spoken by 94% of the population, are known collectively as *hàn-yǔ*. Though a number of these dialects are mutually unintelligible, Chinese from all parts of the country communicate verbally in *pǔ tōng huà*, a kind of *lingua franca*. The written language is everywhere the same, and is understood by all.

After 1949, the Chinese government set up a committee for the reform of Chinese writing. This committee has succeeded in simplifying a large number of characters in everyday use, either by going back to an original form of the ideograms or by reducing the number of strokes involved. In 1958, the National People's Assembly also approved a rational system for the transcription of Chinese characters into the Latin alphabet, called *pinyin* — the transcription you will find in this book. Traditionally, Chinese was written in columns and read from top to bottom, and right to left. Nowadays, however, the policy is to write horizontally from left to right.

PRONUNCIATION

语音

# Guide to pronunciation

If you follow carefully the indications supplied below, you will have no difficulty in reading the transliterations in such a way as to make yourself understood. In addition, listening to the native speakers in China and constant practice will help you to improve your accent. (This book also contains the Chinese script. If, despite your efforts, your listener does not seem to understand you, show him or her the book and indicate what you want to say.)

Chinese is composed less of vowels and consonants than of syllables. The transliteration used in this book is based on the official Chinese phonetic system *(pīn-yīn)*. A transliteration is a representation of the sounds of the language in the Latin (our) alphabet, as opposed to traditional Chinese characters. It can be read quite easily once a few rules have been mastered. Still, any attempt of this kind is open to criticism, for some of the sounds of the Chinese tongue cannot be exactly reproduced by the letters of the English alphabet.

For ease of reading and pronunciation, we have broken down multisyllabic Chinese words by inserting hyphens in the *pīn-yīn* transliteration. For example, *zhōngguó* (China) becomes *zhōng-guó*.

## Tones

Every syllable in Chinese has a definite tone, and therefore tones are as important as vowels and consonants in forming syllables. The difference in tone is the deciding factor in the meaning of words. For example, *mài* with falling tone means "sell" and *mǎi* with falling-rising tone means "buy".

There are four basic tones in Mandarin Chinese:

‾ 1st tone (high level): is spoken high and the voice neither rises nor falls

ˊ 2nd tone (rising): starts with the voice lower but ends up as high as in the first tone

ˇ 3rd tone (falling-rising): starts with the voice lower than the second tone, dips and then rises in a rather drawn-out way

ˋ 4th tone (falling): the voice falls from high to low

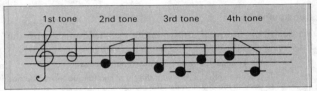

Every syllable is pronounced on one of these four tones, except when it is unstressed. In this case, the tone distinctions disappear, and the unstressed syllable is pronounced light and short. In speech, when two 3rd tones follow one another, the first automatically becomes 2nd tone.

**Vowels**

| Letter | Approximate pronunciation |
| --- | --- |
| a | like **a** in c**a**r (but with no **r**-sound) |
| e | like **e** in h**e**r (but with no **r**-sound) |
| i | 1) like **ee** in b**ee** <br> 2) after **c**, **s**, **z**, **ch**, **sh**, **zh**, **r**, like **e** in h**e**r (with no **r**-sound) |
| o | like **aw** in s**aw** |
| u | like **oo** in sp**oo**n |
| ü | similar to German **ü** or **u** in French "l**u**ne"; round your lips and try to say **ee** |

Though Chinese syllables most often end with a straight vowel, they may also end in a diphthong or a vowel and a consonant. A few of these letter combinations are not pronounced exactly as one would expect, notably the following:

**ou** as in s**ou**l     **ian** like **yen**     **ui** like **way**

In compound vowels (diphthongs and triphthongs) the pronunciation starts from one vowel and "glides" to or towards another vowel; e.g. **i, ia, iao**.

### Consonants

These are pronounced approximately as in English, with the following exceptions:

| | |
|---|---|
| **c** | like **ts** in i**ts**, followed by a strong puff of breath |
| **ch** | like **ch** in **ch**urch, but with the tip of the tongue turned up and back to touch the roof of the mouth |
| **g** | always as in **g**ive |
| **h** | like **ch** in Scottish lo**ch** |
| **j** | like **j** in **j**eer (strongly fronted: pronounced as near to the front of the mouth as possible) |
| **q** | similar to **ch** in **ch**eap |
| **r** | like English **r**, but with the tip of the tongue turned up and back to touch the roof of the mouth, so that it sounds something like the **s** in plea**s**ure |
| **s** | like **s** in **s**it |
| **sh** | like **sh** in **sh**oe, but with the tip of the tongue turned up and back to touch the roof of the mouth |
| **x** | like **sh** in **sh**eep (strongly fronted), but with lips widely spread |
| **y** | like **y** in **y**ard |
| **z** | like **ds** in li**ds** |
| **zh** | like **j** in **j**ug, but with the tip of the tongue turned up and back to touch the roof of the mouth |

The three consonants **p, t** and **k** should be pronounced with a strong puff of breath.

# Some basic expressions

| | | |
|---|---|---|
| Correct/Is.* | 对/是。 | duì/shì |
| Incorrect/Is not.* | 不对/不是。 | bú duì/bú shì |
| Please. | 请。 | qǐng |
| Thank you. | 谢谢。 | xiè-xie |
| Thank you very much. | 十分感谢。 | shí-fēn gǎn-xiè |
| That's all right/ You're welcome. | 不客气。 | bú kè-qi |

## Greetings 问候

| | | |
|---|---|---|
| Good morning/ Good afternoon/ Good evening. | 你好。 | nǐ hǎo** |
| Good night. | 晚安。 | wǎn-ān |
| Goodbye. | 再见。 | zài-jiàn |
| See you soon. | 回头见。 | huí-tóu-jiàn |
| This is Mr. ... | 这是…先生。 | zhè shì ... xiān-sheng |
| This is Mrs. ... | 这是…夫人。 | zhè shì ... fū-rén |
| This is Miss... | 这是…小姐。 | zhè shì ... xiǎo-jie |
| How do you do? (Pleased to meet you.) | 你好，很高兴认识你。 | nǐ-hǎo hěn gāo-xìng néng rèn-shi ni |
| How are you? | 你好吗？ | nǐ hǎo ma |
| Very well, thank you. | 很好，谢谢。 | hěn hǎo xiè-xie |
| And you? | 你呢？ | nǐ ne |
| Fine. | 很好。 | hěn hǎo |
| How's life? | 怎么样，忙吗？ | zěn-me yàng máng ma |
| Not bad/So so. | 还可以。 | hái kě-yǐ |

---

\* The Chinese do not say ''yes'' and ''no'', instead they repeat the verb. E.g. Do you speak Chinese? I speak. or I don't speak. You may also answer with the words ''correct'' or ''incorrect''.

\*\* The *nǐ* form is the general word for ''you''. The special polite form *nín* should be used when talking to an older person, a business partner, or anyone else to whom special respect is due.

| I beg your pardon?/ Sorry! | 对不起。 | duì-bu-qǐ |
| Excuse me. (May I get past?) | 对不起。 | duì-bu-qǐ |
| Excuse me. (Can you tell me...?) | 请问… | qǐng wèn |

## Questions 问话

| Where? | 哪儿？ | nǎr |
| Where is there ...? | 哪儿有… ？ | nǎr yǒu |
| Where is...? | …在哪儿？ | ...zài nǎr |
| Where are...? | …在哪儿？ | ...zài nǎr |
| Where can I buy/ get...? | 我在哪儿能买/找到…？ | wǒ zài nǎr néng mǎi/ zhǎo dào |
| When? (time) | 几点？ | jǐ diǎn |
| When? (date) | 几号？ | jǐ hào |
| When does ... open? | …几点开门？ | ...jǐ diǎn kāi mén |
| When does ... close? | …几点关门？ | ...jǐ diǎn guān mén |
| How? | 怎么？ | zěn-me |
| How far? | 多远？ | duō yuǎn |
| How long? | 多长时间？ | duō cháng shí-jiān |
| How much? (money) | 多少钱？ | duō-shao qián |
| How much/ How many? | 多少/多少个？ | duō-shao/duō-shao ge |
| How much does this cost? | 这要多少钱？ | zhè yào duō-shao qián |
| Who? | 谁？ | shéi |
| Why? | 为什么？ | wèi shén-me |
| Which? | 哪个？ | nǎ ge |
| What? | 什么？ | shén-me |
| What do you call this? | 这叫什么？ | zhè jiào shén-me |
| What do you call that? | 那叫什么？ | nà jiào shén-me |
| What does this mean? | 这是什么意思？ | zhè shì shén-me yì-si |
| What does that mean? | 那是什么意思？ | nà shì shén-me yì-si |

## Do you speak...? 你会说…？

| | | |
|---|---|---|
| Do you speak English? | 你会说英语吗？ | nǐ huì shuō yīng-yǔ ma |
| Does anyone here speak English? | 这儿谁会说英语？ | zhèr shéi huì shuō yīng-yǔ |
| Do you speak...? | 你会说…吗？ | nǐ huì shuō … ma |
| French | 法语 | fǎ-yǔ |
| German | 德语 | dé-yǔ |
| Spanish | 西班牙语 | xī-bān-yá-yǔ |
| I don't speak Chinese. | 我不会说汉语。 | wǒ bú huì shuō hàn-yǔ |
| I only speak a little Chinese. | 我只会说一点儿汉语。 | wǒ zhǐ huì shuō yì-diǎnr hàn-yǔ |
| Could you speak more slowly? | 请说慢点儿。 | qǐng shuō màn dianr |
| Could you repeat that? | 请再说一遍。 | qǐng zài shuō yí-biàn |
| Please write it down. | 请写下来。 | qǐng xiě xià lai |
| Can you translate this for me? | 请把这个翻译出来。 | qǐng bǎ zhèi-ge fān-yì chū lai |
| Please point to the ... in the book. | 请在这本书里找出这个… | qǐng zài zhè běn shū li zhǎo chū zhèi-ge |
| word/phrase | 词/短语 | cí/duǎn-yǔ |
| Please point to the sentence in the book. | 请在这本书里找出这句话。 | qǐng zài zhè běn shū li zhǎo chū zhè jù huà |
| Just a moment. | 请等一下。 | qǐng děng yí-xià |
| I'll see if I can find it in this book. | 看我能否在这本书里找到。 | kàn wǒ néng fǒu zài zhè běn shū li zhǎo dào |
| I understand. | 我懂了。 | wǒ dǒng le |
| I don't understand. | 我不懂。 | wǒ bù dǒng |

## Can/May...? 能…吗？

| | | |
|---|---|---|
| Can I...? | 我能…吗？ | wǒ néng … ma |
| Can we...? | 我们能…吗？ | wǒ-men néng … ma |
| Can I/we have...? | 能给我/我们…吗？ | néng gěi wǒ/wǒ-men … ma |

| Can you show me...? | 你能让我看看…吗？ | nǐ néng ràng wǒ kàn-kan ... ma |
| Can you tell me...? | 你能告诉我…吗？ | nǐ néng gào-su wǒ ... ma |
| Can you help me, please? | 你能帮助我吗？ | nǐ néng bāng-zhù wǒ ma |
| Can you direct me to...? | 去…怎么走？ | qù ... zěn-me zǒu |

## Wanting 需要

| I'd like (to have)... | 我想（要）… | wǒ xiǎng (yào) |
| We'd like (to have)... | 我们想（要）… | wǒ-men xiǎng (yào) |
| Please give me... | 请给我… | qǐng gěi wǒ |
| Give it to me, please. | 请把这个给我。 | qǐng bǎ zhè-ge gěi wǒ |
| Please bring me... | 请给我拿… | qǐng gěi wǒ ná |
| Show me... | 让我看看… | ràng wǒ kàn-kan |
| I'm looking for... | 我找… | wǒ zhǎo |
| I'm hungry. | 我饿了。 | wǒ è le |
| I'm thirsty. | 我渴了。 | wǒ kě le |
| I'd like something to eat. | 我想吃点什么。 | wǒ xiǎng chī diǎn shén-me |
| I'd like something to drink. | 我想喝点什么。 | wǒ xiǎng hē diǎn shén-me |
| I'm tired. | 我累了。 | wǒ lèi le |
| I'm lost. | 我迷路了。 | wǒ mí-lù le |
| It's important. | 这很重要。 | zhè hěn zhòng-yào |
| It's urgent. | 这很紧急。 | zhè hěn jǐn-jí |

## It is/There is... 这是/有…

| It is... | 这是… | zhè shì |
| Is it...? | 这是…吗？ | zhè shì ... ma |
| It isn't... | 这不是… | zhè bú shì |
| There is/There are... | 有… | yǒu |
| Is there/Are there...? | 有…吗？ | yǒu ... ma |

| There isn't/<br>There aren't… | 没有… | méi yǒu |
| There isn't any/<br>There aren't any. | 没有。 | méi yǒu |

## It's… 这…

| big/small | 大/小 | dà/xiǎo |
| quick/slow | 快/慢 | kuài/màn |
| early/late | 早/晚 | zǎo/wǎn |
| cheap/expensive | 便宜/贵 | pián-yi/guì |
| near/far | 近/远 | jìn/yuǎn |
| hot/cold | 热/冷 | rè/lěng |
| full/empty | 满/空 | mǎn/kōng |
| easy/difficult | 容易/难 | róng-yi/nán |
| heavy/light | 重/轻 | zhòng/qīng |
| open/shut | 开/关 | kāi/guān |
| right/wrong | 对/错 | duì/cuò |
| old/new | 旧/新 | jiù/xīn |
| old/young | 年老/年轻 | nián-lǎo/nián-qīng |
| beautiful/ugly | 好看/难看 | hǎo-kàn/nán-kàn |
| good/bad | 好/坏 | hǎo/huài |
| better/worse | 好些/更坏了 | hǎo xiē/gèng huài le |
| long/short | 长/短 | cháng/duǎn |
| free (vacant)/<br>occupied | 没人/有人 | méi rén/yǒu rén |
| here/there | 这儿/那儿 | zhèr/nàr |

## Quantities 数量

| a little/a lot | 一点儿/很多 | yì-diǎnr/hěn duō |
| some | 一些 | yì-xiē |
| few/a few | 很少/有几个 | hěn-shǎo/yǒu jǐ-ge |
| much/many | 很多/很多 | hěn duō/hěn duō |
| more/less | 多些/少些 | duō xiē/shǎo xiē |
| more than/less than | 超过/不到 | chāo-guò/bú dào |
| enough/too | 足够/太 | zú-gòu/tài |

## A few more useful words 一些常用词汇

| | | |
|---|---|---|
| at | 在 | zài |
| on | 在…上 | zài … shàng |
| in | 在…里 | zài … li |
| to | 向 | xiàng |
| from | 从 | cóng |
| for | 为了 | wèi-le |
| with* | 有 | yǒu |
| with (person) | 跟…一起 | gēn … yì-qǐ |
| without | 没有 | méi-yǒu |
| before (place) | 在…前面 | zài … qián-miàn |
| before (time) | 前 | qián |
| after | 后 | hòu |
| through | 经过 | jīng-guò |
| towards | 向 | xiàng |
| until | 直到 | zhí-dào |
| during | 在…的时候 | zài … de shí-hou |
| next to | 在…旁边儿 | zài … páng-biānr |
| near | 在…附近 | zài … fù-jìn |
| behind | 在…后面 | zài … hòu-miàn |
| between | 在…中间 | zài … zhōng-jiān |
| since | 从 | cóng |
| above | 在…上 | zài … shàng |
| below | 在…下 | zài … xià |
| under | 在…下面 | zài … xià-miàn |
| inside | 里边儿 | lǐ-bianr |
| outside | 外边儿 | wài-bianr |
| upstairs | 楼上 | lóu-shàng |
| downstairs | 楼下 | lóu-xià |
| and | 和 | hé |
| or | 还是 | hái-shì |
| but | 但是 | dàn-shì |
| not | 不 | bù |
| never | 从来没有 | cóng-lái méi-yǒu |
| very | 很 | hěn |
| too (also) | 也 | yě |
| yet | 还没有 | hái méi-yǒu |
| soon | 很快就 | hěn kuài jiù |
| now | 现在 | xiàn-zài |
| then | 然后 | rán-hòu |
| perhaps | 也许 | yě-xǔ |
| only | 只 | zhǐ |

---

\* If you want to use the word "with" followed by an object, i.e. room with a view, cup with a handle, then you must say 有 *yǒu*. If you are talking about people, i.e. with my sister, with a friend, you must use a different construction 跟…一起 *gēn … yi-qǐ*.

# Arrival

| Here's my... | 这是我的… | zhè shì wǒ-de |
| passport | 护照 | hù-zhào |
| vaccination certificate | 预防注射证 | yù-fáng-zhù-shè-zhèng |
| visa | 签证 | qiān-zhèng |
| I'll be staying... | 我将停留… | wǒ jiāng tíng-liú |
| a few days | 几天 | jǐ tiān |
| a week | 一星期 | yì xīng-qī |
| a month | 一个月 | yí-ge yuè |
| I don't know yet. | 还不一定。 | hái bù yí-dìng |
| I'm here on holiday. | 我来这里渡假。 | wǒ lái zhè-lǐ dù-jià |
| I'm here on business. | 我因工作来这里。 | wǒ yīn gōng-zuò lái zhè-lǐ |
| I'm a student. | 我是学生。 | wǒ shì xué-sheng |
| I'm here with a group. | 我是团体来的。 | wǒ shì tuán-tǐ lái de |

海关
hǎi-guān
CUSTOMS

Before arriving you will have filled out a baggage-declaration form listing any watches, jewellery, cameras or electronic gadgets in your possession. When you leave China at the end of your stay, you may be asked to prove that you are taking with you all the items on the list.

In general, it is forbidden to carry into the People's Republic of China the following: arms and explosives, radio transmitting equipment, Chinese currency, material deemed morally or ideologically subversive, and habit-forming drugs.

The duty-free allowance for tourists entering China consists of two bottles of alcoholic beverages (neither exceeding ¾ litre), 400 cigarettes, food, clothing and medicine for personal use, and any quantity of foreign currency.

To change money back on departure you must show your exchange receipts.

| I have nothing to declare. | 我没有要报关的东西。 | wǒ méi-yǒu yào bào-guān de dōng-xi |
| I have... | 我带了… | wǒ dài le |
| ...packets of cigarettes | …包香烟 | ...bāo xiāng-yān |
| a bottle of whisky | 一瓶威士忌 | yì-píng wēi-shì-jì |
| Here's my camera. | 这是我的照相机。 | zhè shì wǒ de zhào-xiàng-jī |
| I've brought ... rolls of film with me. | 我带了…卷胶卷。 | wǒ dài le ... juǎn jiāo-juǎn |
| It's not professional equipment. | 这不是专业器材。 | zhè bú shì zhuān-yè qì-cái |
| Here are my valuables. | 这些是我的贵重品。 | zhè xiē shì wǒ de guì-zhòng-pǐn |
| It's (not) gold. | 这（不）是金的。 | zhè (bú) shì jīn de |
| It's a gift. | 这是送人的礼物。 | zhè shì sòng rén de lǐ-wù |
| It has no commercial value. | 这不是要出售的。 | zhè bú shì yào chū-shòu de |
| It's for my personal use/It's not new. | 这是我的私人用品/这不是新的。 | zhè shì wǒ de sī-rén yòng-pǐn /zhè bú shì xīn de |

---

你们的向导在出口等着你们。

这件东西应该上税。

请到那边的办公室去付。

你还有别的行李吗？

Your guide is waiting for you at the exit.

You'll have to pay duty on this.

Please pay at the office over there.

Do you have any more luggage?

## Baggage 行李

You carry your own luggage to the customs checkpoint. At large airports you will find luggage trolleys. Although there are no porters, the coach driver of your tour group will help in carrying and loading up the luggage.

| | | |
|---|---|---|
| Please take my… | 请搬我的… | qǐng bān wǒ de |
| travelling bag | 旅行袋 | lǚ-xíng-dài |
| luggage | 行李 | xíng-li |
| suitcase | 箱子 | xiāng-zi |
| That's mine. | 这是我的。 | zhè shì wǒ de |
| There's one piece missing. | 少了一件。 | shǎo le yí-jiàn |
| Where are the luggage trolleys (carts)? | 哪儿有手推车？ | nǎr yǒu shǒu-tuī-chē |
| Where is the left-luggage office (baggage check)? | 行李寄存处在哪儿？ | xíng-li jì-cún-chù zài nǎr |

## Changing money 兑换外汇

Foreign currency and traveller's cheques can be exchanged or cashed only at authorized exchange offices (there is one at every major airport). Most hotel exchange counters stay open until 7 p.m., or even later. Any money still in your hands when you leave China will be changed back at the same rate as when you entered.

| | | |
|---|---|---|
| Where can I change money? | 在哪儿能兑换外汇？ | zài nǎr néng duì-huàn wài-huì |
| What's the exchange rate? | 兑换率是多少？ | duì-huàn-lǜ shì duō-shao |

---

外汇兑换处
wài-huì duì-huàn-chù
CURRENCY EXCHANGE OFFICE

---

BANK — CURRENCY, see page 129

到达

| I want to change some … | 我想用…兑换。 | wǒ xiǎng yòng … duì-huàn |
| traveller's cheques (checks) | 旅行支票 | lǚ-xíng-zhī-piào |
| U.S. dollars | 美元 | měi-yuán |
| pounds | 英磅 | yīng-bàng |
| Here's my currency declaration form. | 这是我的外汇申报单。 | zhè shì wǒ de wài-huì shēn-bào-dān |

## Where is …? …在哪儿？

| Where is the …? | …在哪儿？ | … zài nǎr |
| duty-free shop | 免税商店 | miǎn-shuì shāng-diàn |
| information office | 问询处 | wèn-xùn-chù |
| newsstand | 售报亭 | shòu-bào-tíng |
| restaurant | 餐厅 | cān-tīng |
| taxi booking-office | 出租汽车站 | chū-zū-qì-chē-zhàn |
| ticket office | 售票处 | shòu-piào-chù |
| How do I get to …? | 去…怎么走？ | qù … zěn-me zǒu |
| Is there a(n) … into town? | 有去城里的…吗？ | yǒu qù chéng-lǐ de … ma |
| airport bus | 机场班车 | jī-chǎng bān-chē |
| bus | 公共汽车 | gōng-gòng qì-chē |
| Where can I get a taxi? | 哪儿有出租汽车？ | nǎr yǒu chū-zū qì-chē |
| Where can I hire (rent) a car?* | 哪儿能租到包车？ | nǎr néng zū dào bāo-chē |

## Hotel reservation 预订房间

| Could you reserve a room for me at a hotel? | 可以给我在旅馆订一间房间吗？ | kě-yǐ gěi wǒ zài lǚ-guǎn dìng yì-jiān fáng-jiān ma |
| a single room | 单人房间 | dān-rén fáng-jiān |
| a double room | 双人房间 | shuāng-rén fáng-jiān |
| not too expensive | 要便宜些的 | yào pián-yi xiē de |
| Is there a student hostel nearby? | 附近有专门接待学生的旅馆吗？ | fù-jìn yǒu zhuān-mén jiē-dài xué-sheng de lǚ-guǎn ma |
| Could you reserve a bed for me? | 可以给我订一张床位吗？ | kě-yǐ gěi wǒ dìng yì-zhāng chuáng-wèi ma |

---

* Self-drive cars cannot be hired in China (see page 22).

HOTEL/ACCOMMODATION, see page 23

| Where is the hotel? | 这家旅馆在哪儿？ | zhè jiā lǚ-guǎn zài nǎr |
| Do you have a street map? | 你有交通图吗？ | nǐ yǒu jiāo-tōng-tú ma |

## Taxi 出租汽车

Many airports and railway stations have special counters at which you can book a taxi. Occasionally they may be hailed on the street; there are no taxi ranks. The easiest way to get a taxi is through your hotel receptionist. All Friendship Stores have a transport officer who will order a taxi for you, and tell the driver where you need to go.

If you're out sightseeing on your own for a few hours, it's wise to take a taxi and keep it waiting for you between stops — a relatively inexpensive investment in convenience. When travelling independently ask someone to write down your destination in Chinese on a piece of paper; drivers rarely speak anything other than Chinese.

Taxis are not metered, but drivers are universally trustworthy and honest. They usually insist on giving receipts; tips should not be offered.

| Where can I get a taxi? | 哪儿有出租汽车？ | nǎr yǒu chū-zū-qì-chē |
| Can you call me a taxi, please? | 能给我叫辆出租汽车吗？ | néng gěi wǒ jiào liàng chū-zū-qì-chē ma |
| Do you know this place? | 你认识这个地方吗？ | nǐ rèn-shi zhè-ge dì-fang ma |
| What's the fare to …? | 到…的车费是多少？ | dào … de chē-fèi shì duō-shao |
| How long does it take to get to …? | 到…要多少时间？ | dào … yào duō-shao shí-jiān |
| Take me to … | 请送我去… | qǐng sòng wǒ qù |
| this address | 地址上写的地方 | dì-zhǐ shàng xiě de dì-fang |
| the airport | 飞机场 | fēi-jī-chǎng |
| the … Hotel | …旅馆 | … lǚ-guǎn |
| the railway station | 火车站 | huǒ-chē-zhàn |
| the town centre | 市中心 | shì-zhōng-xīn |

到达

| Back to the hotel, please. | 请开回旅馆。 | qǐng kāi huí lǚ-guǎn |
| I'm in a hurry. | 我很急。 | wǒ hěn jí |
| Go straight ahead. | 一直走。 | yì-zhí zǒu |
| Turn … at the next corner. | 在前边的路口向…拐。 | zài qián-bian de lù-kǒu xiàng … guǎi |
| left/right | 左/右 | zuǒ/yòu |
| Could you drive more slowly? | 请开慢点儿。 | qǐng kāi màn diǎnr |
| Please stop here. | 请停一下。 | qǐng tíng yí xià |
| Could you help me carry my luggage? | 可以帮我提行李吗？ | kě-yǐ bāng wǒ tí xíng-li ma |
| Could you wait for me? | 请等我。 | qǐng děng wǒ |
| Can you come back and pick me up at … o'clock? | 能在…点回来接我吗？ | néng zài … diǎn huí lái jiē wǒ ma |

## Car hire (rental) 租包车

Self-drive cars cannot be hired in China, but chauffeur-driven cars are readily available. If you don't want to hire a car for the whole day, it's often possible to arrange for a taxi by the hour plus mileage.

| I'd like to hire (rent) a car. | 我想租一辆包车。 | wǒ xiǎng zū yí-liàng bāo-chē |
| I'll be alone. | 我一个人。 | wǒ yí-ge rén |
| There will be … of us. | 我们…个人。 | wǒ-mén … ge rén |
| I'd like it for … | 我想用… | wǒ xiǎng yòng |
| a day/a week | 一天/一星期 | yì-tiān/yì xīng-qī |
| What's the charge per day/per week? | 一天/一星期多少钱？ | yì tiān/yì xīng-qī duō-shao qián |
| Do you charge …? | 是按…计价吗？ | shì àn … jì-jià ma |
| by the hour | 时间 | shí-jiān |
| according to mileage | 里程 | lǐ-chéng |
| What's the deposit? | 押金多少？ | yā-jīn duō-shao |

TELLING THE TIME, see page 155

到达

# Hotel

Whether you are going to China on your own or as part of a group, your hotel accommodation will probably be reserved in advance by the China International Travel Service (CITS). At present, only a few Chinese hotels accept individual reservations, but this will change as computers come into wider use.

Hotels (旅馆 – *lǚ-guǎn*) in China range from first class to grimly spartan. The newest hotels, often built with foreign cooperation and expertise, bear the closest resemblance to their counterparts in Europe and America. More adventurous travellers may prefer the charm of old-fashioned establishments in interesting or scenic locations.

In general, hotels in small or remote towns offer few comforts. Air conditioning is a relatively new feature in China; radios and telephones are usually provided, and ever more hotels are now equipped with small refrigerators and television sets.

In almost every room you'll find cups and a large thermos of hot water for making tea. A small container of tea is often provided as well. The separate carafe of "drinking water" may not always be trusted; *never* drink water from the tap.

Large hotels now have post offices, exchange offices, bars, swimming pools, bookshops, hairdressers, theatres (with shows staged especially for foreign visitors) and Chinese massage parlours.

If staying in a larger hotel you will find a service desk on each floor. The floor monitor will probably speak a little English and be able to handle small problems that may crop up during your stay. The desk also sells cigarettes, snacks, drinks and postcards.

## Checking in — Reception 住宿-接待

The phrases below can be used either in the hotel or at the CITS office if they are organizing your accommodation.

| | | |
|---|---|---|
| My name is … | 我叫… | wǒ jiào |
| I have a reservation. | 我预订了。 | wǒ yù-dìng le |
| Here's the confirmation. | 这是订单。 | zhè shì dìng-dān |
| I don't have a reservation. | 我没预订。 | wǒ méi yù-dìng |
| Do you have any vacancies? | 你这儿有空房间吗？ | nǐ zhèr yǒu kōng fáng-jiān ma |
| I'd like a … | 我想要一间… | wǒ xiǎng-yào yì-jiān |
| single room | 单人房间 | dān-rén fáng-jiān |
| double room | 双人房间 | shuāng-rén fáng-jiān |
| with twin beds | 有两张单人床的 | yǒu liǎng zhāng dān-rén-chuáng de |
| with a double bed | 有一张双人床的 | yǒu yì-zhāng shuāng-rén-chuáng de |
| room with a bath | 有澡盆的房间 | yǒu zǎo-pén de fáng-jiān |
| room with a shower | 有淋浴的房间 | yǒu lín-yù de fáng-jiān |
| We'd like a room … | 我们想要一个…房间。 | wǒ-men xiǎng-yào yí-ge … fáng-jiān |
| with a balcony | 有阳台的 | yǒu yáng-tái de |
| with a view | 窗外风景好看的 | chuāng wài fēng-jǐng hǎo-kàn de |
| at the front | 临街的 | lín-jiē de |
| at the back | 在后面的 | zài hòu-miàn de |
| facing the sea | 朝着海的 | cháo zhe hǎi de |
| It must be quiet. | 要安静的。 | yào ān-jìng de |
| Is there (a) …? | 有…吗？ | yǒu … ma |
| air conditioning | 空调 | kōng-tiáo |
| heating | 暖气 | nuǎn-qì |
| hot water | 热水 | rè-shuǐ |
| laundry service | 洗衣服务 | xǐ-yī fú-wù |
| private toilet | 私人厕所 | sī-rén cè-suǒ |
| room service | 清扫整理服务 | qīng-sǎo zhěng-lǐ fú-wù |
| running water | 自来水 | zì-lái-shuǐ |
| Could you put … in the room? | 可以在房间里加…吗？ | kě-yǐ zài fáng-jiān li jiā … ma |

CHECKING OUT, see page 32

旅馆

| an extra bed | 一张床 | yì-zhāng chuáng |
| a cot | 一张小床 | yì-zhāng xiǎo-chuáng |

## How much? 多少钱？

Meals are not normally included in the price if you aren't part of a tour group. If you eat in the hotel dining room you should pay at the end of each meal.

| What's the price …? | …多少钱？ | … duō-shao qián |
| per night | 一夜 | yí-yè |
| per week | 一星期 | yì xīng-qī |
| Does that include …? | 这包括…吗？ | zhè bāo-kuò … ma |
| breakfast | 早饭 | zǎo-fàn |
| meals | 伙食费 | huǒ-shí fèi |
| Is there any reduction for children? | 儿童有减价吗？ | ér-tóng yǒu jiǎn-jià ma |
| Do you charge for the baby? | 这儿婴儿也要付钱吗？ | zhèr yīng-ér yě yào fù qián ma |
| That's too expensive for me. | 对我来说这太贵了。 | duì wǒ lái shuō zhè tài guì le |
| Don't you have anything cheaper? | 有便宜些的吗？ | yǒu pián-yi xiē de ma |

## How long? 多长时间？

| I'll be staying … | 我打算住… | wǒ dǎ-suan zhù |
| We'll be staying … | 我们打算住… | wǒ-men dǎ-suan zhù |
| overnight only | 一夜 | yí-yè |
| a few days | 几天 | jǐ tiān |
| a week (at least) | （最少）一星期 | (zuì shǎo) yì xīng-qī |
| I don't know yet. | 还不一定。 | hái bù yí-dìng |

## Decision 决定

| May I see the room? | 我可以看看房间吗？ | wǒ kě-yǐ kàn-kan fáng-jiān ma |
| No, I don't like it. | 我不喜欢这间。 | wǒ bù xǐ-huan zhè-jiān |
| It's too … | 这里太… | zhè-li tài |
| cold/hot | 冷/热 | lěng/rè |
| dark/small/noisy | 暗/小/吵 | àn/xiǎo/chǎo |

NUMBERS, see page 149

旅馆

26

| I asked for a room with a bath. | 我要的是一个有澡盆的房间。 | wǒ yào de shì yí-ge yǒu zǎo-pén de fáng-jiān |
| Do you have any-thing …? | 你这儿有…的吗？ | nǐ zhèr yǒu … de ma |
| better/bigger | 好些/大些 | hǎo xiē/dà xiē |
| cheaper/quieter | 便宜些/安静些 | pián-yi xiē/ān-jìng xiē |
| higher up/lower down | 楼层高些/楼层低些 | lóu-céng gāo xiē/lóu-céng dī xiē |
| Do you have a room with a better view? | 你这儿有窗外风景更好些的房间吗？ | nǐ zhèr yǒu chuāng wài fēng-jǐng gèng hǎo xiē de fáng-jiān ma |
| That's fine. | 这间很好。 | zhè jiān hěn hǎo |
| I'll take it. | 我要了。 | wǒ yào le |

## Registration 住宿登记

Upon arrival at a hotel you will be asked to fill in a registration form (住宿登记表 zhù-sù dēng-jì-biǎo).

| 姓/名 | Name/First name |
| 家庭住址/街道/门牌号 | Home address/Street/Number |
| 国籍/职业 | Nationality/Profession |
| 出生年月日/籍贯 | Date/Place of birth |
| 从…来/到…去 | Coming from …/Going to … |
| 护照号码 | Passport number |
| 地点/日期 | Place/Date |
| 签名 | Signature |

| What does this mean? | 这是什么意思？ | zhè shì shén-me yì-si |

| 我可以看看你的护照吗？ | May I see your passport? |
| 请你填写这份住宿登记表。 | Please fill in this registration form. |
| 请在此签名。 | Sign here, please. |
| 你打算住多长时间？ | How long will you be staying? |

| What's my room number? | 我的房间号是多少？ | wǒ de fáng-jiān-hào shì duō-shao |
| Will you have our luggage sent up? | 请把我们的行李送到房间里。 | qǐng bǎ wǒ-men de xíng-li sòng dào fáng-jiān li |
| I'd like to leave this in your safe. | 我想把这个寄存在你们的保险箱里。 | wǒ xiǎng bǎ zhè-ge jì-cún zài nǐ-men de bǎo-xiǎn-xiāng li |

## Hotel staff 旅馆工作人员

| bank clerk | 银行职员 | yín-háng zhí-yuán |
| cashier | 出纳员 | chū-nà-yuán |
| floor supervisor | 楼层负责人 | lóu-céng fù-zé-rén |
| lift attendant | 电梯服务员 | diàn-tī fú-wù-yuán |
| maid/room attendant | 客房服务员 | kè-fáng fú-wù-yuán |
| person in charge (manager) | 经理 | jīng-lǐ |
| porter | 行李员 | xíng-li-yuán |
| postal clerk | 邮局职员 | yóu-jú zhí-yuán |
| receptionist | 接待员 | jiē-dài-yuán |
| switchboard operator | 接线员 | jiē-xiàn-yuán |

There is just one form of address you need to know for anybody you meet in the service sector in China (porters, waiters etc …): 服务员 *fú-wù-yuán*, for both men and women.

## General requirements 一般要求

| The key, please. | 请给我钥匙。 | qǐng gěi wǒ yào-shi |
| Room 1-2-3. | 一二三号房间。 | 123 hào fáng-jiān |
| Will you wake me at …, please? | 请…叫醒我。 | qǐng … jiào-xǐng wǒ |
| Is there a bath room on this floor? | 这楼层有浴室吗？ | zhè lóu-céng yǒu yù-shì ma |
| How does the shower work? | 这个淋浴怎么用？ | zhè-ge lín-yù zěn-me yòng |
| Where's the socket (outlet) for the shaver? | 接电动剃须刀的插座在哪儿？ | jiē diàn-dòng tì-xū-dāo de chā-zuò zài nǎr |

TELLING THE TIME, see page 155

旅馆

| What's the voltage here? | 电压是多少？ | diàn-yā shì duō-shao |
| Can you lend me an adaptor? | 能借我一个多路插座吗？ | néng jiè wǒ yí-ge duō lù chā-zuò ma |
| Can we have breakfast in our room? | 我们可以在房间里用早饭吗？ | wǒ-men kě-yǐ zài fáng-jiān li yòng zǎo-fàn ma |
| Would you serve ... in our room, please? | 请你把…送到我的房间里来。 | qǐng nǐ bǎ ... sòng dào wǒ de fáng-jiān li lái |
| breakfast | 早饭 | zǎo-fàn |
| lunch | 午饭 | wǔ-fàn |
| dinner | 晚饭 | wǎn-fàn |
| I don't want to be disturbed. | 请不要打扰我。 | qǐng bú-yào dǎ-rǎo wǒ |
| Can you find me a ...? | 请帮我找…。 | qǐng bāng wǒ zhǎo |
| babysitter | 一位临时保姆 | yí-wèi lín-shí bǎo-mǔ |
| secretary | 一位秘书 | yí-wèi mì-shū |
| typewriter | 一架打字机 | yí-jià dǎ-zì-jī |
| May I have a/an/some ...? | 请给我… | qǐng gěi wǒ |
| ashtray | 一个烟灰缸 | yí-ge yān-huī-gāng |
| bath towel | 一块浴巾 | yí-kuài yù-jīn |
| boiled water | 一些开水 | yì-xiē kāi-shuǐ |
| extra blanket | 一条毯子 | yì-tiáo tǎn-zi |
| electric fan | 一架电扇 | yí-jià diàn-shàn |
| envelopes | 几个信封 | jǐ ge xìn-fēng |
| hangers | 几个挂钩 | jǐ ge guà-gōu |
| hot-water bottle | 一个暖水袋 | yí-ge nuǎn-shuǐ-dài |
| ice cubes | 一些冰块 | yì-xiē bīng-kuài |
| mosquito net | 一顶蚊帐 | yì-dǐng wén-zhàng |
| needle and thread | 一些针和线 | yì-xiē zhēn hé xiàn |
| extra pillow | 加一个枕头 | jiā yí-ge zhěn-tou |
| reading lamp | 一盏台灯 | yì-zhǎn tái-dēng |
| soap | 一块肥皂 | yí-kuài féi-zào |
| writing paper | 几张信纸 | jǐ zhāng xìn-zhǐ |
| Where's the ...? | …在哪儿？ | ... zài nǎr |
| bathroom | 浴室 | yù-shì |
| dining room | 餐厅 | cān-tīng |
| emergency exit | 太平门 | tài-píng-mén |
| hairdresser's | 理发室 | lǐ-fà-shì |
| lift (elevator) | 电梯 | diàn-tī |
| Where are the toilets? | 厕所在哪儿？ | cè-suǒ zài nǎr |

FOR VOLTAGE, see page 119

## Telephone — Post (mail) 打电话-邮寄

| | | |
|---|---|---|
| Can you get me Beijing 123 4567? | 请接北京一二三—四五六七？ | qǐng jiē běi-jīng 123-4567 |
| Do you have any stamps? | 你这儿卖邮票吗？ | nǐ zhèr mài yóu-piào ma |
| Would you post (mail) this for me? | 请帮我寄出这封信。 | qǐng bāng wǒ jì-chū zhè-fēng xìn |
| Are there any letters for me? | 有我的信吗？ | yǒu wǒ de xìn ma |
| Are there any messages for me? | 有给我的留言吗？ | yǒu gěi wǒ de liú-yán ma |
| What is my telephone bill? | 我的电话费一共多少？ | wǒ de diàn-huà-fèi yí-gòng duō-shao |

## Difficulties 出毛病了

| | | |
|---|---|---|
| The ... doesn't work. | …坏了。 | ... huài le |
| air conditioner | 空调 | kōng-tiáo |
| electric fan | 电扇 | diàn-shàn |
| heating | 暖气 | nuǎn-qì |
| light | 电灯 | diàn-dēng |
| toilet | 厕所 | cè-suǒ |
| radio | 收音机 | shōu-yīn-jī |
| television | 电视机 | diàn-shì-jī |
| The tap (faucet) is dripping. | 水龙头关不紧。 | shuǐ-lóng-tóu guān-bu-jǐn |
| There's no hot water. | 没有热水。 | méi-yǒu rè-shuǐ |
| The washbasin is blocked. | 水池子的下水道堵了。 | shuǐ-chí-zi de xià-shuǐ-dào dǔ le |
| The window is jammed. | 窗户卡住了。 | chuāng-hu qiǎ-zhù le |
| The curtains are stuck. | 窗帘儿拉不动。 | chuāng-liánr lā-bu-dòng |
| The bulb is burned out. | 灯泡儿烧坏了。 | dēng-pàor shāo huài le |
| The mosquito net on my window is torn. | 沙窗破了。 | shā-chuāng pò le |
| My room hasn't been prepared. | 我的房间还没有整理。 | wǒ de fáng-jiān hái méi-yǒu zhěng-lǐ |

POST OFFICE AND TELEPHONE, see page 134

旅馆

| There are some insects in my room. | 我的房间有虫子。 | wǒ de fáng-jiān yǒu chóng-zi |
| The … is broken. | …坏了。 | … huài le |
| blind | 百叶窗 | bǎi-yè-chuāng |
| bulb | 灯泡 | dēng-pào |
| lamp | 电灯 | diàn-dēng |
| plug | 插头 | chā-tóu |
| switch | 开关 | kāi-guān |
| Can you get it repaired? | 你能找人把它修理好吗？ | nǐ néng zhǎo rén bǎ tā xiū-lǐ hǎo ma |

### Laundry — Dry cleaner's 洗衣店－干洗店

Hotels process laundry and dry-cleaning quickly and efficiently. Most hotels provide their guests with laundry bags; if you're in a hurry, deliver the filled bag to the service desk on your floor; otherwise it will be picked up when the room is cleaned. Laundry is usually returned within 24 hours, but dry-cleaning may take an extra day in all but the largest hotels.

| I want these clothes … | 请把这些衣服… | qǐng bǎ zhè-xiē yī-fu |
| cleaned | 弄干净 | nòng gān-jìng |
| ironed/pressed | 熨好 | yùn hǎo |
| washed | 洗干净 | xǐ gān-jìng |
| When will they be ready? | 什么时候能洗好？ | shén-me shí-hou néng xǐ hǎo |
| I need them … | 我…需要。 | wǒ … xū-yào |
| today | 今天 | jīn-tiān |
| tonight | 今晚 | jīn-wǎn |
| tomorrow | 明天 | míng-tiān |
| before Friday | 星期五以前 | xīng-qī-wǔ yǐ-qián |
| I want them as soon as possible. | 请尽早给我洗好。 | qǐng jìn-zǎo gěi wǒ xǐ hǎo |
| Can you … this? | 你能…这个吗？ | nǐ néng … zhè-ge ma |
| mend/stitch | 补/缝 | bǔ/féng |
| Can you sew on this button? | 请帮我把这个钮扣缝上好吗？ | qǐng bāng wǒ bǎ zhè-ge niǔ-kòu féng-shang hǎo ma |
| Can you get this stain out? | 请帮我把这个污点去掉好吗？ | qǐng bāng wǒ bǎ zhè-ge wū-diǎn qù-diào hǎo ma |

| Is my laundry ready? | 我的衣服洗好了吗？ | wǒ de yī-fu xǐ hǎo le ma |
| This isn't mine. | 这不是我的。 | zhè bú shì wǒ de |
| There's one piece missing. | 少了一件。 | shǎo le yí-jiàn |
| There's a hole in this. | 这件衣服上有一个洞。 | zhè-jiàn yī-fu shàng yǒu yí-ge dòng |

## Hairdresser's — Barber's 理发店

The larger hotels usually have a hairdresser and a barber shop. The service is good and extremely cheap by Western standards. The treatment may include a head and neck massage, which is most relaxing. Tipping is not allowed.

| Is there a … in the hotel? | 这个旅馆里有…吗？ | zhè-ge lǚ-guǎn li yǒu … ma |
| barber/hairdresser | 理发室 | lǐ-fà-shì |
| beauty salon | 美容室 | měi-róng-shì |
| Can I make an appointment for …? | 请给我约个…的时间。 | qǐng gěi wǒ yuē ge … de shí-jiān |
| Please give me a head and neck massage. | 请给我按摩一下头部和脖子。 | qǐng gěi wǒ àn-mó yí xià tóu-bù he bó-zi |
| I'd like a haircut, please. | 我想剪发。 | wǒ xiǎng jiǎn fà |
| blow dry | 把头发吹干定型 | bǎ tóu-fa chuī gān dìng-xíng |
| colour rinse | 着色洗发 | zhuó sè xǐ fà |
| dye | 染发 | rǎn fà |
| face pack | 绞脸 | jiǎo liǎn |
| perm(anent) | 烫发 | tàng fà |
| shampoo and set | 洗头和做发 | xǐ tóu hé zuò fà |
| I'd like a shampoo for …. | 我想用一种适用于…的洗发剂。 | wǒ xiǎng yòng yì-zhǒng shì yòng yú … de xǐ-fà-jì |
| normal hair | 普通头发 | pǔ-tōng tóu-fa |
| dry hair | 很干的头发 | hěn gān de tóu-fa |
| greasy (oily) hair | 出油的头发 | chū yóu de tóu-fa |
| Don't cut it too short. | 不要剪得太短。 | bú yào jiǎn de tài duǎn |
| A little more off the … | …再剪短一点。 | … zài jiǎn duǎn yì-diǎn |
| back | 后头的 | hòu tóu de |
| neck | 脖子上的 | bó-zi shàng de |

旅馆

DAYS OF THE WEEK, see page 153

| sides | 两侧的 | liǎng cè de |
| top | 头项上的 | tóu-dǐng shàng de |
| Would you trim my …, please? | 请给我修剪一下我的… ? | qǐng gěi wǒ xiū jiǎn yí-xià wǒ de |
| beard | 下胡子 | xià hú-zi |
| moustache | 上胡子 | shàng hú-zi |
| sideboards (side-burns) | 两侧的胡子 | liǎng cè de hú-zi |
| I'd like a shave. | 我想要刮脸。 | wǒ xiǎng-yào guā liǎn |
| I'd like a … | 我想要… | wǒ xiǎng yào |
| manicure | 修手指甲 | xiū shǒu zhǐ-jia |
| pedicure | 修脚指甲 | xiū jiǎo zhǐ-jia |

**Checking out** 结帐离开

| May I have my bill, please? | 我想要结帐。 | wǒ xiǎng-yào jié-zhàng |
| I'm leaving early in the morning. Please have my bill ready. | 我明天早上要很早离开。请先开好帐单。 | wǒ míng-tiān zǎo-shang yào hěn zǎo lí-kāi. qǐng xiān kāi hǎo zhàng-dān |
| I'll be checking out around noon. | 我想在中午办理结帐离开手续。 | wǒ xiǎng zài zhōng-wǔ bàn-lǐ jié-zhàng lí-kāi shǒu-xù |
| I must leave at once. | 我必须马上走。 | wǒ bì-xū mǎ-shàng zǒu |
| Can I pay by credit card? | 我可以用信用卡付钱吗? | wǒ kě-yǐ yòng xìn-yòng-kǎ fù qián ma |
| I think there's a mistake in the bill. | 这个帐单好象有错吧。 | zhè-ge zhàng-dān hǎo-xiàng yǒu cuò ba |
| Can you get me a taxi? | 请给我叫辆出租汽车好吗? | qǐng gěi wǒ jiào liàng chū-zū qì-chē hǎo ma |
| Would you have our luggage sent down? | 请把行李帮我拿下来可以吗? | qǐng bǎ xíng-li bāng wǒ ná-xia-lai kě-yǐ ma |
| Here's the forwarding address. | 这是通讯地址。 | zhè shì tōng-xùn dì-zhǐ |
| You have my home address. | 你有我家的地址了。 | nǐ yǒu wǒ jiā de dì-zhǐ le |
| It's been a very enjoyable stay. | 这次住得很愉快。 | zhè cì zhù de hěn yú-kuài |

*Note:* Tipping is not customary in the People's Republic, and can only cause embarrassment.

# Eating out

Chinese cuisine, long known and highly appreciated throughout the world by lovers of good food, is gaining an ever broader following. Chinese restaurants continue to spring up and flourish in the towns and cities of Europe and America, affording a mouth-watering insight into the gastronomic riches of the "Middle Kingdom".

The Western visitor may be astonished at the variety, flavour and finesse of the products of Chinese culinary art. It is the culmination of age-old traditions, extending over thousands of years of the world's longest continuous civilization. Cooking techniques have been modified and adapted from one century to the next across the many troubled epochs of China's existence.

In the north, rice is not the staple, and wheat-, corn-, and millet-based dishes are the rule. As a result of long, harsh winters, Northerners have become very skilled in the preparation of dried and pickled foods. The general emphasis is on strongly-flavoured dishes, but Beijing is the exception due to the Imperial influence. This can still be seen in the more complex and spectacular dishes like Peking Duck.

In the western inland provinces of Sichuan and Hunan, food is spicy and hot, with red chillis, Sichuan peppercorns and ginger as principal ingredients. While the East, with its long coastline, excels in the preparation of fish and seafood. The food of Guangdong (Canton) province is probably the best known in the West, with its sweet and sour dishes and exotic delicacies. In this region, visitors will have the pleasure of trying snake, turtle or even dog. Here the emphasis is on the preservation of natural colour and taste, so cooking methods are swift, and avoid using heavy flavourings.

上饭馆儿

At your hotel you'll have no trouble ordering a special meal. All you need to do is indicate the number of dishes you'd like, the number of diners there will be, and the hour.

If you're planning to dine out at a top restaurant, be sure to reserve a table in advance. Comfortably esconced in an armchair, you'll have time for a cup of tea before the meal if you wish. On the round table in front of you, there will be, not the cutlery you are used to, but a pair of chopsticks (see p.36 for how to use them) and a spoon. There will also be a small plate and, to your left, a gravy boat and bowl. Beside each place setting are three glasses, a big one for the beer, a wine glass and a smaller glass for spirits. A word of advice: take care not to over-indulge in the first few dishes; save your appetite so that you are fully able to savour and appreciate all the items on the menu.

### Banquets 宴会

During your stay in China you may be invited to a formal dinner or banquet. Here is a brief guide to etiquette on such occasions.

After welcoming you, your host will invite you to be seated at a low table where the ice will be broken over tea and conversation. After about a quarter of an hour you will move to your place at the customary large round table. The host usually sits facing the entrance, and the guests are seated to his right and left.

You will notice an extra pair of chopsticks on the table. These are for the use of the host, who will serve the guests seated to his right and left with them, thereby giving the signal that the meal may begin.

Toasts regularly punctuate a formal Chinese dinner or banquet, but it is considered bad form to drink before the host has first proposed a toast to his guests' health. He will raise his glass shortly after the dinner begins, and the guest of honour is expected to reply to this opening toast either straight away or when the next dish is served. Though the Chinese generally drink very little, especially in the presence of foreigners (it is considered undignified to show signs of inebriety to those one doesn't know), they do sip the fiery *máo-tái* (53% alcohol) before, during and after the meal. Moderation is advised. Your hosts will not be offended if you prefer to toast in wine, beer, fruit juice or even mineral water. Always raise your glass when a toast is proposed.

If you don't feel like a particular dish, just leave it, and it will soon be removed from the table. But it would be considered polite to try a mouthful in any case.

Fruit marks the end of the meal. The Western custom of rounding off dinner with coffee, cigars and brandy is unknown in China, and the party will break up quite quickly at 9 or 10 p.m. at the latest.

### Courses 上菜顺序

A formal Chinese meal normally follows this pattern: first some highly seasoned cold hors-d'oeuvre such as crab-meat, chicken salad, shark's fin or pork- or shrimp-balls are served. The bowl in front of you is then filled with rice. Next come the "star" dishes, likely to include chicken, duck, pigeon (squab), fish, pork, etc. You help yourself directly from the dishes using chopsticks and can dip your food in the sauces provided (soya, ginger and other spices) to enhance its flavour.

Cheese is virtually unknown in China.

Dessert as such is rarely included in a Chinese meal, though a pie, sweet soup or other sweet dish — walnut purée, for example — is often served between two savoury dishes.

Don't be surprised if the person in charge of the restaurant invites his guests to take the remaining fruit, pies or cigarettes home with them. It's quite customary.

## Chopsticks 筷子

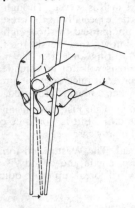

How to use chopsticks can be briefly explained as follows: you hold the upper stick between your thumb and first two fingers, while holding the lower stick stationary with the third, or third and fourth finger. Hold them about one third of the way down their length. Contrary to our own customs, in China you are expected to bring the bowl up to your mouth when eating.

## Mealtimes 用餐时间

Meals in China are taken considerably earlier than in the West. Breakfast (*zǎo-fàn*) is usually served between 6.30 and 9 a.m., while lunch (*wǔ-fàn*) can start as early as 10.30 a.m. and goes on until 1.30 p.m. Dinner (*wǎn-fàn*) is served between 4.30 and 7.30 or 8 p.m., and banquets tend to finish by 9.30 p.m.

## Hungry? 饿吗？

| | | |
|---|---|---|
| I'm hungry/I'm thirsty. | 我饿了/我渴了。 | wǒ è le/wǒ kě le |
| Can you recommend a good restaurant? | 你能介绍一家好的饭馆吗？ | nǐ néng jiè-shào yì-jiā hǎo de fàn-guǎn ma |

If you want to be sure of getting a table in a well-known restaurant, it is better to book in advance.

| I'd like to reserve a table for 4. | 我想预订一张桌子，四个人。 | wǒ xiǎng yù-dìng yì-zhāng zhuō-zi sì-ge rén |
| We'll come at 7. | 我们七点来。 | wǒ-men qī-diǎn lái |
| Could we have a table ...? | 能给我们定一张…的桌子吗？ | néng gěi wǒ-men dìng yì-zhāng ... de zhuō-zi ma |
| | | |
| in the corner | 在屋角 | zài wū-jiǎo |
| by the window | 靠窗户 | kào chuāng-hu |
| outside | 在室外 | zài shì wài |
| in a non-smoking area | 在禁止吸烟的地方 | zài jìn-zhǐ xī-yān de dì-fang |
| in a private room | 在单间里 | zài dān-jiān li |

### Ordering 点菜

Although you can't normally get a set menu, a good way of having a cheap meal with plenty of variety is to join a table where there is a set price per diner. The restaurant waits until the table is full (around 8 people), and then puts between 5 and 8 dishes in the centre of the table, which everybody shares.

| Waiter/Waitress! | 服务员！ | fú-wù-yuán |
| May I have the menu, please? | 能给我看看菜单吗？ | néng gěi wǒ kàn-kan cài-dān ma |
| Do you have local dishes? | 你们这儿有地方风味菜吗？ | nǐ-men zhèr yǒu dì-fāng fēng-wèi cài ma |
| Is there a set-price table? | 你们这儿有包桌吗？ | nǐ-men zhèr yǒu bāo-zhuō ma |
| What do you recommend? | 你能介绍些什么菜吗？ | nǐ néng jiè-shào xiē shén-me cài ma |
| I'd like ... | 我想要… | wǒ xiǎng-yào |
| Could we have a/ an ..., please? | 请给我们… | qǐng gěi wǒ-men |
| | | |
| ashtray | 一个烟灰缸 | yí-ge yān-huī-gāng |
| cup | 一个茶杯 | yí-ge chá-bēi |
| fork | 一把叉子 | yì-bǎ chā-zi |
| glass | 一个杯子 | yí-ge bēi-zi |
| knife | 一把刀子 | yì-bǎ dāo-zi |
| napkin (serviette) | 一条餐巾 | yì-tiáo cān-jīn |
| plate | 一个盘子 | yí-ge pán-zi |
| spoon | 一把勺子 | yì-bǎ sháo-zi |

上饭馆儿

| May I have some ...? | 能给我些…吗？ | néng gěi wǒ xiē ... ma |
| bread | 面包 | miàn-bāo |
| butter | 黄油 | huáng-yóu |
| green tea | 绿茶 | lǜ-chá |
| jasmine tea | 茉莉花茶 | mò-lì huā-chá |
| lemon | 柠檬 | níng-méng |
| pepper | 胡椒 | hú-jiāo |
| salt | 盐 | yán |
| seasoning | 调料 | tiáo-liào |
| soy sauce | 酱油 | jiàng-yóu |
| sugar | 糖 | táng |
| toothpicks | 牙签 | yá-qiān |
| vinegar | 醋 | cù |

## Some useful expressions for dieters and special requirements:

| I am on a special diet. | 我必须遵守特别的食谱。 | wǒ bì-xū zūn-shǒu tè-bié de shí-pǔ |
| I mustn't eat food containing ... | 我不能吃含有…的食物。 | wǒ bù néng chī hán-yǒu ... de shí-wù |
| fat/flour | 脂肪/面粉 | zhī-fáng/miàn-fěn |
| monosodium glutamate | 味精 | wèi-jīng |
| salt/sugar | 盐/糖 | yán/táng |
| I can't eat spicy food. | 我不能吃味厚的食物。 | wǒ bù néng chī wèi-hòu de shí-wù |
| Do you have ... for diabetics? | 你这儿有给糖尿病人吃的…吗？ | nǐ zhèr yǒu gěi táng-niào bìng-rén chī de ... ma |
| fruit juice | 果汁 | guǒ-zhī |
| a special menu | 特别的食物 | tè-bié de shí-wù |
| Do you have vegetarian dishes? | 你这儿有素菜吗？ | nǐ zhèr yǒu sù-cài ma |

## And ...

| I'd like some more. | 我还想要。 | wǒ hái xiǎng-yào |
| Can I have more ..., please? | 请再给我些…？ | qǐng zài gěi wǒ xiē |
| Just a small portion. | 就要一点儿。 | jiù yào yì-diǎnr |
| Nothing more, thanks. | 不要了，谢谢。 | bú yào le. xiè-xie |
| Where are the toilets? | 厕所在哪儿？ | cè-suǒ zài nǎr |

### Breakfast 早饭

Chinese breakfasts don't differ substantially from any other meal of the day. A typical breakfast might consist of some tea cakes, a plate of meat and vegetables, pickles, a kind of doughnut, rice porridge, bean-curd gruel and maybe a fish-flavoured omelet. Most tourist hotels will serve both Western and Chinese breakfasts.

| | | |
|---|---|---|
| I'd like a … breakfast, please. | 我想吃…早饭。 | wǒ xiǎng chī … zǎo-fàn |
| Chinese | 中式 | zhōng-shì |
| Western | 西式 | xī-shì |
| I'll have a/an/ some … | 我要… | wǒ yào |
| bacon and eggs | 咸肉和鸡蛋 | xián-ròu hé jī-dàn |
| boiled egg | 煮鸡蛋 | zhǔ jī-dàn |
| soft/hard | 嫩的/老的 | nèn-de/lǎo-de |
| eggs | 鸡蛋 | jī-dàn |
| fried eggs | 煎鸡蛋 | jiān jī-dàn |
| scrambled eggs | 炒鸡蛋 | chǎo jī-dàn |
| fruit juice | 果汁 | guǒ-zhī |
| grapefruit juice | 西柚汁 | xī-yòu-zhī |
| orange juice | 桔子汁 | jú-zi-zhī |
| ham and eggs | 火腿和鸡蛋 | huǒ-tuǐ hé jī-dàn |
| jam | 果酱 | guǒ-jiàng |
| marmalade | 桔子酱 | jú-zi-jiàng |
| toast | 烤面包片 | kǎo miàn-bāo piàn |
| yoghurt | 酸奶 | suān-nǎi |
| May I have some …? | 能给我些…吗。 | néng gěi wǒ xiē … ma |
| (hot) chocolate | （热）巧克力 | (rè) qiǎo-kē-lì |
| coffee | …咖啡 | … kā-fēi |
| decaffeinated | 不带咖啡因的 | bú dài kā-fēi-yīn de |
| black/with milk | 纯的/加牛奶的 | chún de/jiā niú-nǎi de |
| honey | 蜂蜜 | fēng-mì |
| milk | 牛奶 | niú-nǎi |
| cold/hot | 冷/热 | lěng/rè |
| pepper | 胡椒 | hú-jiāo |
| rolls (bread) | 小圆面包 | xiǎo yuán miàn-bāo |
| salt | 盐 | yán |
| tea | …茶 | … chá |
| with milk | 加牛奶的 | jiā niú-nǎi de |
| with lemon | 加柠檬的 | jiā níng-méng de |
| (hot) water | （热）水 | (rè) shuǐ |

**What's on the menu?** 菜单上有什么？

Most restaurants display their menus just inside the door, and some, particularly those that cater to tourists, also have English translations alongside. In places where restaurateurs have experience of foreign visitors, a set menu may be on offer, but if not, you can tell the waiter how much you would like to spend, and he will be able to suggest an appropriate menu for you.

Under the headings below you'll find lists of dishes that might be offered on a Chinese menu, with their English equivalent. You can simply show the book to the waiter. If you want some fruit, for instance, let *him* point to what's available on the list. Use pages 36 and 37 for ordering in general.

**Cooking methods** 烹调方法

If you go to China expecting to find food prepared according to Western methods, then you will probably be disappointed. You will see very few chops, steaks and chips, unless you eat in a Western restaurant. However, if you approach this ancient and fascinating cuisine with an open mind you are unlikely to come away dissatisfied.

One very important aspect of Chinese cookery is the preparation time. This will usually be longer than the actual cooking time. Most food will be chopped to a uniform size so that no one element takes any longer to cook than any other. Another important aspect is the visual one; the finished dish should satisfy the eye as well as the stomach.

The chopping of the food is in itself an art, and each food will be chopped, sliced, diced, minced or shredded differently, according to its shape, size and texture. The point of this is not only decorative but practical, to present the largest surface area for swift cooking and absorption of spices.

| barbecued | 炭火烤 | tàn-huǒ-kǎo |
| blanched (vegetables) | 焯 | chāo |
| braised | 干烧 | gān-shāo |
| crystal cooked* | 白斩 | bái-zhǎn |
| deep-fried | 焦炸 | jiāo-zhá |
| fried | 炸 | zhá |
| marinaded | 腌 | yān |
| red-braised (red-cooked)** | 红烧 | hóng-shāo |
| steamed | 清蒸 | qīng-zhēng |
| stir-fried | 爆炒 | bào-chǎo |

* Meat cooked in boiling stock for a short length of time (1-3 minutes), then taken off the heat and left to continue cooking in the cooling stock.

** Food cooked for a long time in a dark liquid, like soy sauce, giving the food a reddish-brown appearance.

## Starter (appetizers) 凉菜拼盘儿

Nibbling while sipping an aperitif is not customary in China. However, a good meal always includes a wide variety of hors d'oeuvres. Here is a selection of what you are likely to come across.

| | | |
|---|---|---|
| I'd like a starter. | 我想要一个拼盘儿 | wǒ xiǎng-yào yí-ge pīn-pánr |
| What do you recommend? | 你能介绍些什么凉菜吗？ | nǐ néng jiè-shào xiē shén-me liáng-cài ma |

| | | |
|---|---|---|
| 酱鸡 | jiàng jī | chicken in soy sauce |
| 盐水鸡 | yán-shuǐ jī | salted chicken |
| 拌鸭掌 | bàn yā-zhǎng | ducks' feet |
| 盐水鸭 | yán-shuǐ yā | salted duck |
| 糟鸭片 | zāo yā-piàn | duck slices in wine |
| 叉烧肉 | chā-shāo ròu | pork barbecue |
| 陈皮牛肉 | chén-pí niú-ròu | beef with dried orange peel |
| 酱牛肉 | jiàng niú-ròu | beef in soy sauce |
| 盐水虾 | yán-shuǐ xiā | salted prawns |
| 干贝松翠丝 | gān-bèi sōng-cuì sī | shredded scallop with spring onion |
| 田鸡腿 | tián-jī tuǐ | frogs legs |
| 炸花生米 | zhá huā-shēng-mǐ | fried peanuts |
| 酸辣泡菜 | suān-là pào-cài | sour and hot pickles |

| | |
|---|---|
| 炸鱼仔<br>(zhá yú-zǐ) | Five small fish, such as sardines or herrings, that have been slowly simmered in a mixture of garlic, onions, soy sauce, vinegar, ginger and tangerine or lemon peel. |
| 茶鸡蛋<br>(chá jī-dàn) | Tea eggs. Hard-boiled eggs that have been marinaded overnight in a tea and cane-sugar marinade. |
| 牛肉干<br>(niú-ròu-gān) | Spiced, salted beef (jerky). The beef is oven-dried and eaten at any time of day with beer or tea. |
| 鸡珍肝<br>(jī-zhēn-gān) | Giblets in soy sauce, boiled together with aniseed, soy sauce and cinnamon sticks. The Chinese are very fond of giblets which were formerly considered only a rich man's food. |
| 炸铁雀<br>(zhá tiě-què) | Marinaded sparrow, fried until crunchy. |

## Eggs 蛋类

The Chinese invest a great deal of imagination in egg preparations. Probably the best known dish is "thousand-year eggs" (松花蛋 *sōng-huā-dàn*): duck eggs buried in lime for 60 days, with a resulting cheese-like taste. Apart from serving eggs hard-boiled, they are also stir-fried or steamed.

Steamed eggs (鸡蛋羹 *jī-dàn-gēng*) look rather like a wobbly egg custard and go well with rice. The basic mixture can also be combined with "extras" like chopped or minced meat, flaked fish or vegetables. This mixture of beaten eggs, stock and seasonings is steamed, with or without the extras. And the finished article is garnished with spring onions or chives.

If steamed eggs sound a little exotic, then it's worth trying stir-fried eggs — the nearest thing to an omelet. The eggs are beaten with seasoning and thrown into a very hot pan. Just before the eggs set, a dash of rice wine is added, giving the "omelet" a very special flavour. This recipe can be combined with a variety of other ingredients like seafood, fish or vegetables.

| | |
|---|---|
| 爆腌鸡蛋<br>(bào-yān jī-dàn) | Soya eggs. Shelled hard-boiled eggs simmered in soy sauce. Served cold in quarters. |
| 芙蓉虾仁儿<br>(fū-róng xiā-rénr) | Stir-fried eggs with prawns. Prawns are stir-fried and set aside. Eggs are mixed with sesame oil, rice wine, soy sauce and stock. The egg mixture is stir-fried and the prawns are added at the last moment. |
| 芙蓉蛋<br>(fū-róng dàn) | Egg yolks mixed with monosodium glutamate and salt. Milk is added to the whites which are then beaten until stiff. The flesh of a crab is crumbled and added to the yolk mixture. This preparation is then fried and served sprinkled with coriander and accompanied by the egg whites which have also been fried. |
| 芙蓉牡蛎<br>(fū-róng mǔ-lì) | Eggs with oysters. The flesh of oysters is mixed with spring onions and soy sauce. Eggs and soy sprouts are added, and the mixture is shaped into little cakes. |

## Soup 汤类

Soup is not served at the beginning of a meal. Instead it accompanies the main course or it can be served separately at a banquet to cleanse the palate between courses. There are two basic types of soup: clear and thicker ones. The latter often constitute a meal in themselves.

| What do you recommend? | 你能介绍些什么汤吗？ | nǐ néng jiè-shào xiē shén-me tāng ma |
| --- | --- | --- |
| 蟹肉汤 | xiè-ròu tāng | crab soup |
| 扇贝汤 | shàn-bèi tāng | scallop soup |
| 鸡汤 | jī-tāng | chicken soup |
| 鸡蛋汤 | jī-dàn tāng | egg drop soup |
| 猪脚汤 | zhū-jiǎo tāng | pig's trotter (feet) soup |
| 豆腐腰花汤 | dòu-fu yāo-huā tāng | kidney and beancurd soup |
| 榨菜汤 | zhà-cài tāng | hot pickled mustard tuber soup |
| 白菜汤 | bái-cài tāng | cabbage soup |
| 黄瓜汤 | huáng-guā tāng | cucumber soup |
| 芦笋汤 | lú-sǔn tāng | asparagus soup |
| 酸辣汤 | suān-là tāng | hot and sour soup |
| 鸡汤面 | jī tāng-miàn | chicken noodle soup |
| 长寿汤面 | cháng-shòu tāng-miàn | long-life noodle soup |
| 莲蓬豌豆 | lián-peng wān-dòu | pea and lotus-seed soup |
| 竹笋汤 | zhú-sǔn tāng | bamboo shoot soup |
| 鱼肚汤 | yú-dǔ tāng | fish maw soup |
| 云片鸽蛋 | yún-piàn gē-dàn | pigeon's egg soup |
| 西红柿鸡蛋汤 | xī-hóng-shì jī-dàn tāng | tomato and egg soup |
| 什锦火锅 | shí-jǐn huǒ-guō | Chinese hot pot |

| | |
| --- | --- |
| 燕窝汤 (yàn-wō tāng) | Bird's nest soup (renowned for its delicate taste). The nests of a certain type of small swift are collected, then boiled. It's the mucus from the bird's salivary glands that flavours the soup. |
| 鱼翅汤 (yú-chì tāng) | Shark's fin soup. This rare and famous soup is prepared with shark's fin, shredded chicken and crabmeat or pork in chicken stock. |
| 馄饨 (hún-tun) | Wuntun soup. Savoury dumplings are wrapped in wafer-thin wuntun wrappers and served in a rich broth. |

**Fish and seafood** 鱼和海鲜

The Chinese eat their fish as fresh as possible, and also like to serve it whole rather than filleted as they believe this way it retains its natural juices better. For the same reason fish and seafood are steamed and quick-braised or stir-fried.

| | | |
|---|---|---|
| I'd like a fish dish. | 我想要一个鱼。 | wǒ xiǎng-yào yí-ge yú |
| What kinds of sea-food do you serve? | 你们这儿都有些什么海鲜？ | nǐ-men zhèr dōu yǒu xiē shén-me hǎi-xiān |
| What do you recommend? | 你能介绍些什么鱼类菜吗？ | nǐ néng jiè-shào xiē shén-me yú-lèi cài ma |

| | | |
|---|---|---|
| 鲍鱼 | bào-yú | abalone |
| 鳊鱼 | biān-yú | bream |
| 大黄鱼 | dà huáng-yú | large yellow croaker |
| 大马哈鱼 | dà mǎ-hā-yú | dog salmon |
| 带鱼 | dài-yú | hairtail |
| 真鲷 | zhēn-diāo | porgy |
| 鳜鱼 | guì-yú | mandarin fish |
| 鳇鱼 | huáng-yú | sturgeon |
| 鲫鱼 | jì-yú | crucian carp |
| 鲤鱼 | lǐ-yú | carp |
| 鲢鱼 | lián-yú | silver carp |
| 鲈鱼 | lú-yú | perch |
| 鳗鱼 | màn-yú | eel |
| 鮸鱼 | miǎn-yú | slate cod croaker |
| 墨斗鱼 | mò-dǒu-yú | cuttlefish |
| 鲇鱼 | nián-yú | catfish |
| 鲆鱼 | píng-yú | flounder |
| 鲭鱼 | qīng-yú | mackerel |
| 鳝鱼 | shàn-yú | yellow eel |
| 鲥鱼 | shí-yú | reeves shad |
| 鳎鱼 | tǎ-yú | sole |
| 武昌鱼 | wǔ-chāng yú | blunt snout bream |
| 鱿鱼 | yóu-yú | squid |
| 对虾 | duì-xiā | prawns |
| 龙虾 | lóng-xiā | lobster |
| 虾 | xiā | shrimp |
| 螃蟹 | páng-xiè | crab |
| 蚝 | háo | oyster |
| 扇贝 | shàn-bèi | scallop |

| | |
|---|---|
| 带子炒什锦 (dài-zi chǎo shí-jǐn) | Marinated scallops, gratineed and served with a distinctive sauce. Garnished with cucumber, celery, carrots and ham. |

核桃虾
(hé-tao xiā)

Prawns with nuts (a delicious recipe from the Guangzhou region): the prawns are prepared in a mixture of cashew nuts, peanuts, peppers, ginger and spring onions.

蘑菇鱼片
(mó-gu yú-piàn)

Fillet of fish with mushrooms: chunks of fish served with flavoured mushrooms, bamboo shoots and ginger.

蒜味鱼
(suàn-wèi yú)

Fried fish with garlic. The fish is fried whole in oil for 4 to 6 minutes. Generally served with a garlic, soy and sugar sauce.

咖喱鱼
(gā-lí yú)

Curried fish. Browned in oil for 3 to 4 minutes and served together with carrots, chillies, peppers, cabbage etc …

熏鱼
(xūn yú)

Smoked fish, accompanied by a seasoning consisting of tea, cane-sugar and a spirit; it will have previously been marinaded for half an hour in a soy-based marinade.

清蒸鱼
(qīng-zhēng yú)

Steamed black sea bream. Bream stuffed with onions and ginger, seasoned with sugar, vinegar and soy sauce, and garnished with sliced mushroom caps and bamboo shoots.

炒龙虾
(chǎo lóng-xiā)

Guangzhou-style lobster. This dish is accompanied by black beans mixed with finely-chopped pork sprinkled with garlic.

蟹肉豆腐
(xiè-ròu dòu-fu)

Fresh crabmeat mixed with soy paste, seasoned with black pepper and sprinkled with finely-chopped spring onion.

鲜贝腰花
(xiān bèi yāo-huā)

Scallops served on the half-shell with pork kidneys fried and glazed in rice wine, seasoned with ginger and spring onions.

虾饺儿
(xiā-jiǎor)

Prawn pouches. Prawns sealed into tiny omelets and steamed, then doused with a soy and chicken-stock sauce.

鱼丸子
(yú-wán-zi)

Fishballs with broccoli. Poached fishballs served with florets of broccoli in a light sauce.

干烧鲤鱼
(gān-shāo lǐ-yú)

Carp in hot sauce. Fried carp with spring onions and garlic served in a hot sauce flavoured with chilli bean sauce, yellow bean sauce, rice wine and soy sauce.

### Meat 肉类

When the Chinese talk about meat they are usually referring to pork. This is the most popularly-used meat in Chinese cookery, contrasted with veal which is almost unknown in China. You will come across beef and lamb but these are also rather rare.

| I'd like some ... | 我想要些… | wǒ xiǎng-yào xiē |
|---|---|---|
| beef | 牛肉 | niú-ròu |
| mutton | 羊肉 | yáng-ròu |
| pork | 猪肉 | zhū-ròu |

### Pork dishes 猪肉菜肴

| | |
|---|---|
| 狮子头<br>(shī-zi-tóu) | ''Lion's head'' meatballs, a favourite dish of the Chinese. Made of chopped pork, shrimp, ginger, egg, soy sauce and wine, mixed together and formed into balls. These are then browned in oil. |
| 卤猪脚<br>(lǔ zhū-jiǎo) | Steamed pig's trotters (feet). Cut into pieces, the trotters are served after having simmered three to four hours. They're deliciously enhanced with ginger and aniseed. |
| 古老肉<br>(gǔ-lǎo ròu) | Sweet and sour pork. Chunks of pork are dipped into egg yolk and then deep fried. The pork is then mixed with pineapple, sweet pepper, carrots and spring onion, and dressed with a spicy sauce. |
| 白云猪手<br>(bái-yún zhū-shǒu) | Marinaded pig's trotters (feet), served chilled after being marinaded the night before in sugar, salt and vinegar. A delicious aspic, made from the cooking broth, celery, ham and coriander, generally garnishes the platter on which the trotters are served. |
| 回锅肉<br>(huí-guō ròu) | Sichuan-style pork. The pork is cut into chunks which are browned in oil. They're served with garlic, chilli paste, soy sauce and cubes of bean curd. |
| 猪肉炖豆腐<br>(zhū-ròu dùn dòu-fu) | Braised pork with bean curd. Stir-fried minced pork braised together with yellow bean sauce, soy sauce, rice wine, chilli bean sauce, spring onion and bean curd. |
| 宫爆肉丁<br>(gōng-bào ròu-dīng) | Stir-fried cubed pork with fried peanuts. |

## Beef dishes 牛肉菜肴

卤水牛肉
(lǔ-shuǐ niú-ròu)

Beef with four spices. This dish is considered by the Chinese as one that can be eaten anytime, anywhere, and is usually served chilled or as a snack. It keeps a long time and its taste only improves. Chunks of meat are placed in a marinade of salt, aniseed, powdered ginger, candied sugar and soy sauce. Then chicken thighs, hard-boiled eggs and a slice of liver are added. It all marinades overnight.

芦笋牛肉
(lú-sǔn niú-ròu)

Jade beef. Thinly-sliced beef accompanied by sautéed asparagus.

洋葱牛肉
(yáng-cōng niú-ròu)

Beef with onions. Finely-sliced beef in a soy-sauce marinade.

西片炒牛肉
(xī-piàn chǎo niú-ròu)

Beef with celery. Finely-sliced beef is marinated in soy sauce, vinegar and egg white. The celery is cut into julienne strips which are blanched. The dish is served with a spicy sauce.

牛肉丸子
(niú-ròu wán-zi)

Meatballs. They're served as a first course. Fillets of fish are minced, then mixed with beef, spring onion and a seasoning of soy sauce and ginger.

干㸆牛肉丝
(gān biān niú-ròu-sī)

Slowly fried shredded beef with sesame seeds.

## Lamb dishes 羊肉菜肴

涮羊肉
(shuàn yáng-ròu)

Mongolian hot pot. Each diner gets a plate of thinly-sliced lamb, fresh spinach and Chinese cabbage leaves, small pieces of which are dipped into a communal pot of stock with garlic, ginger, spring onions and coriander. The cooked morsels are then dipped in a sauce. At the end transparent noodles are thrown into the stock which is drunk as a soup.

烧羊肉
(shāo yáng-ròu)

Beijing braised lamb. Cubes of lamb are first blanched then stir-fried with onions, ginger and spring onions. They are then braised in stock, rice wine, sesame paste, soy sauce and cinnamon.

葱爆羊肉
(cōng bào yáng-ròu)

Stir-fried slices of mutton with spring onion.

## Game and poultry 野味及禽类

Chicken almost rivals pork in its popularity and versatility. You'll also find duck and game. As the flavour of game is rather strong, it is usually served stewed or used as a base for soups.

| | | |
|---|---|---|
| I'd like some game. | 我想吃点儿野味。 | wǒ xiǎng chī diǎnr yě-wèi |
| What poultry dishes do you serve? | 你们有什么禽类菜肴？ | nǐ-men yǒu shén-me qín-lèi cài-yáo |
| 鹌鹑 | ān-chún | quail |
| 雏鸽 | chú gē | squab |
| 雏鸭 | chú yā | duckling |
| 鹅 | é | goose |
| 鸽子 | gē-zi | pigeon |
| 火鸡 | huǒ-jī | turkey |
| 鸡 | jī | chicken |
| 鸡胸脯 | jī xiōng-pú | chicken breast |
| 麻雀 | má-què | sparrow |
| 烧鸡 | shāo-jī | braised chicken |
| 鸭子 | yā-zi | duck |
| 野鸡 | yě-jī | pheasant |
| 野猪 | yě-zhū | wild boar |

| | |
|---|---|
| 烤鸭 (kǎo yā) | Glazed duck. This succulent dish, a Beijing speciality, is renowned the world over. A young crammed duck is coated with a salt-malt-sugar syrup, hung up for a few hours, and then half-filled with water. It is cooked for about 40 minutes. As it roasts on the outside, it is boiled on the inside. The duck is served with a sauce made from sesame oil, sugar, stock and chives. |
| 四川香酥鸭 (sìchuān xiāng-sū yā) | Crispy Sichuan duck. A duck is stuffed with ginger and spring onions, steamed and then deep fried. |
| 五香鸽子 (wǔ-xiāng gē-zi) | Five-spice braised pigeons. Pigeons are braised in a sauce of soy sauce, five spice powder, rice wine and sugar. After cooking, the pigeons are cooled and served cold. |
| 冬笋鹌鹑 (dōng-shǔn ān-chún) | Stir-fried quails. Marinaded quail stir fried with spring onions and bamboo shoots, and coated with a sauce flavoured with chicken stock and oyster sauce. |

上饭馆儿

## Chicken dishes 鸡类菜肴

| | | |
|---|---|---|
| I'd like a chicken dish. | 我想要一个鸡做的菜。 | wǒ xiǎng-yào yí-ge jī zuò de cài |
| 酱鸡 | jiàng-jī | chicken with soy sauce |
| 花菇鸡 | huā-gū jī | with wild rice-stems |
| 辣鸡 | là jī | with several spices |
| 芝麻鸡 | zhī-ma jī | with sesame seeds |
| 青椒鸡丁 | qīng-jiāo jī-dīng | with sweet peppers |
| 菠萝鸡 | bō-luó jī | with pineapple |
| 莲子鸡 | lián-zǐ jī | with lotus seeds |
| 炸酱鸡 | zhá jiàng-jī | sautéed chicken Sichuan-style |
| 熏鸡 | xūn-jī | smoked chicken |
| 咖喱鸡 | gā-lí jī | curried chicken |
| 双冬鸡 | shuāng dōng jī | Empress chicken |
| 棒棒鸡 | bàng-bàng jī | Sichuan-style cold chicken |
| 辣凤爪 | là fèng-zhuǎ | spiced chicken feet |
| 甜酸鸡 | tián-suān jī | sweet and sour chicken |

炸子鸡
(zhá zǐ-jī)

Deep-fried chicken. Chicken legs are marinaded in a soy, wine and pepper mixture. They're then dusted with flour, fried in oil and garnished with chopped shallots.

核桃炸鸡片
(hé-tao zhá jī-piàn)

Deep-fried chicken with walnuts. Chicken breasts are cut into little pieces and seasoned with wine and condiments. The chicken portions are dipped in beaten egg whites, rolled in chopped walnuts and deep-fried.

香酥鸡
(xiāng-sū jī)

Crispy chicken. Simmered chicken halves, glazed and deep-fried.

炒鸡肝
(chǎo jī-gān)

Chicken livers with ginger. Marinaded livers are fried in a sauce of ginger, soy sauce, rice wine, rice vinegar and sesame oil. This dish can be eaten hot or cold.

宫爆鸡丁
(gōng-bào jī-dīng)

Spicy chicken with peanuts. Cubed chicken and peanuts are stir-fried with chillies and then simmered for a short time in rice wine, soy sauce and stock.

### Vegetables 蔬菜

Vegetables are certainly tops in China where vegetarianism is widespread. Some vegetables are served cold but they are normally cooked first and then allowed to cool. There is no direct equivalent to the Western salad.

| | | |
|---|---|---|
| What vegetables do you recommend? | 你能介绍些什么蔬菜吗？ | nǐ néng jiè-shào xiē shén-me shū-cài ma |
| 白菜 | bái-cài | Chinese cabbage |
| 油菜 | yóu-cài | rape |
| 菠菜 | bō-cài | spinach |
| 芹菜 | qín-cài | celery |
| 韭菜 | jiǔ-cài | Chinese leeks |
| 菜花 | cài-huā | cauliflower |
| 葱 | cōng | spring onions |
| 蒜 | suàn | garlic |
| 姜 | jiāng | ginger |
| 蒜薹 | suàn-tái | garlic stems |
| 柿子椒 | shì-zi-jiāo | sweet pepper |
| 辣椒 | là-jiāo | pimento |
| 茄子 | qié-zi | aubergine (eggplant) |
| 西红柿 | xī-hóng-shì | tomatoes |
| 豆芽儿 | dòu-yár | bean sprouts |
| 竹笋 | zhú-sǔn | bamboo shoots |
| 芦笋 | lú-sǔn | asparagus |
| 藕 | ǒu | lotus root |
| 蘑菇 | mó-gu | mushrooms |
| 西葫芦 | xī-hú-lu | summer squash |
| 白萝卜 | bái luó-bo | radish (white) |
| 小萝卜 | xiǎo luó-bo | radish (red) |
| 东瓜 | dōng-guā | wax gourd |
| 南瓜 | nán-guā | pumpkin |
| 黄瓜 | huáng-guā | cucumber |
| 小黄瓜 | xiǎo huáng-guā | gherkins |
| 苦瓜 | kǔ-guā | bitter gourd |
| 芥菜 | jiè-cài | mustard plant |
| 甜玉米 | tián yù-mǐ | corn |
| 扁豆 | biǎn-dòu | French (green) beans |
| 豌豆 | wān-dòu | peas |
| 蚕豆 | cán-dòu | broad beans |
| 土豆 | tǔ-dòu | potatoes |
| 米 | mǐ | rice |
| 豆腐 | dòu-fu | bean curd |
| 花茎甘蓝 | huā-jìng gān-lán | broccoli |
| 青葱 | qīng-cōng | shallots |
| 红豆 | hóng-dòu | aduki beans |

## Vegetable dishes 蔬菜类

炒什锦蔬菜
(chǎo shí-jǐn shū-cài)

Mixed vegetables. A selection of vegetables stir-fried and then braised in soy sauce, salt and sugar.

烧茄子
(shāo qié-zi)

Braised aubergines. Deep-fried sliced aubergine with spring onions and mushrooms in a sauce of ginger, garlic, soy sauce, rice wine and chilli sauce — with a sprinkle of Sichuan pepper.

炒甘蓝
(chǎo gān-lán)

Stir-fried broccoli with ginger. Blanched broccoli florets are stir-fried with shredded ginger in sesame oil.

炒冬笋
(chǎo dōng-sǔn)

Stir-fried bamboo shoots. Sliced bamboo shoots fried in soy sauce with a little rice wine, stock and sugar.

芙蓉菜花
(fú-róng cài-huā)

Steamed cauliflower in an egg-white sauce. Cauliflower florets fried in stock and soy sauce, coated in egg-white sauce, and steamed.

甜酸新菜
(tián-suān xīn-cài)

Sweet and sour cabbage. Shredded cabbage stir fried with carrots and served in a sweet and sour sauce.

## Bean curd 豆腐类

Although bean curd has been known in the east for many thousands of years it has only recently made its debut in the west. Many people dismiss it as tasteless, but it is, in fact, a very versatile food, and delicious when imaginatively prepared.

Bean curd is made from yellow soya beans that have been ground and cooked, then pressed into a mould. It is a valuable source of protein that contains no cholesterol, and is much cheaper than steak.

Its texture is similar to that of blancmange and it is used in chunks, perhaps marinaded and stir-fried, or as a base for soups and sauces.

炸豆腐
(zhá dòu-fu)

Fried bean curd. Cakes of bean curd are fried until golden and then served in a sauce of soy sauce, chilli oil, rice wine and coriander.

## Spices and seasonings 作调和调料

The aim of the Chinese chef is to design a menu in which the sensations of sight, smell and taste are in perfect harmony. To this end he will use a wide range of seasonings, many of which were originally used for their medicinal properties.

| 葱 | cōng | spring onion |
| 丁香 | dīng-xiāng | cloves |
| 干蘑菇 | gān mó-gu | dried mushrooms |
| 桂皮 | guì-pí | cinnamon |
| 姜 | jiāng | ginger |
| 酱油 | jiàng-yóu | soy sauce |
| 辣椒 | là-jiāo | chillies |
| 蒜 | suàn | garlic |
| 味精 | wèi-jīng | monosodium glutamate |
| 香菜 | xiāng-cài | coriander |
| 小茴香 | xiǎo huí-xiāng | fennel seeds |

大料
(dà-liào)
Chinese aniseed (star anise). The fruit of a Chinese evergreen that opens up into a star shape and contains one very pungent seed, faintly reminiscent of aniseed.

陈皮
(chén-pí)
Citrus peel. Dried lemon, orange or even tangerine peel which imparts a strong citrus flavour.

蚝油
(háo-yóu)
Oyster sauce. Oyster concentrate in soy sauce.

黄酱
(huáng-jiàng)
Yellow bean sauce. An aromatic sauce of yellow beans fermented with flour and salt.

辣酱油
(là jiàng-yóu)
Chilli bean sauce. A hot and spicy sauce made from chillies and soya beans.

五香粉
(wǔ-xiāng fěn)
Five-spice powder. A mixture of aniseed, fennel, cinnamon, cloves and Sichuan pepper.

虾酱
(xiā-jiàng)
Shrimp sauce. A very savoury golden sauce.

香油
(xiāng-yóu)
Sesame oil. A pungent oil made from toasted sesame seeds.

芝麻酱
(zhī-ma jiàng)
Sesame paste. Sesame seeds ground into a creamy paste.

**Rice** 饭类

China is far and away the world's foremost producer of rice, the staple of two-thirds of the country's population. It is considered such a precious foodstuff that the Chinese would never leave even a few grains at the bottom of their bowl.

Rice growing occupies a major share of Chinese agriculture and demands important irrigational and hoeing-up care. After soaking the rice grain 24 hours in water, the rice is sown broadcast in a region of good earth, and takes root in three to four days. Then the plant is trimmed back when it reaches about a foot in height. As soon as the grain is planted, water is slowly let into the paddy and remains until the rice buds. Irrigation is then regulated to permit the maturing of the shaft. The harvest takes place, depending on the region, anywhere from four to five months after the seeding, which allows a new seeding and hence two crops annually.

Here are some dishes found in China which use a rice base:

| | |
|---|---|
| 炒饭<br>(chǎo fàn) | Fried rice. Gammon, pork and chicken are diced, then mixed with rice, peas, marinaded shrimp and an omelet cut into thin strips, served with soy sauce. This dish is usually prepared ahead of time, and reheated before serving. |
| 珍珠肉丸<br>(zhēn-zhū ròu-wán) | "Pearl meatballs". Made of prawns, spring onions, pork, eggs, and spices, mixed together and covered with sticky rice, steamed and served lukewarm. |
| 菠菜花生炒饭<br>(bō-cài huā-shēng chǎo fàn) | Jade rice. This dish is accompanied by chopped spinach, diced ham and finely chopped garlic. |
| 江米粥<br>(jiāng-mǐ zhōu) | Sticky rice. Boiled rice porridge often eaten for breakfast. |
| 米粉肉<br>(mí-fěn-ròu) | Steamed pork in ground rice. Marinaded cubed pork steamed, and served mixed with heated ground rice. |

**Noodles** 面条及粉丝菜肴

The best known of Chinese noodles (which, together with rice, are staples in the Chinese diet) are *fěn-sī*, also called Chinese vermicelli or cellophane noodles. *Fěn-sī* are made from mung bean starch. Noodles are also made from wheat and rice flour. They absorb the aroma of the seasoning and spices cooked with them perfectly.

The Chinese are very fond of ravioli which they eat steamed, boiled, lightly fried or in soup.

| | |
|---|---|
| 蚂蚁上树<br>(mǎ-yǐ shàng shù) | ''Ants climbing the tree''. Braised *fěn-sī* coated with grains of fried minced meat. |
| 凉拌粉丝<br>(liáng-bàn fěn-<br>sī) | Noodle salad. An ''Imperial sauce'' made of soy sauce, spring onion, slivers of ginger, sesame oil, lemon juice and pimento paste which accompanies the noodles as a garnish to chicken, ham, soy sprouts, peas and bamboo shoots. |
| 粉丝炒羊肉<br>(fěn-sī chǎo yáng-<br>ròu) | Lamb with *fěn-sī*. 2-inch lengths of *fěn-sī* served with turnips, lamb, ginger, leeks and a seasoning of soy sauce, alcohol and candied sugar. |
| 菊花芙蓉块<br>(jú-huā fú-róng<br>kuài) | ''Chrysanthemum flowers''. Finely chopped prawns mixed with egg white and pork fat. Square patties are formed and covered with sliced *fěn-sī*. This is served with spring carrots and some pimento sauce. |
| 猪肉炒面<br>(zhū-ròu chǎo miàn) | Pork with noodles. Egg noodles are served with pork cut into strips, cabbage, carrots, celery and chicken broth. |
| 什锦炒面<br>(shí-jǐn chǎo miàn) | Chow mein. Boiled egg noodles, fried and then combined with shredded meat and chopped vegetables. |
| 阳春面<br>(yáng-chūn miàn) | A light chicken broth Shanghai-style, with vegetables and noodles. |
| 鸡丝面<br>(jī-sī miàn) | Shredded chicken with noodles in stock. |

### Fruit 水果

Thanks to its geographical location, extending from the Siberian steppes in the north to tropical jungles in the south, China has an incomparable range of fruits to offer. If you can, try an Ice Mountain fruit salad. It is a simple but effective arrangement of a variety of fresh fruit, peeled and sliced, and served on a bed of crushed ice.

| Do you have any fruit? | 你们这儿有水果吗？ | nǐ-men zhèr yǒu shuǐ-guǒ ma |
| I'd like a (fresh) fruit salad. | 我想要一个（鲜）什锦水果。 | wǒ xiǎng-yào yí-ge (xiān) shí-jǐn shuǐ-guǒ |
| 荸荠 | bí-qi | water chestnuts |
| 槟榔 | bīng-lang | areca nuts, betel nuts |
| 菠萝 | bō-luó | pineapple |
| （干）橄榄 | (gān) gǎn-lǎn | (dried) olives |
| 甘蔗 | gān-zhe | sugar cane |
| 桔子 | jú-zi | tangerine |
| 核桃 | hé-tao | walnuts |
| 柑子 | gān-zi | orange |
| 梨 | lí | pear |
| 栗子 | lì-zi | chestnuts |
| 李子 | lǐ-zi | plum |
| 荔枝 | lì-zhī | lychees |
| 莲子 | lián-zǐ | lotus seeds |
| 龙眼 | lóng-yǎn | longan |
| 芒果 | máng-guǒ | mango |
| 梅子 | méi-zi | prune |
| 木莓 | mù-méi | raspberries |
| 柠檬 | níng-méng | lemon |
| 枇杷 | pí-pa | loquat |
| 苹果 | píng-guǒ | apple |
| 葡萄 | pú-táo | grapes |
| 桑葚儿 | sāng-rènr | mulberries |
| 石榴 | shí-liù | pomegranate |
| 柿子 | shì-zi | persimmon |
| 桃子 | táo-zi | peach |
| 甜瓜 | tián-guā | sweet melon |
| 无花果 | wú-huā-guǒ | figs |
| 西瓜 | xī-guā | watermelon |
| 香蕉 | xiāng-jiāo | banana |
| 杏 | xìng | apricot |
| 草莓 | cǎo-méi | strawberry |
| 椰子 | yē-zi | coconut |
| 樱桃 | yīng-táo | cherries |
| 枣 | zǎo | Chinese dates |

### Dessert 糕点甜食

Desserts are rarely served in China except at banquets, where they come as very sweet, minor dishes interposed between savouries. If you enjoy something sweet between meals, try some caramel walnuts or chunks of banana in toffee.

If you are invited to dinner in a Chinese home, you will probably be offered seasonal fruit such as oranges, kumquats, longans, cherries or lychees.

| | | |
|---|---|---|
| I'd like a dessert, please. | 我想要一个甜食。 | wǒ xiǎng-yào yí-ge tián-shí |
| What do you recommend? | 你能介绍些什么甜食吗？ | nǐ néng jiè-shào xiē shén-me tián-shí ma |
| Something light, please. | 要清口点儿的。 | yào qīng-kǒu diǎnr de |
| Just a small portion, please. | 就要一点儿。 | jiù yào yì-diǎnr |
| Nothing more, thanks. | 不要了，谢谢。 | bú yào le. xiè-xie |
| 冰镇果羹 | bīng-zhèn guǒ-gēng | fruit jelly |
| 菠萝醪糟 | bō-luó láo-zāo | pineapples marinaded in rice wine |
| 什锦瓜瓶 | shí-jǐn guā-píng | water melon with fruit |
| 西米桔羹 | xī-mǐ jú-gēng | hot orange cakes |
| 拔丝苹果 | bá-sī píng-guǒ | caramelized apple |
| 八宝饭 | bā-bǎo-fàn | rice cake with eight treasures |
| 杏仁儿酥 | xìng-rénr sū | almond biscuits (cookies) |
| 杏仁儿豆腐 | xìng-rénr dòu-fu | almond flavoured custard |
| 芝麻糊 | zhī-ma hú | sesame cream |
| 杏仁儿糊 | xìng-rénr hú | almond cream |
| 花生糊 | huā-shēng hú | peanut cream |
| 千层糕 | qiān-céng gāo | thousand layer cake |
| 甜蛋羹 | tián dàn-gēng | egg custard |
| 冰糖蒸梨 | bīng-táng zhēng lí | steamed pears |
| 莲子羹 | lián-zǐ gēng | lotus root custard |
| 枣泥饼 | zǎo-ní bǐng | date paste pancakes |
| 果子羹 | lì-zi-gēn | chestnuts in jelly |
| 元宵 | yuán-xiāo | sweet rice dumplings |

## Drinks 酒类

As a general rule, the Chinese take neither aperitifs before a meal nor spirits after it. The powerful *máo-tái*, a wheat-and-sugarcane-based spirit, is widely drunk at banquets and when toasts are proposed. The uninitiated should beware of its punch. You will also come across *shào-xīng*, a red rice-wine served hot in tiny cups. Regional wines are generally rather sweet, and the white wines are often reminiscent of certain resinated wines encountered in southern Europe. The inexpensive local sparkling wines tend to be very sweet.

Beer is very similar to Western brews. The most popular brand comes from the city of Qingdao and is known by that city's old-style transliterated name, Tsingtao.

China imports alcohol for its foreign residents, and home-brewed whisky, gin and brandy are also available. In certain regions, spirits are produced in which snakes, lizards and stag's antlers have been steeped. These brews are credited with special, often medical, properties.

| | | |
|---|---|---|
| I don't drink alcohol. | 我不喝酒。 | wǒ bù hē jiǔ |
| I'd like a *máo-tái* | 我想要一小杯茅台。 | wǒ xiǎng-yào yì xiǎo bēi máo-tái |
| aperitif | 开胃酒 | kāi-wèi-jiǔ |
| brandy | 白兰地 | bái-lán-dì |
| gin | 金酒 | jīn-jiǔ |
| gin and tonic | 金酒和奎宁水 | jīn-jiǔ hé kuí-níng-shuǐ |
| sherry | 雪利酒 | xuě-lì jiǔ |
| vermouth | 味美思 | wèi-měi-sī |
| vodka | 伏特加 | fú-tè-jiā |
| whisky | 威士忌 | wēi-shì-jì |
| neat (straight) | 纯的 | chún de |
| on the rocks | 加冰块 | jiā bīng-kuài |

干杯！
gān-bēi
YOUR HEALTH!/ CHEERS!

| Do you have ... beer? | 你这儿有…啤酒吗？ | nǐ zhèr yǒu ... pí-jiǔ ma |
| bottled | 瓶装的 | píng-zhuāng de |
| draught | 散装的 | sǎn-zhuāng de |
| imported | 进口的 | jìn-kǒu de |
| light/dark | 清爽型/黑 | qīng-shuǎng xíng/hēi |
| I'd like (a) ... | 我想要… | wǒ xiǎng-yào |
| half a bottle | 半瓶 | bàn píng |
| half a glass | 半杯 | bàn bēi |
| litre | 一升 | yì-shēng |
| Bring me another ..., please. | 请再拿…来。 | qǐng zài ná ... lái |
| glass/bottle | 一杯/一瓶 | yì bēi/yì píng |
| I'd like a bottle of wine. | 我想要一瓶葡萄酒。 | wǒ xiǎng-yào yì-píng pú-táo-jiǔ |
| What's the name of this wine? | 这是什么葡萄酒？ | zhè shì shén-me pú-táo-jiǔ |
| Where does this wine come from? | 这葡萄酒是哪儿出产的？ | zhè pú-táo-jiǔ shì nǎr chū-chǎn de |

| red | 红 | hóng |
| dry white/sweet white | 干白/甜白 | gān bái/tián bái |
| sparkling | 带气的 | dài qì de |

## Tea 茶

The Chinese drink tea all day long. The history of tea-drinking in China goes back to the year 2737 B.C. and the reign of Shen Nong. This emperor treated some of his ailments with herbal remedies. One of these was tea, which is now claimed to contain 300 chemical constituents, many of them of acknowledged medical value. In A.D. 730, in the Tang dynasty, Lu Yu wrote a "Book of Tea" in which he described the cultivation of the shrub and how to prepare an infusion from its leaves. The beverage was exported to Japan in the thirteenth century and was known in England by the seventeenth. Today, as many as 250 varieties can be distinguished. The Chinese obtain the delicious aroma of their tea by leaving it in the proximity of aromatic plants for some time.

Chinese tea is taken without sugar or milk. Among the varieties available are black (fermented) tea, fragrant green tea, tea scented with jasmine or magnolia, or blends of flowers, and slightly fermented oolong tea.

Every national minority has its own special way of making tea. The Tibetans, for instance, boil it in a pot with salt. Special occasions, such as a visit by a long-absent friend, are celebrated by adding yak's milk to the tea which is served with great ceremony. Mongolian herdsmen of the northern steppes and deserts boil tea leaves together with cow's or goat's milk and add salt. The Moslem Huis welcome their guests with hot tea served in covered cups to which brown sugar and dates are added to bring good luck.

| I'd like some … | 我想要一杯… | wǒ xiǎng-yào yì-bēi |
| tea | 茶 | chá |
| green tea | 绿茶 | lù-chá |
| jasmine tea | 茉莉花茶 | mò-lì huā-chá |
| oolong tea | 乌龙茶 | wū-lóng chá |

## Nonalcoholic drinks 饮料

| apple juice | 苹果汁 | píng-guǒ zhī |
| (hot) chocolate | （热）巧克力 | (rè) qiǎo-kè-lì |
| coffee | 咖啡 | kā-fēi |
| black | 纯的 | chún de |
| with cream | 加奶油的 | jiā nǎi-yóu de |
| with milk | 加牛奶的 | jiā niú-nǎi de |
| decaffeinated | 不带咖啡因的 | bú dài kā-fēi-yīn de |
| fruit juice | 果汁 | guǒ-zhī |
| grapefruit juice | 西柚汁 | xī-yòu-zhī |
| iced tea | 冰茶 | bīng-chá |
| lemon juice | 柠檬汁 | níng-méng zhī |
| lemonade | 柠檬汽水 | níng-méng qì-shuǐ |
| milk | 牛奶 | niú-nǎi |
| mineral water | 矿泉水 | kuàng-quán-shuǐ |
| fizzy | 带汽的 | dài qì de |
| still | 不带汽的 | bú dài qì de |
| orange juice | 桔子汁 | jú-zi-zhī |
| orangeade | 桔子汽水 | jú-zi qì-shuǐ |
| tomato juice | 西红柿汁 | xī-hóng-shì-zhī |
| tonic water | 奎宁水 | kuí-níng shuǐ |

### Complaints 有意见

| There is a plate/ glass missing. | 少一个盘子/杯子。 | shǎo yí-ge pán-zi/ bēi-zi |
| I have no knife/ fork/spoon. | 我没有刀子/叉子/ 勺子。 | wǒ méi yǒu dāo-zi/ chā-zi/sháo-zi |
| I have no chopsticks. | 我没有筷子。 | wǒ méi yǒu kuài-zi |
| That's not what I ordered. | 这不是我点的。 | zhè bú shì wǒ diǎn de |
| I asked for … | 我要的是… | wǒ yào de shì |
| There must be some mistake. | 一定是搞错了。 | yí-dìng shì gǎo cuò le |
| May I change this? | 可以换这个吗？ | kě-yǐ huàn zhè-ge ma |
| I asked for a small plate (for the child). | 我要的是小盘的（给这 个孩子吃的）。 | wǒ yào de shì xiǎo-pán de (gěi zhè-ge hái-zi chī de) |
| The meat is … | 这肉… | zhè ròu |
| underdone | 没熟 | méi shóu |
| overdone | 火太过了 | huǒ tài guò le |
| I'm afraid this is too … for me. | 我觉得这菜太…了。 | wǒ jué-de zhè cài tài … le |
| bitter | 苦 | kǔ |
| oily | 油腻 | yóu-nì |
| salty | 咸 | xián |
| spicy (hot) | 辣 | là |
| sweet | 甜 | tián |
| I don't like this. | 我不喜欢这个。 | wǒ bù xǐ-huan zhè-ge |
| This dish is cold. | 这个菜是凉的。 | zhè-ge cài shì liáng de |
| I don't think this is fresh. | 我觉得这不新鲜。 | wǒ jué-de zhè bù xīn-xiān |
| There is something wrong with this dish. | 这个菜味不对。 | zhè ge cài wèi bú duì |
| What's taking so long? | 做什么需要这么长的 时间？ | zuò shén-me xū-yào zhè-me cháng de shí-jiān |
| Have you forgotten our drinks? | 你忘了我们要的饮料 了吧？ | nǐ wàng-le wǒ-men yào de yǐn-liào le ba |
| This isn't clean. | 这不干净。 | zhè bù gān-jìng |
| Would you ask the manager to come over? | 请叫你们经理来。 | qǐng jiào nǐ-men jīng-lǐ lái |

### The bill (check) 帐单

Even if you have enjoyed your meal very much, you should not attempt to press a tip on the waiter, as this custom is strongly discouraged in the People's Republic. If, at a special dinner or banquet, you would like to express your satisfaction with the meal, you can invite the chef over for a drink and offer him a toast.

| I'd like to pay. | 我想付钱。 | wǒ xiǎng fù qián |
| We'd like to pay separately. | 我们想各付各的。 | wǒ-men xiǎng gè fù gè de |
| May I have the bill (check), please? | 请给我帐单。 | qǐng gěi wǒ zhàng-dān |
| I think there's a mistake in the bill. | 这个帐单好象有错吧。 | zhè-ge zhàng-dān hǎo-xiàng yǒu cuò ba |
| What is this amount for? | 这项是付什么的钱？ | zhè xiàng shì fù shén-me de qián |
| Is everything included? | 都包括了吗？ | dōu bāo-kuò le ma |
| Do you accept traveller's cheques? | 你们这儿收旅行支票吗？ | nǐ-men zhèr shōu lǚ-xíng zhī-piào ma |
| Can I pay with this credit card? | 我能用这个信用卡付款吗？ | wǒ néng yòng zhè-ge xìn-yòng-kǎ fù-kuǎn ma |
| That was a very good meal. | 这顿饭吃得很好。 | zhè dùn fàn chī-de hěn hǎo |
| We enjoyed it, thank you. | 我们吃得很满意，谢谢。 | wǒ-men chī-de hěn mǎn-yì. xiè-xie |
| Where should we pay? | 我们该在哪儿付钱？ | wǒ-men gāi zài nǎr fù qián |

### Snacks — picnic 小吃－野餐

Snacks can be found in every city and all over the city. The Chinese are inveterate snackers and the roadside stalls selling steamed savoury buns and other "fast food" have been in business for a very long time. If you're thirsty you can have a beer from a corner beer shop, and at the same time maybe try a small dish of sliced kidneys or a spring roll.

If you're in the South then it's worth having at least one meal in a dim sum (点心) restaurant. In the North you would go to a "small snack" (小吃) restaurant. This is where people meet, from mid-morning until mid-afternoon, to catch up on the latest news or even to discuss business. These restaurants are usually large, noisy and friendly. In dim sum restaurants waiters course around the room pushing trolleys loaded down with delicious bite-sized snacks, and you simply stop them and take your pick. In the North, more prosaically, you pick your snacks up at the counter. The food is normally quite light and non-greasy, and usually steamed rather than fried.

| I'll have ..., please. | 我要… | wǒ yào |
| one of those | 一个那的 | yí-ge nà zhǒng de |
| some of those | 几个那种的 | jǐ-ge nà zhǒng de |

| 炒面条 (chǎo miàn-tiáo) | Fried noodles. |
| 汤面 (tāng miàn) | Noodles tossed in gravy or soup. |
| 锅贴 (guō-tiē) | Parcels of thin pastry stuffed with a meat filling, or, in the south, with seafood. They are crispy at the bottom with a steamed filling. |
| 元宵 (yuán-xiāo) | Tiny glutinous rice-flour balls with sweet fillings, usually served in soup. |
| 烧卖 (shāo-mai) | Small open-topped dumplings that are stuffed with meat and steamed. |
| 春卷儿 (chūn-juǎnr) | Spring rolls. A mixture of vegetables and meat, including water chestnuts, bean sprouts and spring onions, which is stir-fried and then wrapped in a thin pancake and deep-fried. |
| 包子 (bāo-zi) | Steamed savoury buns. Meat and gravy are sealed in a yeast dough and then steamed. |
| 江米饭 (jiāng-mǐ fàn) | Glutinous rice steamed with various dried fruit. |

Here's a list of food and drink that might be useful if you want to organise a picnic.

| Please give me a/an/some ... | 请给我拿… | qǐng gěi wǒ ná |
|---|---|---|
| apples | 几个苹果 | jǐ-ge píng-guǒ |
| bananas | 几个香蕉 | jǐ-ge xiāng-jiāo |
| biscuits | 一包饼干 | yì-bāo bǐng-gān |
| bottle opener | 一个开瓶器 | yí-ge kāi-píng-qì |
| cake | 一个蛋糕 | yí-ge dàn-gāo |
| can opener | 一个开罐器 | yí-ge kāi-guàn-qì |
| chocolate bar | 一块巧克力 | yí-kuài qiǎo-kè-lì |
| coffee | 一筒咖啡 | yì-tǒng kā-fēi |
| cold cuts | 一些熟肉 | yì-xiē shóu-ròu |
| cookies (Am.) | 一包饼干 | yì-bāo bǐng-gān |
| cucumbers | 几条黄瓜 | jǐ tiáo huáng-guā |
| eggs | 几个鸡蛋 | jǐ-ge jī-dàn |
| ham | 一些火腿 | yì-xiē huǒ-tuǐ |
| ice cream | 几个冰淇淋 | jǐ-ge bīng-qí-lín |
| lemons | 几个柠檬 | jǐ-ge níng-méng |
| matches | 几盒火柴 | jǐ-hé huǒ-chái |
| milk | 一瓶牛奶 | yì-píng niú-nǎi |
| mustard | 一些芥末 | yì-xiē jiè-mo |
| oranges | 几个柑子 | jǐ-ge gān-zi |
| (paper) napkins | 一打（纸）餐巾 | yì-dá (zhǐ) cān-jīn |
| pepper | 一些胡椒 | yì-xiē hú-jiāo |
| potatoes | 几个土豆 | jǐ-ge tǔ-dòu |
| rolls (bread) | 几个小圆面包 | jǐ-ge xiǎo yuán miàn-bāo |
| salt | 一些盐 | yì-xiē yán |
| sandwiches | 几个三明治 | jǐ-ge sān-míng-zhì |
| soft drink | 一瓶不带酒精的饮料 | yì-píng bú dài jiǔ-jīng de yǐn-liào |
| soy sauce | 一瓶酱油 | yì-píng jiàng-yóu |
| sugar | 一包糖 | yì-bāo táng |
| tea | 一包茶叶 | yì-bāo chá-yè |
| tin opener | 一个开罐器 | yí-ge kāi-guàn-qì |
| tomatoes | 几个西红柿 | jǐ-ge xī-hóng-shì |
| wine | 一瓶葡萄酒 | yì-píng pú-táo-jiǔ |
| yoghurt | 一瓶酸奶 | yì-píng suān-nǎi |

| bottle | 瓶 | píng |
|---|---|---|
| box | 盒 | hé |
| carton | 箱 | xiāng |
| jar | 筒 | tǒng |
| packet | 包 | bāo |

# Travelling around

## Plane 飞机

| Is there a flight to Beijing? | 有去北京的航班吗？ | yǒu qù běijīng de háng-bān ma |
| Is it a direct flight? | 这是直达的航班吗？ | zhè shì zhí-dá de háng-bān ma |
| When's the next flight to Shanghai? | 下一班去上海的航班什么时间起飞？ | xià yì-bān qù shànghǎi de háng-bān shén-me shí-jiān qǐ-fēi |
| Is there a connection to Guangzhou? | 有去广州的联程航班吗？ | yǒu qù guǎngzhōu de lián-chéng háng-bān ma |
| I'd like a ticket to Nanjing. | 我想买一张去南京的机票。 | wǒ xiǎng mǎi yì-zhāng qù nánjīng de jī-piào |
| single (one-way) | 单程票 | dān-chéng piào |
| return (roundtrip) | 往返票 | wǎng-fǎn piào |
| What time do we take off? | 什么时间起飞？ | shén-me shí-jiān qǐ-fēi |
| What time do I have to check in? | 我什么时间到机场办登机手续？ | wǒ shén-me shí-jiān dào jī-chǎng bàn dēng-jī shǒu-xù |
| Is there a bus to the airport? | 有去机场的班车吗？ | yǒu qù jī-chǎng de bān-chē ma |
| What's the flight number? | 航班班次是多少？ | háng-bān bān-cì shì duō-shao |
| What time do we arrive? | 我们什么时间到？ | wǒ-men shén-me shí-jiān dào |
| I'd like to … my reservation on flight no. 123. | 我想…我在一二三号航班的预定。 | wǒ xiǎng … wǒ zài 123 hào háng-bān de yù-dìng |
| cancel | 取消 | qǔ-xiāo |
| change | 更换 | gēng-huàn |
| confirm | 确认 | què-rèn |
| What's the rate for excess baggage? | 超重的行李怎么计价？ | chāo-zhòng de xíng-li zěn-me jì-jià |

| 到达 | 出发 | 候机室 |
| dào-dá | chū-fā | hòu-jī-shì |
| ARRIVAL | DEPARTURE | WAITING ROOM |

旅行

## Trains 火车

The train system is well developed in China, however, independent train travel is not easy. Spur-of-the-moment journeys are almost impossible, as tickets can rarely be bought immediately before departure. All the seats will have been sold out, and the train will be full. Tickets are normally bought well in advance.

There are a number of possibilities when buying a ticket. You can choose between hard and soft seating, and, on longer journeys, between hard and soft sleeping. In practice, the choice is more limited as the Chinese prefer that foreign visitors travel "soft", together with the high-ranking Chinese. The main difference between the two categories lies, as the names suggest, in the degree of comfort. But price is also an important factor — soft sleeping can cost almost as much as an airline seat.

| 慢车<br>màn-chē<br>SLOW TRAIN | 快车<br>kuài-chē<br>FAST TRAIN | 特快车<br>tè-kuài-chē<br>EXPRESS TRAIN |
| --- | --- | --- |

There are three types of train in terms of speed. The first are local trains, stopping at all the stations; these travel quite regularly. The second type — fast trains — stop only at larger towns and cities. Express trains are generally long-distance and connect major cities as well as providing the international service.

All trains are numbered and are referred to primarily by this number. However, both number and destination are mentioned in loudspeaker announcements.

Although independent travel is possible, it is extremely complicated and time-consuming to make the necessary arrangements. You would be advised to take advantage of the service provided by CITS.

## To the railway station 去火车站

| Where's the railway station? | 火车站在哪儿？ | huǒ-chē-zhàn zài nǎr |
| I'd like a taxi. | 我想要一辆出租汽车。 | wǒ xiǎng yào yí-liàng chū-zū qì-chē |
| Please take me to the railway station. | 请送我去火车站。 | qǐng sòng wǒ qù huǒ-chē-zhàn |
| What's the fare? | 车费多少？ | chē-fèi duō-shao |
| Can I have a receipt, please? | 请开一张收据。 | qǐng kāi yì-zhāng shōu-jù |

| 入口 | 出口 | 至站台 |
|------|------|--------|
| rù-kǒu | chū-kǒu | zhì zhàn-tái |
| ENTRANCE | EXIT | TO THE PLATFORMS |

## Where's the …? …在哪儿？

| Where is/are the …? | …在哪儿？ | … zài nǎr |
| information office | 问讯处 | wèn-xùn-chù |
| left-luggage office (baggage check) | 行李寄存处 | xíng-li jì-cún-chù |
| lost property (lost-and-found) office | 失物招领处 | shī-wù zhāo-lǐng-chù |
| newsstand | 售报亭 | shòu-bào-tíng |
| platform 7 | 七号站台 | qī hào zhàn-tái |
| restaurant | 饭馆儿 | fàn-guǎnr |
| ticket office | 售票处 | shòu-piào-chù |
| waiting room | 候车室 | hòu-chē-shì |
| Where are the toilets? | 厕所在哪儿？ | cè-suǒ zài nǎr |

| 请勿吸烟 |
|---------|
| qǐng wù xī-yān |
| NO SMOKING |

Smokers beware: on 1st June 1987 the whole of Beijing station officially became a non-smoking area.

**Inquiries** 问讯

When making inquiries about departure and arrival times of a particular train, refer to it by its number as well as its destination.

| | | |
|---|---|---|
| When is the … train to Tianjin? | 去天津的…列车几点开车? | qù tiānjīn de … liè-chē jǐ diǎn kāi chē |
| last/next | 最后一班/下一班 | zuì-hòu yì-bān/xià yì-bān |
| What time does train no. 19 leave? | 十九次列车什么时间开车? | 19 cì liè-chē shén-me shí-jiān kāi chē |
| What's the fare to Shanghai? | 去上海的票价是多少? | qù shànghǎi de piào-jià shì duō-shao |
| Is it an express train? | 是特快列车吗? | shì tè-kuài liè-chē ma |
| Do I have to change trains? | 我需要换车吗? | wǒ xū-yào huàn chē ma |
| How long will the train stop in Suzhou? | 列车在苏州停多长时间? | liè-chē zài sūzhōu tíng duō-cháng shí-jiān |
| Is there enough time to change? | 有足够的时间换车吗? | yǒu zú-gòu de shí-jiān huàn chē ma |
| Is the train running on time? | 列车正点吗? | liè-chē zhèng-diǎn ma |
| What time does the train arrive in Nanjing? | 列车什么时间到南京? | liè-chē shén-me shí-jiān dào nánjīng |
| Is there a … on the train? | 车上有…吗? | chē-shang yǒu … ma |
| dining-car sleeping-car | 餐车 卧铺车厢 | cān-chē wò-pù chē-xiāng |
| Does the train stop in Jinan? | 列车在济南停吗? | liè-chē zài jǐnán tíng ma |
| What platform does train no. 16 from Guangzhou arrive at? | 从广州来的十六次列车在几号站台停? | cóng guǎngzhōu lái de 16 cì liè-chē zài jǐ hào zhàn-tái tíng |
| What platform does the train to Beijing leave from? | 去北京的列车从哪个站台发车? | qù běi-jīng de liè-chē cóng nǎ-ge zhàn-tái fā chē |
| I'd like to buy a time-table. | 我想买一本列车时刻表。 | wǒ xiǎng mǎi yì-běn liè-chē shí-kè-biǎo |

| | |
|---|---|
| 对不起，这次车的座位买完了。 | I'm sorry, there are no seats left on that train. |
| …次列车客满。 | Train no. … is full. |
| 这是直达列车。 | It's a through train. |
| 你得在…换车。 | You have to change at … |
| 在…下车后换乘慢车。 | Change at … and get a local train. |
| 七号站台在… | Platform 7 is … |
| 那边/左边/右边 | over there/ on the left/ on the right |
| 二次列车将于八号站台发车。 | Train no. 2 will leave from platform 8. |
| 列车将晚点…分钟。 | There will be a delay of … minutes. |

## Tickets 车票

You can only buy single (one-way) tickets for the trains. If you should want to break your journey, go to the ticket office and enquire if there are any free seats on the train you would like to continue on.

| | | |
|---|---|---|
| I want a ticket to Nanjing. | 我要一张去南京的车票。 | wǒ yào yì-zhāng qù nánjīng de chē-piào |
| hard seating | 硬座 | yìng-zuò |
| soft seating | 软座 | ruǎn-zuò |
| hard sleeping | 硬卧 | yìng-wò |
| soft sleeping | 软卧 | ruǎn-wò |
| Is it cheaper for the child? | 儿童票便宜吗？ | ér-tóng-piào pián-yi ma |
| I want a … | 我要一个… | wǒ yào yí-ge |
| seat (by the window) | （靠窗的）座位 | (kào chuāng de) zuò-wèi |
| berth in the sleeping car | 卧铺 | wò-pù |
| upper berth | 上铺 | shàng-pù |
| middle berth | 中铺 | zhōng-pù |
| lower berth | 下铺 | xià-pù |

## All aboard 开车啦

Tickets are checked on entering and leaving the station, but there are also occasional checks on board.

| | | |
|---|---|---|
| Is this the platform for the train to Shanghai? | 去上海是在这个站台上车吗？ | qù shànghǎi shì zài zhèi-gè zhàn-tái shàng chē ma |
| Is this the train to Jinan? | 这是去济南的列车吗？ | zhè shì qù jǐnán de liè-chē ma |
| Excuse me. May I get past? | 对不起，我可以过去吗？ | duì-bu-qǐ. wǒ kě-yǐ guò qu ma |
| Is this seat taken? | 这个座位有人吗？ | zhèi-ge zuò-wèi yǒu rén ma |
| I think that's my seat. | 这是我的座位吧。 | zhè shì wǒ de zuò-wèi ba |
| Would you let me know before we get to Suzhou? | 到苏州前请告诉我好吗？ | dào sūzhōu qián qǐng gào-su wǒ hǎo ma |
| What station is this? | 这是哪站？ | zhè shì něi zhàn |
| How long does the train stop here? | 列车在这儿停多长时间？ | liè-chē zài zhèr tíng duō-cháng shí-jiān |
| When do we get to Suzhou? | 列车什么时间到苏州？ | liè-chē shén-me shí-jiān dào sūzhōu |

| 硬席 | 软席 |
|---|---|
| (yìng-xí) | (ruǎn-xí) |
| HARD SEATS | SOFT SEATS |

## Sleeping 卧铺

| | | |
|---|---|---|
| Are there any free berths in the sleeping car? | 请问还有空着的卧铺吗？ | qǐng wèn hái yǒu kōng-zhe de wò-pù ma |
| Where's the sleeping car? | 卧铺车厢在哪儿？ | wò-pù chē-xiāng zài nǎr |
| Where's my berth? | 我的卧铺在哪儿？ | wǒ de wò-pù zài nǎr |
| I'd like a lower berth. | 我想要下铺。 | wǒ xiǎng yào xià-pù |
| Would you make up our berths? | 请把我们的卧铺整理一下。 | qǐng bǎ wǒ-men de wò-pù zhěng-lǐ yí xià |
| Would you wake me at 7 o'clock? | 请在七点叫醒我。 | qǐng zài 7 diǎn jiào-xǐng wǒ |

## Eating 就餐

All long-distance trains have dining-cars in which you will be able to enjoy Chinese cuisine patterned after that which you would find in a good restaurant in Guangzhou or Beijing.

The dining-car is only open at meal times, but there is also often a snack bar trolley which supplies hot lunches, usually rice with fried meat and vegetables. Boiling water is brought around to make tea but the custom of providing tea leaves is dying out.

During station stops you will see platform carts selling local specialities: fruit, boiled eggs and very often a kind of hot steamed bread filled with meat and known as *bāo-zi*.

| | | |
|---|---|---|
| Where's the dining-car? | 餐车在哪儿？ | cān-chē zài nǎr |
| Can I have a lunch box? | 请给我一盒盒饭。 | qǐng gěi wǒ yì-hé hé-fàn |
| Please give me two of these and one of those. | 请给我拿两个这种的和一个那种的。 | qǐng gěi wǒ nā liǎng-ge zhè zhǒng de he yí-ge nà zhǒng de |

## Baggage 行李

Chinese railway stations do not normally supply luggage trolleys, so if you have to carry your own luggage it would be wise to invest in a suitcase with wheels.

| | | |
|---|---|---|
| Where's the left-luggage office (baggage check)? | 行李寄存处在哪儿？ | xíng-li jì-cún-chù zài nǎr |
| I'd like to leave my luggage, please. | 我想寄存我的行李。 | wǒ xiǎng jì-cún wǒ de xíng-li |
| I'd like to register (check) my luggage? | 我想托运我的行李。 | wǒ xiǎng tuō-yùn wǒ de xíng-li |

---

**行李托运处**
xíng-li tuō-yùn-chù
REGISTERING (CHECKING) LUGGAGE

---

### Coach (long-distance bus) 长途汽车

Coaches are not a practical alternative to trains as they are slow and not very comfortable. But you may need to travel by coach if you want to visit some of the less accessible sights.

| When's the next coach to …? | 下趟去…的长途汽车什么时间开车？ | xià tàng qù … de cháng-tú qì-chē shén-me shí-jiān kāi chē |
| Does this coach stop in …? | 这趟长途汽车在…停吗？ | zhèi tàng cháng-tú qì-chē zài … tíng ma |
| How long does the journey (trip) take? | 路上要用多长时间？ | lù-shang yào yòng duō cháng shí-jiān |

### Bus — Tram (streetcar) 公共汽车–电车

Public transport is generally very crowded and it's not unusual to see passengers clinging onto the outside windows of buses. You buy your ticket from the conductor who will tell you when to get off if you give him or her a note of your destination written in Chinese characters. If a Chinese person offers you a seat, accept with a smile.

| Which tram (streetcar) goes to the National Art Gallery? | 哪路电车去美术馆？ | nǎ lù diàn-chē qù měi-shù-guǎn |
| Where can I get a bus to …? | 我去…到哪儿去坐公共汽车？ | wǒ qù … dào nǎr qù zuò gōng-gòng qì-chē |
| What bus do I take for …? | 我去…乘哪路公共汽车？ | wǒ qù … chèng nǎ lù gōng-gòng qì-chē |
| Where's the …? | …在哪儿？ | … zài nǎr |
| bus stop | 公共汽车站 | gōng-gòng qì-chē-zhàn |
| terminus | 终点站 | zhōng-diǎn-zhàn |

公共汽车站
gōng-gòng qì-chē-zhàn
BUS STOP

| When is the … bus to the zoo? | 去动物园的…公共汽车几点开？ | qù dòng-wù-yuán de… gōng-gòng qì-chē jǐ-diǎn kāi |
| first/last | 头班/末班 | tóu-bān/ mò-bān |
| How often do the buses to the airport run? | 去机场的公共汽车多长时间一趟？ | qù jī-chǎng de gōng-gòng qì-chē duō cháng shí-jiān yí-tàng |
| How much is the fare to …? | 去…的票价多少？ | qù …de piào-jià duō-shao |
| Do I have to change buses? | 我得换车吗？ | wǒ děi huàn chē ma |
| How many bus stops are there to …? | 去…得坐几站？ | qù … děi zuò jǐ zhàn |
| How long does the journey (trip) take? | 路上要用多长时间？ | lù-shang yào yòng duō cháng shí-jiān |
| Will you tell me when to get off? | 你能在该下车的时候告诉我吗？ | nǐ néng zài gāi xià chē de shí-hou gào-su wǒ ma |
| I want to get off at the next stop. | 我下站下车。 | wǒ xià-zhàn xià chē |

## Underground (subway) 地铁

The Beijing underground — whose stations are recognized by the sign 地铁 (dì-tiě) — operates daily between 6 a.m. and 9 p.m., carrying more than 70 million passengers each year. Trains and stations are maintained in spotless condition.

Each station is visibly quite different from all the others by virtue of its colour scheme, the shape of the columns or other lesser details. Station names are written in Pinyin as well as Chinese, which also helps.

At present, the single-line system only covers 24km., but more lines are being built. An underground system is also under construction in Shanghai.

| Where's the nearest underground station? | 离这儿最近的地铁站在哪儿？ | lí zhèr zuì jìn de dì-tiě-zhàn zài nǎr |
| Does this train go to …? | 这趟列车去…吗？ | zhèi tàng liè-chē qù … ma |
| Is the next station …? | 下站是…吗？ | xià zhàn shì … ma |

## Boat service 水路

If you have the chance, try to spend a few hours exploring the Shanghai waterfront, with its golden-sailed junks and big steamers, or go for a cruise down the Chang Jiang. Better still on a warm summer afternoon in Beijing you might like to go boating on one of the serene lakes that grace the capital's many parks.

If taking a longer cruise you will probably be more comfortable in second class, where there are two to four beds in each cabin, and often the use of a collective sitting room. Third and fourth classes are much more crowded, being based on dormitory-style accommodation.

| | | |
|---|---|---|
| Can I hire a rowing boat? | 我可以租条游船吗？ | wǒ kě-yǐ zū tiáo yóu-chuán ma |
| There are … of us. | 我们…个人。 | wǒ-men … ge rén |
| I'd like it for … | 我想租… | wǒ xiǎng zū |
| half an hour | 半小时 | bàn xiǎo-shí |
| 1 hour | 一小时 | yì xiǎo-shí |
| What's the charge per hour? | 每小时多少钱？ | měi xiǎo-shí duō-shao qián |
| When does a boat for … leave? | 去…的船几点开？ | qù … de chuán jǐ diǎn kāi |
| Where's the embarkation point? | 在哪儿上船？ | zài nǎr shàng chuán |
| I'd like to take a tour of the harbour. | 我想坐船游览一下儿港湾。 | wǒ xiǎng zuò chuán yóu-lǎn yí xiàr gǎng-wān |
| boat | 船 | chuán |
| cabin | 客舱 | kè-cāng |
|   second class | 二等 | èr-děng |
|   third class | 三等 | sān-děng |
| cruise | 坐船游览 | zuò chuán yóu-lǎn |
| deck | 甲板 | jiǎ-bǎn |
| life belt | 救生衣 | jiù-shēng-yī |
| life boat | 救生艇 | jiù-shēng-tǐng |
| port | 码头 | mǎ-tou |
| river cruise | 河上坐船游览 | hé shàng zuò chuán yóu-lǎn |
| ship | 轮船 | lún-chuán |
| I'd like to take a short cruise. | 我想短途坐船游览。 | wǒ xiǎng duǎn-tú zuò chuán yóu-lǎn |

### Pedicabs 三轮车

Pedicabs can still be encountered in certain large cities such as Shanghai, and are an ideal way of sightseeing. These man-powered three-wheelers take two passengers.

| I'd like visit to the town centre. | 我想去市区观光。 | wǒ xiǎng qù shì-qū guān-guāng |
| How much do you charge? | 要付多少钱？ | yào fù duō-shao qián |

### Car 包车

You will not be able to hire a self-drive car, but you can hire a car and driver for the day or longer.

| I'd like to hire a car with a guide and driver. | 我想租一辆有导游和司机的汽车。 | wǒ xiǎng zū yí-liàng yǒu dǎo-yóu hé sī-jī de qì-chē |
| I'd like it for ... | 我想用… | wǒ xiǎng yòng |
| a day/ ... days | 一天/…天 | yì-tiān/ ... tiān |
| a week/ ... weeks | 一个星期/…个星期 | yí-ge xīng-qī/ ... ge xīng-qī |
| What's the charge per day? | 一天多少钱？ | yì-tiān duō-shao qián |

### Accidents — Police 事故-警察

Here are a few phrases that may be useful should you be involved in or witness an accident.

| Please call a doctor, quickly. | 请快叫一位大夫来。 | qǐng kuài jiào yí-wèi dài-fu lái |
| Please call the police. | 请叫警察来。 | qǐng jiào jǐng-chá lái |
| There's been an accident. | 出事了。 | chū shì le |
| There are people injured. | 有人受伤了。 | yǒu rén shòu shāng le |
| I'd like an interpreter. | 我想请一位口译。 | wǒ xiǎng qǐng yí-wèi kǒu-yì |
| Here's my name and address. | 这是我的姓名和地址。 | zhè shì wǒ de xìng-míng hé dì-zhǐ |

### Bicycle hire 租自行车

Even on a tightly-scheduled tour, you may be able to fit in a bike ride around town. Machines can be hired at Friendship Stores and large bicycle repair shops.

| | | |
|---|---|---|
| I'd like to hire a bicycle … | 我想租一辆自行车… | wǒ xiǎng zū yí-liàng zì-xíng-chē |
| for … hours | 骑…小时 | qí … xiǎo-shí |
| for 1 day | 骑一天 | qí yì tiān |
| for a ride around the town | 在市区骑 | zài shì-qū qí |
| What is the hire charge? | 租金多少？ | zū-jīn duō-shao |
| How much is the deposit? | 押金多少？ | yā-jīn duō-shao |
| When must I return the bicycle? | 我该在什么时候还自行车？ | wǒ gāi zài shén-me shí-hou huán zì-xíng-chē |

| | |
|---|---|
| 行，我能租给你一辆自行车。 | Yes, I can rent you a bicycle. |
| 不行，我不能把自行车租给你。 | No, I can't rent you a bicycle. |
| 请交…块钱押金。 | Please leave a deposit of … yuan. |
| 这辆自行车你能用… | You can keep the bicycle … |
| …小时 | for … hours |
| 到…点钟为止 | until … o'clock |
| 到明天 | until tomorrow |

### Other means of transport 其它交通工具

| | | |
|---|---|---|
| helicopter | 直升飞机 | zhí-shēng fēi-jī |
| moped | 小摩托车 | xiǎo mó-tuō-chē |
| motorbike | 摩托车 | mó-tuō-chē |

Or perhaps you prefer:

| | | |
|---|---|---|
| to hike | 徒步旅行 | tú-bù lǚ-xíng |
| to hitchhike | 搭车 | dā chē |
| to walk | 走路 | zǒu lù |

## Asking the way – Street directions 问路-指路

| Excuse me. | 请问 | qǐng wèn |
| What is the name of this street? | 这条街叫什么名字？ | zhèi tiáo jiē jiào shén-me míng-zi |
| Could you show me on this map where I am? | 你能在这张地图上指出我在哪儿吗？ | nǐ néng zài zhèi zhāng dì-tú shang zhǐ-chū wǒ zài nǎr ma |
| Where can I find this address? | 我怎么才能找到这个地方？ | wǒ zěn-me cái néng zhǎo dào zhèi-ge dì-fang |
| Can you tell me the way to …? | 你能告诉我去…的路吗？ | nǐ néng gào-su wǒ qù … de lù ma |
| How do I get to …? | 去…怎么走？ | qù … zěn-me zǒu |
| How long does it take on foot? | 走路去要用多少时间？ | zǒu lù qù yào yòng duō-shao shí-jiān |
| Where can I find this place? | 我怎么能找到这个地方？ | wǒ zěn-me néng zhǎo dào zhèi-ge dì-fang |
| Where's this? | 这在哪儿？ | zhèi zài nǎr |
| How far is it to … from here? | …离这儿有多远？ | … lí zhèr yǒu duō yuǎn |
| Which bus should I take? | 我该坐几路汽车？ | wǒ gāi zuò jǐ-lù qì-chē |

| 你走错路了。 | You're going the wrong way. |
| 一直走。 | Go straight ahead. |
| 往那边走，在马路… | It's down there on the … |
| 左边/右边 | left/right |
| 对面/在…后面 | opposite/behind … |
| 在…旁边儿/过了…之后 | next to/after … |
| 北/南/东/西 | north/south/east/west |
| 走到第一个/第二个十字路口。 | Go to the first/second crossroads (intersection). |
| 在红绿灯处向左拐。 | Turn left at the traffic lights. |
| 在下一个路口往右拐。 | Turn right at the next corner. |

SIGHTSEEING

# Sightseeing

| Is there a Lüxingshe (CITS) office here? | 旅行社在哪儿？ | lǚ-xíng-shè zài nǎr |
| What are the main points of interest? | 这儿都有些什么名胜古迹？ | zhèr dōu yǒu xiē shén-me míng-shèng gǔ-jī |
| We're here for … | 我们在这里停留… | wǒ-men zài zhè-li tíng-liú |
| a few hours | 几小时 | jǐ xiǎo-shí |
| a day | 一天 | yì-tiān |
| a week | 一星期 | yì xīng-qī |
| Can you recommend a sightseeing tour? | 请推荐一个集体游览路线。 | qǐng tuī-jiàn yí-ge jí-tǐ yóu-lǎn lù-xiàn |
| Where do we leave from? | 从哪儿出发？ | cóng nǎr chū-fā |
| Will the bus pick us up at the hotel? | 汽车来旅馆接我们吗？ | qì-chē lái lǚ-guǎn jiē wǒ-men ma |
| How much does the tour cost? | 游览一趟要花多少钱？ | yóu-lǎn yí-tàng yào huā duō-shao qián |
| What time do we leave? | 我们什么时间出发？ | wǒ-men shén-me shí-jiān chū-fā |
| Is lunch included? | 包括午饭吗？ | bāo-kuò wǔ-fàn ma |
| What time do we get back? | 我们什么时间回来？ | wǒ-men shén-me shí-jiān huí-lai |
| Do we have free time in …? | 我们在…有自由活动的时间吗？ | wǒ-men zài … yǒu zì-yóu huó-dòng de shí-jiān ma |
| I'd like to hire an English-speaking private guide for … | 我想请一位私人英语导游，工作… | wǒ xiǎng qǐng yí-wèi sī-rén yīng-yǔ dǎo-yóu gōng-zuò |
| half a day | 半天 | bàn-tiān |
| a day | 一天 | yì-tiān |

and if you'd like a close-up of someone on your travels it's polite to ask:

| May I take a photo of you, please? | 我可以给你照像吗？ | wǒ kě-yǐ gěi nǐ zhào-xiàng ma |

游览

## Admission 入场

| Is ... open on Sundays? | …星期天开门吗？ | … xīng-qī-tiān kāi mén ma |
| When does it open? | 几点开门？ | jǐ diǎn kāi mén |
| When does it close? | 几点关门？ | jǐ diǎn guān mén |
| How much is the entrance fee? | 门票多少钱？ | mén-piào duō-shao qián |

---

免费入场
miǎn-fèi rù chǎng
ADMISSION FREE

---

禁止摄影
jìn-zhǐ shè-yǐng
NO CAMERAS ALLOWED

---

| Is there any reduction for ...? | …买票减价吗？ | … mǎi piào jiǎn-jià ma |
| children | 儿童 | ér-tóng |
| the disabled | 残废人 | cán-fèi-rén |
| groups | 团体 | tuán-tǐ |
| pensioners | 退休的 | tuì-xiū de |
| students | 学生 | xué-sheng |
| Do you have a guidebook (in English)? | 你这儿有（英文）旅游指南吗？ | nǐ zhèr yǒu (yīng-wén) lǚ-yóu zhǐ-nán ma |
| Can I buy a catalogue? | 可以买一份简介吗？ | kě-yǐ mǎi yí-fèn jiǎn-jiè ma |
| Is it all right to take pictures? | 可以照相吗？ | kě-yǐ zhào-xiàng ma |
| Is there an English-speaking guide? | 有会说英语的导游吗？ | yǒu huì shuō yīng-yǔ de dǎo-yóu ma |

## Where is ...? …在哪儿？

| Where is/ Where are the ...? | …在哪儿？ | … zài nǎr |
| aquarium | 水族馆 | shuǐ-zú-guǎn |
| art gallery | 画店 | huà-diàn |
| botanical gardens | 植物园 | zhí-wù-yuán |
| bridge | 桥 | qiáo |
| building | 建筑 | jiàn-zhù |

| cathedral | 大教堂 | dà-jiào-táng |
|---|---|---|
| cave | 岩洞 | yán-dòng |
| cemetery | 公墓 | gōng-mù |
| church | 教堂 | jiào-táng |
| city centre | 市中心 | shì zhōng-xīn |
| commune | 公社 | gōng-shè |
| concert hall | 音乐厅 | yīn-yuè-tīng |
| courtyard | 庭院 | tíng-yuàn |
| department store | 百货商店 | bǎi-huò shāng-diàn |
| docks | 码头 | mǎ-tou |
| downtown area | 市中心 | shì zhōng-xīn |
| exhibition | 展览会 | zhǎn-lǎn-huì |
| factory | 工厂 | gōng-chǎng |
| fortress | 要塞 | yào-sài |
| fountain | 泉 | quán |
| gardens | 园林 | yuán-lín |
| grotto | 小岩洞 | xiǎo yán-dòng |
| harbour | 港湾 | gǎng-wān |
| island | 岛 | dǎo |
| lake | 湖 | hú |
| market | 农贸市场 | nóng-mào shì-chǎng |
| memorial (museum) | 纪念馆 | jì-niàn-guǎn |
| memorial (stone) | 纪念碑 | jì-niàn-bēi |
| monument | 纪念碑 | jì-niàn-bēi |
| mosque | 清真寺 | qīng-zhēn-sì |
| museum | 博物馆 | bó-wù-guǎn |
| observatory | 天文台 | tiān-wén-tái |
| old town | 老城 | lǎo chéng |
| opera house (Chinese) | 戏院 | xì-yuàn |
| pagoda | 宝塔 | bǎo-tǎ |
| palace | 宫殿 | gōng-diàn |
| park | 公园 | gōng-yuán |
| pavilion | 亭子 | tíng-zi |
| planetarium | 天文馆 | tiān-wén-guǎn |
| river | 河 | hé |
| ... ruins | …旧址 | ... jiù-zhǐ |
| shopping area | 商业区 | shāng-yè-qū |
| square | 广场 | guǎng-chǎng |
| stadium | 体育场 | tǐ-yù-chǎng |
| statue | 雕像 | diāo-xiàng |
| temple (Buddhist) | 佛寺 | fó-sì |
| (Taoist) | 道观 | dào-guàn |
| theatre | 剧场 | jù-chǎng |
| tomb | 陵墓 | líng-mù |
| tower | 塔 | tǎ |
| university | 大学 | dà-xué |
| zoo | 动物园 | dòng-wù-yuán |

## What are your special interests? 你对什么特别感兴趣？

| | | |
|---|---|---|
| I'd like to see a/ the ... | 我想看… | wǒ xiǎng kàn |
| Buddhist temple | 佛寺 | fó-sì |
| carved lacquerware factory | 雕漆厂 | diāo-qī chǎng |
| cloisonné factory | 景泰蓝厂 | jǐng-tài-lán chǎng |
| hot springs | 温泉 | wēn-quán |
| jade factory | 玉器厂 | yù-qì chǎng |
| Mao Zedong Memorial Hall | 毛主席纪念堂 | máo zhǔ-xí jì-niàn-táng |
| National Art Gallery | 中国美术馆 | zhōng-guó měi-shù-guǎn |
| Nationalities' Cultural Palace | 民族文化宫 | mín-zú wén-huà-gōng |
| rock carvings | 石雕 | shí-diāo |
| silk factory | 丝绸厂 | sī-chóu chǎng |
| Summer Palace | 颐和园 | yí-hé-yuán |
| Taoist temple | 道观 | dào-guàn |
| Temple of Heaven | 天坛 | tiān-tán |
| We're interested in ... | 我们对…感兴趣。 | wǒ-men duì ... gǎn xìng-qu |
| acupuncture | 针灸 | zhēn-jiǔ |
| antiques | 古董 | gǔ-dǒng |
| archaeology | 考古学 | kǎo-gǔ-xué |
| architecture | 建筑学 | jiàn-zhù-xué |
| art | 艺术 | yì-shù |
| botany | 植物学 | zhí-wù-xué |
| calligraphy | 书法 | shū-fǎ |
| ceramics | 陶瓷 | táo-cí |
| furniture | 家具 | jiā-jù |
| geology | 地质学 | dì-zhì-xué |
| handicrafts | 手工艺品 | shǒu-gōng-yì-pǐn |
| history | 历史 | lì-shǐ |
| ivory carvings | 牙雕 | yá-diāo |
| jade carvings | 玉器 | yù-qì |
| medicine | 医学 | yī-xué |
| musical instruments | 乐器 | yuè-qì |
| natural history | 自然博物 | zì-rán bó-wù |
| painting | 画儿 | huàr |
| porcelain | 细瓷器 | xì-cí-qì |
| sculpture | 雕塑 | diāo-sù |
| silk painting | 绢画 | juàn-huà |
| zoology | 动物学 | dòng-wù-xué |
| Where's the ... department? | …部在哪儿？ | ... bù zài nǎr |

### Who — What — When? 哪位－什么－什么时代？

| What's that building? | 那个建筑是什么？ | nà-ge jiàn-zhù shì shén-me |
| When was it built? | 是什么时候建的？ | shì shén-me shí-hou jiàn de |
| Who was the ...? | 是哪位…的作品？ | shì nǎ-wèi ... de zuò-pǐn |
| architect | 建筑师 | jiàn-zhù-shī |
| artist | 艺术家 | yì-shù-jiā |
| painter | 画家 | huà-jiā |
| sculptor | 雕塑家 | diāo-sù-jiā |
| When did he live? | 他是什么时代的人？ | tā shì shén-me shí-dài de rén |
| Who painted this? | 这是谁画的？ | zhè shì shéi huà de |
| It's ... | 这真… | zhè zhēn |
| beautiful | 美丽 | měi-lì |
| interesting | 有趣 | yǒu qù |
| magnificent | 雄伟 | xióng-wěi |
| strange | 奇怪 | qí-guài |

### Religious services 作礼拜

If you want to attend a religious service, give your guide advance warning so that your request can be accommodated in the general schedule.

| Is there a ... near here? | 附近有…吗？ | fù-jìn yǒu ... ma |
| Catholic church | 天主教教堂 | tiān-zhǔ-jiào jiào-táng |
| mosque | 清真寺 | qīng-zhēn-sì |
| Protestant church | 新教教堂 | xīn-jiào jiào-táng |
| synagogue | 犹太教堂 | yóu-tài jiào-táng |
| Is it open to visitors? | 对旅游者开放吗？ | duì lǚ-yóu-zhě kāi-fàng ma |
| What time is mass/the service? | 几点作弥撒/礼拜？ | jǐ diǎn zuò mí-sa/lǐ-bài |
| Where can I find a priest/minister who speaks English? | 哪儿有说英语的神父/牧师？ | nǎr yǒu shuō yīng-yǔ de shén-fù/mù-shī |

The table of dynasties and major events, opposite, provides a useful frame of reference for Chinese history.

## Chinese dynasties and major events

夏     *Xià* (approx. 21st–16th centuries B.C.): Legendary first Chinese dynasty.

商     *Shāng* (16th–11th centuries B.C.): Cultivation of silkworm first documented.

周     *Zhōu* (11th–5th centuries B.C.): *Zhōu* establish a state near Xi'an, later relocating their capital at Luoyang.

战国     *Zhàn Guó* (Warring States, 403–221 B.C.): Development of iron-working.

秦     *Qín* (221–206 B.C.): Building of the Great Wall as protection against the Huns.

汉     *Hàn* (206 B.C.–A.D. 220): Great advance in agriculture, commerce, learning and historical writing.

三国     *Sān Guó* (Three Kingdoms, 220–265): Taoism and Buddhism spread throughout China.

晋     *Jìn* (265–420): Following partition of empire under previous dynasty, China now enjoys a brief period of unification.

南北朝     *Nán Běi Cháo* (Southern and Northern dynasties, 386–581): North splinters into numerous small states, while South makes spectacular progress.

隋     *Suí* (581–618): Imperial Canal started, for transport of cereals from Yangtze.

唐     *Táng (618–907): China is paramount power in eastern Asia; highest flowering of Chinese culture and science. Gunpowder invented.*

五代十国     *Wǔ Dài — Shí Guó* (Five Dynasties and Ten Kingdoms, 907–960): Expansion of trade in China.

宋     *Sòng* (960–1279): Printing promotes communications. Paper currency in circulation.

元     *Yuán* (1279–1368): Moslem and European explorers and traders link China with the West.

明     *Míng* (1368–1644): Empire reaches new heights. Power is further centralized. Bureaucracy, the economy and agriculture are reorganized.

清     *Qīng* (1644–1911): Population explosion. Opium War (1839–1842). Hong Kong ceded to British. War with Japan, 1894. Advent of the republic in 1912.

### In the countryside 在农村

| | | |
|---|---|---|
| Is there a scenic route to …? | 去…有风景好的路吗？ | qù … yǒu fēng-jǐng hǎo de lù ma |
| How far is it to …? | 到…有多远？ | dào … yǒu duō yuǎn |
| Can we get there on foot? | 能走路去吗？ | néng zǒu-lù qù ma |
| How high is that mountain? | 那座山有多高？ | nà-zuò shān yǒu duó gāo |
| What's the name of that …? | 那是什么…？ | nà shì shén-me |
| animal/bird | 动物/鸟儿 | dòng-wù/niǎor |
| flower/tree | 花儿/树 | huār/shù |

### Landmarks 风景

| | | |
|---|---|---|
| bridge | 桥 | qiáo |
| canal | 运河 | yùn-hé |
| cliff | 山崖 | shān-yá |
| farm (state run) | （国营）农场 | (guó-yíng) nóng-chǎng |
| field | 农田 | nóng-tián |
| footpath | 小路 | xiǎo lù |
| forest | 森林 | sēn-lín |
| garden | 花园 | huā-yuán |
| Great Wall | 长城 | cháng-chéng |
| hill | 小山 | xiǎo shān |
| house | 房屋 | fáng-wū |
| island | 岛 | dǎo |
| lake | 湖 | hú |
| meadow | 草场 | cǎo-chǎng |
| mountain (pass) | 山（口） | shān (kǒu) |
| paddy field | 稻田 | dào-tián |
| path | 小路 | xiǎo lù |
| peak | 山峰 | shān-fēng |
| plantation | 种植园 | zhòng-zhí-yuán |
| pond | 池塘 | chí-táng |
| river | 河 | hé |
| road | 路 | lù |
| sea | 海 | hǎi |
| spring | 泉 | quán |
| swamp | 沼泽 | zhǎo-zé |
| valley | 山谷 | shān-gǔ |
| village | 村庄 | cūn-zhuāng |
| vineyard | 葡萄园 | pú-táo-yuán |
| waterfall | 瀑布 | pù-bù |
| wood | 树林 | shù-lín |

ASKING THE WAY, see page 77

游览

# Relaxing

Whether you are visiting China on your own or as part of a group your travel schedule will be worked out in advance down to the last detail. Your days will be well filled: a visit to a people's commune, a trip to the Great Wall, a shopping expedition to a Friendship Store, etc. Back at the hotel, you will certainly be happy to take things easy for a while.

However, for the benefit of those who don't want to waste a minute of their precious time, hotels sometimes put on typical Chinese shows of interest to tourists. Table-tennis and billiards buffs will often find facilities for these sports in their hotel. Savvy travellers will have brought a chess or scrabble set or pack of cards along with which to while away idle evening hours.

In all probability, your visit to China will include an evening or two of organized entertainment. Popular items are concerts, acrobat shows, Chinese ballet and opera, the circus, and, of course, the banquets which will be unforgettable highlights of your trip.

### Theatre — Opera, etc.

If your places have been booked in advance, all you have to do is to turn up at the appointed meeting place on time. However, if you are travelling alone or for some other reason find yourself left to your own devices, the phrases given on the following pages will enable you to communicate your wishes – preferably to your hotel receptionist who will then make the appropriate reservations for you.

A number of favourites from the traditional Chinese theatre have resurfaced over recent years, and modern plays are often staged depicting heroic episodes from the Long March or the setting up of a people's commune; but the star attraction of the Beijing (Peking) stage is the renowned Peking Opera. You will be enchanted by the sumptuous costumes, the daring leaps, the virtuoso performances. The action takes place on a sparsely decorated stage where it is the actor's gestures which indicate whether he is opening a door, riding a horse or travelling aboard a vessel on a river.

These works are rich in intrigue and surprise developments, and in the simplest and often most touching plots the focal point may be a brief argument, a quarrel, a unique situation such as a chance meeting, a misunderstanding or a reconciliation. What's more, the libretto is extremely adaptable: it gets rewritten, developed, abbreviated — to the delight and pleasure of connoisseurs.

The roles can be categorized according to sex, age and type of character. One of the leading male parts is generally that of *lǎo shēng*, a venerable gentleman with a long beard and a fine baritone voice. *Xiǎo shēng* is a young lover or a student. His make-up is like that of a girl and he often speaks in a high-pitched voice. *Wǔ shēng* is a soldier who appears in a great number of operas of the classical repertoire. He is led to perform acrobatic feats that will leave you breathless. One of the main female roles you'll notice is that of *qīng yī* ("blue dress"), a lady with a falsetto voice who represents either a mistress or the faithful and virtuous wife. Her movements are graceful and she sings with her eyes modestly lowered. *Huā dàn* ("flower") is agile and alert. The actress playing this part wears some of the most elegant costumes; her gestures are seductive and coquettish. A wide range of other characters represent valiant warriers, dishonest government ministers, ruthless bandits, incorruptible judges and loyal servants of the state, not to mention deities and other supernatural beings.

You will certainly not understand all of the actors' gestures, let alone the songs and the words, but the rhythm, the colours, the mime and the music will capture your imagination as little else can.

## Theatre 戏剧

| | | |
|---|---|---|
| What's playing at the Capital Theatre? | 首都剧场现在正上演什么？ | shǒu-dū jù-chǎng xiàn-zài zhèng shàng-yǎn shén-me |
| What sort of play is it? | 这是哪种戏剧？ | zhè shì nǎ zhǒng xì-jù |
| Who's it by? | 剧作者是谁？ | jù-zuò-zhě shì shéi |
| Who's playing the lead? | 主角是谁？ | zhǔ-jué shì shéi |
| Are there any tickets for tonight? | 还有今晚的票吗？ | hái yǒu jīn wǎn de piào ma |
| How much are the tickets? | 这些票多少钱？ | zhè xiē piào duō-shao qián |
| What time does it begin? | 什么时间开演？ | shén-me shí-jiān kāi yǎn |
| Can I have a ticket for the matinée? | 我想买一张早场的票。 | wǒ xiǎng mǎi yì-zhāng zǎo-chǎng de piào |
| I want a seat in the stalls (orchestra). | 我要一张楼下的票。 | wǒ yào yì-zhāng lóu-xià de piào |
| Not too far back. | 不要太后边。 | bú yào tài hòu-bian |
| Somewhere in the middle. | 要中间的。 | yào zhōng-jiān de |
| May I have a programme, please? | 请给我一份节目单。 | qǐng gěi wǒ yí-fèn jié-mù-dān |
| Where's the cloakroom? | 衣帽间在哪儿？ | yī-mào-jiān zài nǎr |

| | |
|---|---|
| 对不起，票卖完了。 | I'm sorry, we're sold out. |
| 只剩几张楼上的票了。 | There are only a few seats left in the circle (mezzanine). |
| 我可以看看你的票吗？ | May I see your ticket? |

## Opera — Ballet — Concert 歌剧–芭蕾舞–音乐会

| | | |
|---|---|---|
| Can you recommend a/an …? | 你能推荐一场…吗？ | nǐ néng tuī-jiàn yì-chǎng … ma |
| ballet | 芭蕾舞 | bā-léi-wǔ |
| concert | 音乐会 | yīn-yuè-huì |
| opera | 歌剧 | gē-jù |
| Where's the opera house/concert hall? | 歌剧院/音乐厅在哪儿？ | gē-jù-yuàn/yīn-yuè-tīng zài nǎr |
| Is the Beijing Opera putting on a performance? | 北京京剧团现在演出吗？ | běi-jīng jīng-jù-tuán xiàn-zài yǎn-chū ma |
| Who's the singer/ dancing the lead? | 独唱/跳主角的是谁？ | dú-chàng/tiào zhǔ-jué de shì shéi |
| Which orchestra is playing? | 是由哪个乐队演奏的？ | shì yóu nǎ-ge yuè-duì yǎn-zòu de |
| Who's the conductor/ soloist? | 指挥/独奏演员是谁？ | zhǐ-huī/dú-zòu yǎn-yuán shì shéi |

## Cinema 电影院

| | | |
|---|---|---|
| What's on at the cinema tonight? | 这个电影院今晚有什么电影？ | zhè-ge diàn-yǐng-yuàn jīn-wǎn yǒu shén-me diàn-yǐng |
| Can you recommend a …? | 你能推荐一个…吗？ | nǐ néng tuī-jiàn yí-ge … ma |
| good film | 好电影 | hǎo diàn-yǐng |
| comedy | 喜剧片 | xǐ-jù piàn |
| Who's in it? | 有些什么演员？ | yǒu xiē shén-me yǎn-yuán |
| Who's the director? | 导演是谁？ | dǎo-yǎn shì shéi |
| What time does it begin? | 几点开演？ | jǐ diǎn kāi yǎn |

## Nightclubs — Discos 夜总会–迪斯科舞会

| | | |
|---|---|---|
| Where is there a nightclub/disco? | 哪儿有夜总会/迪斯科舞会？ | nǎr yǒu yè-zǒng-huì/dí-sī-kē wǔ-huì |
| Where can we go dancing? | 我们可以去什么地方跳舞？ | wǒ-men kě-yǐ qù shén-me dì-fang tiào-wǔ |
| Is evening.dress required? | 要穿晚礼服吗？ | yào chuān wǎn-lǐ-fú ma |

## Sports 体育运动

Early-risers taking their morning stroll along the city streets are likely to encounter numerous groups of Chinese earnestly engaged in practising tai chi chuan (太极拳 *tài-jí-quán*). To the casual observer it may look as though the participants are merely shadow-boxing or performing slow dance movements, but the adept will tell you that tai chi chuan is, in effect, a physical-philosophical discipline that tones up all the body's muscles and composes the mind and spirit.

Swimming is another popular pastime, and many swimming pools have been housed in converted excavation sites. For most public swimming pools you will need a health certificate from a Chinese clinic, but your tour guide can organise this quite easily.

| | | |
|---|---|---|
| Is it possible to play tennis? | 这儿能打网球吗？ | zhèr néng dǎ wǎng-qiú ma |
| Where are the tennis courts? | 网球场在哪儿？ | wǎng-qiú-chǎng zài nǎr |
| Can I hire (rent) ...? | 我能租用…吗？ | wǒ néng zū-yòng ... ma |
| equipment | 体育器材 | tǐ-yù qì-cái |
| rackets | 球拍 | qiú-pāi |

| | | |
|---|---|---|
| badminton | 羽毛球 | yǔ-máo-qiú |
| basketball | 蓝球 | lán-qiú |
| boxing | 拳击 | quán-jī |
| cycling | 骑自行车 | qí zì-xíng-chē |
| football (soccer) | 足球 | zú-qiú |
| gymnastics | 体操 | tǐ-cāo |
| skating | 滑冰 | huá-bīng |
| swimming | 游泳 | yóu-yǒng |
| table-tennis | 乒乓球 | bīng-bāng-qiú |
| tennis | 网球 | wǎng-qiú |
| volleyball | 排球 | pái-qiú |

| | | |
|---|---|---|
| What's the charge per hour/per day? | 一小时/一天的租金多少？ | yì xiǎo-shí/yì-tiān de zū-jīn duō-shao |

| I'd like to see a ... | 我想看一场… | wǒ xiǎng kàn yì-chǎng |
| table-tennis match | 乒乓球比赛 | bīng-bāng-qiú bǐ-sài |
| gymnastics display | 体操表演 | tǐ-cāo biǎo-yǎn |
| What's the admission charge? | 门票多少钱？ | mén-piào duō-shao qián |
| Is a national team playing? | 有国家队上场吗？ | yǒu guó-jiā-duì shàng-chǎng ma |
| Can you get me a ticket? | 你能帮我搞张票吗？ | nǐ néng bāng wǒ gǎo zhāng piào ma |
| Is there a skating-rink near here? | 这附近有滑冰场吗？ | zhè fù-jìn yǒu huá-bīng-chǎng ma |
| Can I hire skates? | 我能租到冰鞋吗？ | wǒ néng zū-dào bīng-xié ma |
| Is there any good fishing around here? | 附近有可以钓鱼的地方吗？ | fù-jìn yǒu kě-yǐ diào-yú de dì-fang ma |
| Do I need a permit to fish? | 钓鱼需要争得许可吗？ | diào-yú xū-yào zhēng-dé xǔ-kě ma |

---

**禁止钓鱼**
jìn-zhǐ diào-yú
NO FISHING ALLLOWED

---

| Can one swim in the lake/river? | 可以在这个湖/河里游泳吗？ | kě-yǐ zài zhè-ge hú/hé li yóu-yǒng ma |
| Is there a swimming pool here? | 这儿有游泳池吗？ | zhèr yǒu yóu-yǒng-chí ma |
| Is it open-air or indoor? | 是室外的还是室内的？ | shì shì-wài de hái-shì shì-nèi de |
| Is it heated? | 是温水的吗？ | shì wēn-shuǐ de ma |
| What's the temperature of the water? | 水温多少度？ | shuǐ-wēn duō-shao dù |
| Is there a sandy beach? | 有沙滩吗？ | yǒu shā-tān ma |

---

**禁止入内**
jìn-zhǐ rù nèi
NO ENTRANCE

---

**On the beach** 在海滩上

As Chinese women are rather modest, bikinis are rarely seen at swimming pools or on the beach, and they aren't encouraged. It's a good idea to pack a discreet one-piece suit.

| | | |
|---|---|---|
| Is it safe to swim here? | 这儿游泳安全吗？ | zhèr yóu-yǒng ān-quán ma |
| Is there a lifeguard? | 有救生员吗？ | yǒu jiù-shēng-yuán ma |
| Are there any dangerous currents? | 有危险的潮流吗？ | yǒu wēi-xiǎn de cháo-liú ma |
| When does the tide come in/go out? | 什么时间涨/落潮？ | shén-me shí-jiān zhǎng/luò cháo |
| Is it safe for children? | 儿童在这儿游泳安全吗？ | ér-tóng zài zhèr yóu-yǒng ān-quán ma |
| There are some big waves. | 有大浪。 | yǒu dà-làng |
| The sea is very calm. | 海上风平浪静。 | hǎi-shang fēng-píng làng-jìng |
| Is it deep here? | 这儿水深吗？ | zhèr shuǐ shēn ma |
| Can I hire a/an/some ...? | 我能租用…吗？ | wǒ néng zū-yòng ... ma |
| air mattress | 一条汽褥子 | yì-tiáo qì-rù-zi |
| bathing suit | 一件游泳衣 | yí-jiàn yóu-yǒng-yī |
| deck chair | 一把躺椅 | yì-bǎ tǎng-yǐ |
| motorboat | 汽艇 | qì-tǐng |
| pedalo | 脚踏游艇 | jiǎo-tà yóu-tǐng |
| rowing boat | 游船 | yóu-chuán |
| sailing boat | 帆船 | fān-chuán |
| skin-diving equipment | 潜水装备 | qián-shuǐ zhuāng-bèi |
| sunshade (umbrella) | 遮阳伞 | zhē-yáng-sǎn |
| water skis | 滑水板 | huá-shuǐ-bǎn |
| What's the charge per hour? | 一小时租金多少？ | yì xiǎo-shí zū-jīn duō-shao |

---

禁止游泳
jìn-zhǐ yóu-yǒng
NO BATHING

---

# Making friends

### Introductions 互相介绍

| Let me introduce you to each other. | 让我来介绍一下。 | ràng wǒ lái jiè-shào yí xià |
| John, this is … | 约翰，这是… | yuē-hàn zhè shì |
| My name is … | 我叫… | wǒ jiào |
| How do you do? | 你好，很高兴能认识你。 | nǐ hǎo. hěn gāo-xìng néng rèn-shi nǐ |
| What's your name? | 你叫什么名字？ | nǐ jiào shén-me míng-zi |
| How are you? | 你好吗？ | nǐ hǎo ma |
| Fine, thanks. And you? | 很好，谢谢。你呢？ | hěn hǎo xiè-xie. nǐ ne |

### Follow up 进一步交谈

| How long have you been here? | 你来这儿有多久了？ | nǐ lái zhèr yǒu duō-jiǔ le |
| We've been here a week. | 我们来了一个星期了。 | wǒ-men lái le yí-ge xīng-qī le |
| Is this your first visit? | 这是你们第一次来吗？ | zhè shì nǐ-men dì-yī-cì lái ma |
| No, we came here last year. | 不，我们去年来过。 | bù wǒ-men qù-nián lái guò |
| Are you enjoying your stay? | 你们在这儿过得愉快吗？ | nǐ-men zài zhèr guò-de yú-kuài ma |
| Yes, I like it very much. | 过得很愉快。 | guò de hěn yú-kuài |
| I like the landscape a lot. | 我非常喜欢这儿的风景。 | wǒ fēi-cháng xǐ-huan zhèr de fēng-jǐng |
| Do you travel a lot? | 你经常旅行吗？ | nǐ jīng-cháng lǚ-xíng ma |
| Where do you come from? | 你是从哪儿来的？ | nǐ shì cóng nǎr lái de |
| I'm from … | 我从…来的。 | wǒ cóng … lái de |
| What nationality are you? | 你是哪国人？ | nǐ shì nǎ guó rén |

COUNTRY, see page 148

| I'm … | 我是… | wǒ shì |
| American | 美国人 | měi-guó rén |
| British | 英国人 | yīng-guó rén |
| Canadian | 加拿大人 | jiā-ná-dà rén |
| Irish | 爱尔兰人 | ài-ěr-lán rén |
| Where are you staying? | 你住在哪儿？ | nǐ zhù zài nǎr |
| Are you on your own? | 你是一个人来的吗？ | nǐ shì yí-ge rén lái de ma |
| I'm with my … | 我和我…一同来的。 | wǒ hé wǒ … yì-tóng lái de |
| wife | 妻子 | qī-zi |
| husband | 丈夫 | zhàng-fu |
| family | 家属 | jiā-shǔ |
| children | 孩子 | hái-zi |
| parents | 父母 | fù-mǔ |
| boyfriend/girlfriend | 男朋友/女朋友 | nán-péng-you/ nǚ-péng-you |

| father/mother | 父亲/母亲 | fù-qin/mǔ-qin |
| son/daughter | 儿子/女儿 | ér-zi/nǚ-er |
| older brother/ younger brother | 哥哥/弟弟 | gē-ge/dì-di |
| older sister/younger sister | 姐姐/妹妹 | jiě-jie/mèi-mei |

| Are you married? | 你已经结婚了吗？ | nǐ yǐ-jīng jié-hūn le ma |
| Are you single? | 你还没有结婚吗？ | nǐ hái méi-yǒu jié-hūn ma |
| Do you have children? | 你有孩子吗？ | nǐ yǒu hái-zi ma |
| What do you think of the country? | 你觉得这个国家怎么样？ | nǐ jué-de zhè-ge guó-jiā zěn-me yàng |
| What do you do? (work) | 你是做什么工作的？ | nǐ shì zuò shén-me gōng-zuò de |
| I'm a student. | 我是学生。 | wǒ shì xué-sheng |
| What are you studying? | 你在学什么？ | nǐ zài xué shén-me |
| I'm here on a business trip. | 我来这儿出差。 | wǒ lái zhèr chū-chāi |
| Do you play cards? | 你会玩儿牌吗？ | nǐ huì wánr pái ma |

### The weather 天气

The weather in China tends not to be as changeable as in Europe and parts of America, so there is less opportunity to discuss it. Nevertheless, a few of these phrases could be used to break the ice.

| | | |
|---|---|---|
| What a lovely day! | 天气真好！ | tiān-qì zhēn hǎo |
| What awful weather! | 天气真坏！ | tiān-qì zhēn hùai |
| Is it usually as warm as this? | 这儿的天气总是这么热吗？ | zhèr de tiān-qì zǒng-shì zhè-me rè ma |
| Do you think it's going to ... tomorrow? | 你觉得明天会…吗？ | nǐ jué-de míng-tiān huì ... ma |
| be a nice day | 是晴天 | shì qíng-tiān |
| rain | 下雨 | xià yǔ |
| snow | 下雪 | xià xuě |
| What is the weather forecast? | 天气预报怎么说的？ | tiān-qì yù-bào zěn-me shuō de |

| | | |
|---|---|---|
| cloud | 云 | yún |
| fog | 雾 | wù |
| frost | 霜 | shuāng |
| ice | 冰 | bīng |
| lightning | 闪电 | shǎn-diàn |
| monsoon | 季风 | jì-fēng |
| moon | 月亮 | yuè-liang |
| rain | 雨 | yǔ |
| sky | 天空 | tiān-kōng |
| snow | 雪 | xuě |
| star | 星星 | xīng-xing |
| sun | 太阳 | tài-yáng |
| thunder | 雷 | léi |
| thunderstorm | 暴风雨 | bào-fēng-yǔ |
| typhoon | 台风 | tái-fēng |
| wind | 风 | fēng |

### Invitations 邀请

| | | |
|---|---|---|
| Would you like to have dinner with us on ...? | 咱们…一起吃晚饭好吗？ | zán-men ... yì-qǐ chī wǎn-fàn hǎo ma |
| May I invite you to lunch? | 我可以请你吃午饭吗？ | wǒ kě-yǐ qǐng nǐ chī wǔ-fàn ma |

DAYS OF THE WEEK, see page 153

| Can you come over for a drink this evening? | 今晚你能来喝一杯吗？ | jīn-wǎn nǐ néng lái hē yì-bēi ma |
| There's a party. Are you coming? | 今晚有个晚会，你来吗？ | jīn-wǎn yǒu ge wǎn-huì. nǐ lái ma |
| That's very kind of you. | 你真客气。 | nǐ zhēn kè-qi |
| Great. I'd love to come. | 太好了，我很愿意。 | tài hǎo le. wǒ hěn yuàn-yì |
| What time shall we come? | 我们该几点到？ | wǒ-men gāi jǐ-diǎn dào |
| May I bring a friend? | 我能带个朋友吗？ | wǒ néng dài ge péng-you ma |
| May I bring my girlfriend/boyfriend? | 我能带我的女朋友/男朋友吗？ | wǒ néng dài wǒ-de nǚ-péng-you/nán-péng-you ma |
| I'm afraid we have to leave now. | 对不起，我们得走了。 | duì-bu-qǐ. wǒ-men děi zǒu le |
| Next time you must come to visit us. | 下次你一定来我们这儿玩儿。 | xià-cì nǐ yí-dìng lái wǒ-men zhèr wánr |
| Thanks for the evening. It was great. | 今晚过得很高兴，十分感谢。 | jīn-wǎn guò de hěn gāo-xìng. shí-fēn gǎn-xiè |

## Dating 约会

| Do you mind if I smoke? | 我可以吸烟吗？ | wǒ kě-yǐ xī yān ma |
| Would you like a cigarette? | 你吸烟吗？ | nǐ xī yān ma |
| Do you have a light, please? | 你有火儿吗？ | nǐ yǒu huǒr ma |
| Why are you laughing? | 你笑什么？ | nǐ xiào shén-me |
| Is my Chinese that bad? | 我汉语说得那么糟糕吗？ | wǒ hàn-yǔ shuō de nà-me zāo-gāo ma |
| Do you mind if I sit here? | 我能坐这儿吗？ | wǒ néng zuò zhèr ma |
| Can I get you a drink? | 你要喝什么？ | nǐ yào hē shén-me |

| Are you waiting for someone? | 你在等人吗？ | nǐ zài děng rén ma |
| Are you free this evening? | 你今晚有空吗？ | nǐ jīn-wǎn yǒu kòng ma |
| Would you like to go out with me tonight? | 今晚你愿意和我一起去玩儿吗？ | jīn-wǎn nǐ yuàn-yì hé wǒ yì-qǐ qù wánr ma |
| Would you like to go dancing? | 你想去跳舞吗？ | nǐ xiǎng qù tiào-wǔ ma |
| Would you like to dance? | 你想跳舞吗？ | nǐ xiǎng tiào-wǔ ma |
| Shall we go to the cinema (movies)? | 咱们去看电影好吗？ | zán-men qù kàn diàn-yǐng hǎo ma |
| Where shall we meet? | 咱们在什么地方见面？ | zán-men zài shén-me dì-fang jiàn-miàn |
| Let's meet in the hotel bar. | 咱们在旅馆酒吧见面吧。 | zán-men zài lǚ-guǎn jiǔ-bā jiàn-miàn ba |
| I'll pick you up at … | 我…点来接你。 | wǒ … diǎn lái jiē nǐ |
| I'll call for you at 8. | 我八点来找你。 | wǒ bā-diǎn lái zhǎo nǐ |
| May I take you home? | 我可以送你回家吗？ | wǒ kě-yǐ sòng nǐ huí jiā ma |
| Can I see you again tomorrow? | 咱们明天能再见面吗？ | zán-men míng-tiān néng zài jiàn-miàn ma |
| What's your telephone number? | 你的电话号码是多少？ | nǐ-de diàn-huà hào-mǎ shì duō-shao |

## and you might answer:

| I'd love to, thank you. | 我很愿意，谢谢。 | wǒ hěn yuàn-yì xiè-xie |
| No. I'm not interested, thank you. | 我不感兴趣，谢谢。 | wǒ bù gǎn xìng-qu xiè-xie |
| Thank you, but I'm busy. | 谢谢，但我很忙 | xiè-xie dàn wǒ hěn máng |
| Leave me alone, please. | 请别管我。 | qǐng bié guǎn wǒ |
| Thank you, it's been a wonderful evening. | 谢谢，这个晚上过得真痛快。 | xiè-xie zhè-ge wǎn-shang guò de zhēn tòng-kuai |
| I've enjoyed myself. | 我玩得很痛快。 | wǒ wánr de hěn tòng-kuai |

# Shopping guide

This shopping guide is designed to help you find what you want with ease, accuracy and speed. It features:

1. A list of all major shops, stores and services (p. 98).
2. Some general expressions required when shopping to allow you to be specific and selective (p.100).
3. Full details of the shops and services most likely to concern you. Here you'll find advice, alphabetical lists of items, and conversion charts listed under the headings below.

LAUNDRY, see page 30/HAIRDRESSER'S, see page 31

采购指南

**Shops, stores and services** 商店，百货商店及服务行业

Most of your shopping will be done in Friendship Stores which offer certain Western goods as well as a wide range of Chinese goods made for export. They are generally open every day between 9 a.m. and 7 or 8 p.m. You should also try a Chinese department store, these are normally open from 9 a.m. to 6 or 7 p.m.

Some shops may be organised a little differently from Western shops. You will find jewellery sold in antique shops, and watches at the optician's. And if you're looking for a baker's you will probably have no luck at all — bread simply isn't as common in China.

As a general rule prices are fixed so don't try bargaining for anything.

Since the distribution system is unpredictable, old China hands say you shouldn't take a chance: if you find something you like, buy it, for it may be on sale nowhere else in China.

| 营业<br>yíng-yè<br>OPEN | 休息<br>xiū-xi<br>CLOSED |
|---|---|

| Where's the nearest ...? | 离这儿最近的…在哪儿？ | lí zhèr zuì jìn de ... zài nǎr |
|---|---|---|
| antique shop | 古董店 | gǔ-dǒng-diàn |
| baker's | 面包店 | miàn-bāo-diàn |
| bank | 银行 | yín-háng |
| barber's | 理发店 | lǐ-fà-diàn |
| beauty salon | 美容院 | měi-róng-yuàn |
| bookshop | 书店 | shū-diàn |
| butcher's | 肉店 | ròu-diàn |
| cake shop | 糕点店 | gāo-diǎn-diàn |
| camera shop | 照相器材商店 | zhào-xiàng qì-cái shāng-diàn |
| chemist's | 药店 | yào-diàn |
| dairy | 奶制品店 | nǎi-zhì-pǐn-diàn |

| delicatessen | 地方风味食品店 | dì-fāng fēng-wèi shí-pǐn-diàn |
| dental clinic | 牙科门诊部 | yá-kē mén-zhěn-bù |
| department store | 百货商店 | bǎi-huò shāng-diàn |
| dressmaker's | 裁缝店 | cái-feng-diàn |
| drugstore | 药店 | yào-diàn |
| electrician | 电器修理部 | diàn-qì xiū-lǐ-bù |
| fishmonger's | 鱼店 | yú-diàn |
| florist's | 花店 | huā-diàn |
| Friendship Store | 友谊商店 | yǒu-yì shāng-diàn |
| furrier's | 皮货店 | pí-huò-diàn |
| greengrocer's | 蔬菜店 | shū-cài-diàn |
| grocery | 副食店 | fù-shí-diàn |
| hairdresser's (ladies/men) | 理发店（女/男） | lǐ-fà-diàn (nǚ/nán) |
| hardware store | 五金商店 | wǔ-jīn shāng-diàn |
| hospital | 医院 | yī-yuàn |
| ironmonger's | 五金商店 | wǔ-jīn shāng-diàn |
| jeweller's | 珠宝首饰店 | zhū-bǎo shǒu-shì diàn |
| laundry | 洗衣店 | xǐ-yī-diàn |
| library | 图书馆 | tú-shū-guǎn |
| market | 农贸市场 | nóng-mào shì-chǎng |
| optician's | 眼镜店 | yǎn-jìng-diàn |
| pastry shop | 糕点店 | gāo-diǎn-diàn |
| photographer's | 照像馆 | zhào-xiàng-guǎn |
| police station | 公安局 | gōng-ān-jú |
| post office | 邮电局 | yóu-diàn-jú |
| shoemaker's (repair) | 补鞋店 | bǔ-xié-diàn |
| shoe shop | 鞋店 | xié-diàn |
| shopping centre | 商场 | shāng-chǎng |
| souvenir shop | 旅游纪念品商店 | lǚ-yóu jì-niàn-pǐn shāng-diàn |
| sporting goods shop | 体育用品商店 | tǐ-yù yòng-pǐn shāng-diàn |
| stationer's | 文具店 | wén-jù-diàn |
| supermarket | 自选商场 | zì-xuǎn shāng-chǎng |
| tailor's | 裁缝店 | cái-feng-diàn |
| toy shop | 玩具店 | wán-jù-diàn |
| travel agency | 旅行社 | lǚ-xíng-shè |
| vegetable store | 蔬菜店 | shū-cài-diàn |
| veterinarian | 兽医 | shòu-yī |
| watchmaker's | 钟表店 | zhōng-biǎo diàn |

| 入口 | 出口 | 太平门 |
| rù-kǒu | chū-kǒu | tài-píng-mén |
| ENTRANCE | EXIT | EMERGENCY EXIT |

## General expressions 一般语汇

### Where? 哪儿？

| | | |
|---|---|---|
| Where's there a good …? | 哪儿有好的…？ | nǎr yǒu hǎo de |
| Where's the nearest …? | 离这儿最近的…在哪儿？ | lí zhèr zuì jìn de … zài nǎr |
| Where can I find a …? | 哪儿有…？ | nǎr yǒu |
| Where do they sell …? | 哪儿卖…？ | nǎr mài |
| Where's the main shopping area? | 主要商业区在哪儿？ | zhǔ-yào shāng-yè-qū zài nǎr |
| Is it far from here? | 离这儿远吗？ | lí zhèr yuǎn ma |
| How do I get there? | 我怎么去那儿？ | wǒ zěn-me qù nàr |

### Service 服务

| | | |
|---|---|---|
| Can you help me? | 你能帮助我吗？ | nǐ néng bāng-zhù wǒ ma |
| I'm just looking. | 我先看看。 | wǒ xiān kàn-kan |
| Do you sell …? | 你这儿卖…吗？ | nǐ zhèr mài … ma |
| I'd like … | 我想要… | wǒ xiǎng-yào |
| Can you show me some …? | 请拿些…给我看看。 | qǐng ná xiē … gěi wǒ kàn-kan |
| Do you have any …? | 你这儿有…？ | nǐ zhèr yǒu |
| Where's the … department? | …部在哪儿？ | … bù zài nǎr |
| Where's the lift (elevator)? | 电梯在哪儿？ | diàn-tī zài nǎr |

### That one 那个

| | | |
|---|---|---|
| Can you show me …? | 请你把…拿来看看。 | qǐng nǐ bǎ … ná lai kàn-kan |
| this one/that one | 这个/那个 | zhè-ge/nà-ge |
| the one in the window | 橱窗里的那个 | chú-chuāng li de nà-ge |

### Defining the article 说明所要物

| | | |
|---|---|---|
| I'd like a ... | 我想要… | wǒ xiǎng-yào |
| I want a ... one. | 我要…的。 | wǒ yào ... de |
| big | 大 | dà |
| cheap | 便宜 | pián-yi |
| dark | 深色 | shēn sè |
| good | 好 | hǎo |
| heavy | 重 | zhòng |
| light (weight) | 轻 | qīng |
| light (colour) | 浅色 | qiǎn sè |
| oval | 椭圆 | tuǒ-yuán |
| rectangular | 长方 | cháng-fāng |
| round | 圆 | yuán |
| small | 小 | xiǎo |
| square | 方 | fāng |
| sturdy | 结实 | jiē-shi |
| wide | 宽 | kuān |
| I don't want anything too expensive. | 太贵的我不要。 | tài guì de wǒ bú yào |

### Preference 喜好

| | | |
|---|---|---|
| I'd prefer something of better quality. | 我喜欢质量好些的。 | wǒ xǐ-huan zhì-liàng hǎo xiē de |
| Can you show me some others? | 请再拿几个给我看看。 | qǐng zài ná jǐ ge gěi wǒ kàn-kan |
| Do you have anything ...? | 你这儿有…的吗？ | nǐ zhèr yǒu ... de ma |
| cheaper/better | 便宜些/好些 | pián-yi xiē/hǎo xiē |
| larger/smaller | 大些/小些 | dà xiē/xiǎo xiē |

### How much? 多少？

| | | |
|---|---|---|
| How much is this? | 这个多少钱？ | zhè-ge duō-shao qián |
| How much are they? | 这些有多少？ | zhè xiē yǒu duō-shao |
| I don't understand. Please write it down. | 我不懂。请写下来。 | wǒ bù dǒng. qǐng xiě xia lai |
| I don't want to spend more than ... yuan. | 我不想买…块钱以上的东西。 | wǒ bù xiǎng mǎi ... kuài qián yǐ-shàng de dōng-xi |

COLOURS, see page 112

### Decision 决定

| It's not quite what I want. | 这个不太理想。 | zhè-ge bú tài lǐ-xiǎng |
| No, I don't like it. | 我不喜欢这个。 | wǒ bù xǐ-huan zhè-ge |
| I'll take it. | 我决定买这个。 | wǒ jué-dìng mǎi zhè-ge |

### Ordering 订购

| Can you order it for me? | 我能订购吗？ | wǒ néng dìng-gòu ma |
| How long will it take? | 要多长时间？ | yào duō cháng shí-jiān |

### Delivery 寄送

| I'll take it with me. | 我带走。 | wǒ dài zǒu |
| Please deliver it to the … Hotel. | 请把这个送到…旅馆。 | qǐng bǎ zhè-ge sòng dào … lǚ-guǎn |
| Please send it to this address. | 请寄到地址上的地方。 | qǐng jì dào dì-zhǐ shang de dì-fang |
| Will I have any difficulty with the customs? | 在海关会有麻烦吗？ | zài hǎi-guān huì yǒu má-fan ma |

### Paying 付款

| How much is it? | 多少钱？ | duō-shao qián |
| Can I pay by traveller's cheque? | 能用旅行支票付款吗？ | néng yòng lǚ-xíng zhī-piào fù kuǎn ma |
| Do you accept credit cards? | 能用信用卡付款吗？ | néng yòng xìn-yòng-kǎ fù kuǎn ma |
| I think there's a mistake in the bill. | 这个帐单好象有错吧。 | zhè-ge zhàng-dān hǎo xiàng yǒu cuò ba |
| Can I have a receipt? | 请开张收据。 | qǐng kāi zhāng shōu-jù |

### Anything else? 还要别的吗？

| | | |
|---|---|---|
| No, thanks, that's all. | 不要了，谢谢，就这些。 | bú yào le. xiè-xie jiù zhè-xiē |
| Yes, I'd like … | 对，我要… | duì. wǒ yào |
| Can you wrap it up, please? | 请包一下。 | qǐng bāo yí xià |
| May I have a bag, please? | 能给我一个袋子吗？ | néng gěi wǒ yí-ge dài-zi ma |
| Thank you. Goodbye. | 谢谢。再见。 | xiè-xie. zài-jiàn |

### Dissatisfied? 不满意？

| | | |
|---|---|---|
| Can you exchange this, please? | 可以换一个吗？ | kě-yǐ huàn yí-ge ma |
| I want to return this. | 我想退掉这个。 | wǒ xiǎng tuì diào zhè-ge |
| I'd like a refund. | 我要求退款。 | wǒ yāo-qiú tuì kuǎn |
| Here's the receipt. | 这是收据。 | zhè shì shōu-jù |

---

| | |
|---|---|
| 我能为你做点什么？ | Can I help you? |
| 你要什么？ | What would you like? |
| 你要什么…的？ | What … would you like? |
| 颜色/样子 | colour/shape |
| 质量/数量 | quality/quantity |
| 对不起，我们这儿没有。 | I'm sorry, we don't have any. |
| 我们这儿卖完了 | We're out of stock. |
| 要我们寄去吗？ | Shall we send it? |
| 还要别的吗？ | Anything else? |
| 请付…元钱。 | That's … yuan, please. |
| 我们不收… | We don't accept … |
| 信用卡 旅行支票 | credit cards traveller's cheques |
| 收款处在那儿。 | The cash desk is over there. |

## Antiques 古董

Antique shops specialize in old pottery, jewellery, carvings and calligraphy, as well as high quality reproductions. Chinese customs regulations prohibit the export of any cultural relics except those marked with special wax seals. And only fairly recent objects are given the seal. (As in all other shops, do not forget your receipt if you buy anything). The no-haggling rule applies in the case of antiques, too — prices are fixed.

| Do you have any …? | 你们这儿有…吗？ | nǐ-men zhèr yǒu … ma |
| --- | --- | --- |
| ancient coins | 古币 | gǔ-bì |
| bronzeware | 青铜制品 | qīng-tóng zhì-pǐn |
| calligraphy | 书法 | shū-fǎ |
| carpets | 地毯 | dì-tǎn |
| ceramics | 陶瓷 | táo-cí |
| camel | 骆驼 | luò-tuo |
| dog | 狗 | gǒu |
| horse | 马 | mǎ |
| pig | 猪 | zhū |
| chinaware | 瓷器 | cí-qì |
| cloisonné-ware | 景泰蓝 | jǐng-tài-lán |
| folding screens | 折叠屏风 | zhé-dié píng-fēng |
| ivory | 象牙制品 | xiàng-yá zhì-pǐn |
| jade | 玉石制品 | yù-shí zhì-pǐn |
| jewels | 珠宝首饰 | zhū-bǎo shǒu-shi |
| lacquerware | 漆器 | qī-qì |
| pearls | 珍珠 | zhēn-zhū |
| porcelain | 细瓷器 | xì cí-qì |
| scrolls | 卷轴 | juàn-zhóu |
| snuff bottles | 鼻烟壶 | bí-yān-hú |
| What period does this date from? | 这是哪个时期的？ | zhè shì nǎ-ge shí-qī de |
| How old is it? | 这东西有多长的历史？ | zhè dōng-xi yǒu duō cháng de lì-shǐ |
| Who made it? | 这是谁的作品？ | zhè shì shéi de zuò-pǐn |
| There's a fault here. | 这里有一个残痕。 | zhè-li yǒu yí-ge cán-hén |
| I'd like to see some other items. | 我想看看别的品种。 | wǒ xiǎng kàn-kan bié de pǐn-zhǒng |
| I like this one. | 我喜欢这件。 | wǒ xǐ-huan zhè jiàn |
| How much is it? | 这要多少钱？ | zhè yào duō-shao qián |

### Bookshop — Stationer's 书店-文具店

Those fortunate travellers with a reading knowledge of Chinese will, of course, have no problem finding a book to interest them in a bookshop. Works published in translation are on sale in foreign-language bookshops found in the main cities. Foreign newspapers and magazines are only sold in Friendship Stores and in major hotels.

| | | |
|---|---|---|
| Where's the nearest …? | 离这儿最近的…在哪儿？ | lí zhèr zuì jìn de … zài năr |
| (foreign language) bookshop | （外文）书店 | (wài-wén) shū-diàn |
| stationer's | 文具店 | wén-jù-diàn |
| newsstand | 售报亭 | shòu-bào-tíng |
| Where can I buy an English-language newspaper? | 哪儿能买到英文报纸？ | năr néng mǎi dào yīng-wén bào-zhǐ |
| Do you sell stationery? | 你这儿卖文具吗？ | nǐ zhèr mài wén-jù ma |
| Where's the guidebook section? | 哪儿卖旅游指南？ | năr mài lǚ-yóu zhǐ-nán |
| Where do you keep the English books? | 英文书在哪儿？ | yīng-wén shū zài năr |
| Is there an English translation of …? | 有…的英译本吗？ | yǒu … de yīng-yì-běn ma |
| Do you have second-hand books? | 这儿卖旧书吗？ | zhèr mài jiù-shū ma |
| I want to buy a/an/some … | 我想买… | wǒ xiǎng mǎi … |
| abacus | 一把算盘 | yì-bǎ suàn-pan |
| address book | 一本通讯簿 | yì-běn tōng-xùn-bù |
| adhesive tape | 一卷胶条 | yì-juǎn jiāo-tiáo |
| ball-point pen | 一支圆珠笔 | yì-zhī yuán-zhū-bǐ |
| book | 一本书 | yì-běn shū |
| calendar | 一本日历 | yì-běn rì-lì |
| carbon paper* | 一盒复写纸 | yì-hé fù-xiě-zhǐ |
| colouring pencils | 一盒彩色铅笔 | yì-hé cǎi-sè qiān-bǐ |

* Where in English we can use the general word "some", the Chinese language is more specific. For example, the English "some carbon paper" is translated by "a box of carbon paper" to indicate quantity. Some other qualifiers used are "a pad of …" and "a bottle of …".

| crayons | 一盒腊笔 | yì-hé là-bǐ |
| dictionary | 一本…字典 | yì-běn … zì-diǎn |
| Chinese-English | 汉英 | hàn-yīng |
| English-Chinese | 英汉 | yīng-hàn |
| pocket | 袖珍 | xiù-zhēn |
| drawing paper | 一本图画纸 | yì-běn tú-huà-zhǐ |
| drawing pins | 一盒图钉 | yì-hé tú-dīng |
| envelopes | 一打信封 | yì-dá xìn-fēng |
| eraser | 一块橡皮 | yí-kuài xiàng-pí |
| exercise book | 一本练习本 | yì-běn liàn-xí-běn |
| felt-tip pen | 一支软芯笔 | yì-zhī ruǎn-xīn-bǐ |
| fountain pen | 一支钢笔 | yì-zhī gāng-bǐ |
| glue | 一瓶胶水儿 | yì-píng jiāo-shuǐr |
| guidebook | 一本旅游指南 | yì-běn lǚ-yóu zhǐ-nán |
| ink | 一瓶…墨水儿 | yì-píng … mò-shuǐr |
| black/red/blue | 黑/红/蓝 | hēi/hóng/lán |
| labels | 一盒签条 | yì-hé qiān-tiáo |
| magazine | 一本杂志 | yì-běn zá-zhì |
| map | 一张地图 | yì-zhāng dì-tú |
| map of the city | 市区地图 | shì-qū dì-tú |
| map of China | 中国地图 | zhōng-guó dì-tú |
| mechanical pencil | 一支自动铅笔 | yì-zhī zì-dòng qiān-bǐ |
| notebook | 一本笔记本 | yì-běn bǐ-jì-běn |
| note paper | 一本信纸 | yì-běn xìn-zhǐ |
| paintbox | 一个油画箱 | yí-ge yóu-huà-xiāng |
| paper | 一张纸 | yì-zhāng zhǐ |
| paperback | 一本简装本 | yì-běn jiǎn-zhuāng-běn |
| paperclips | 一盒曲别针 | yì-hé qū-bié-zhēn |
| pen | 一支钢笔 | yì-zhī gāng-bǐ |
| pencil | 一支铅笔 | yì-zhī qiān-bǐ |
| pencil sharpener | 一个转笔刀 | yí-ge zhuàn-bǐ-dāo |
| playing cards | 一副扑克 | yí-fù pū-kè |
| pocket calculator | 一个袖珍计算器 | yí-ge xiù-zhēn jì-suàn-qì |
| postcards | 几张明信片 | jǐ-zhāng míng-xìn-piàn |
| propelling pencil | 一支自动铅笔 | yì-zhī zì-dòng qiān-bǐ |
| refill (for a pen) | 一个钢笔芯 | yí-ge gāng-bǐ-xīn |
| rubber | 一块橡皮 | yí-kuài xiàng-pí |
| rubber bands | 几根橡皮筋儿 | jǐ-gēn xiàng-pí-jīnr |
| ruler | 一把尺子 | yì-bǎ chǐ-zi |
| staples | 一盒钉书钉 | yì-hé dīng-shū-dīng |
| string | 一根绳子 | yì-gēn shéng-zi |
| thumbtacks | 一盒图钉 | yì-hé tú-dīng |
| travel guide | 一本旅游指南 | yì-běn lǚ-yóu zhǐ-nán |
| typewriter ribbon | 一卷打字机色带 | yì-juǎn dǎ-zì-jī sè-dài |
| typing paper | 一打打字纸 | yì-dá dǎ-zì-zhǐ |
| wrapping paper | 一张包装纸 | yì-zhāng bāo-zhuāng-zhǐ |
| writing pad | 一本拍纸薄 | yì-běn pāi-zhǐ-bù |

## Chemist's (drugstore) 药店

There are two types of pharmacy in China: those dealing with Western medicine and those specializing in traditional Chinese medicine. Some shops have counters for both services. Though the range of pharmaceutical goods to be found in China should generally be sufficient for your trip, it would be wise to take along a supply of any drugs that you use regularly. Products that you may not find readily available include tampons, sanitary towels, cold and indigestion remedies, insect repellent and adhesive plasters.

If trying a traditional pharmacy then you should describe your pain or problem to the person in charge who will sell you a herb-based remedy.

Toiletries cannot be bought at the chemist's; for these you should go to a department store.

This section has been divided into two parts:

1. Pharmaceutical — medicine, first-aid etc.
2. Toiletry — toilet articles, cosmetics

### General 一般询问

| Where's the nearest (all-night) chemist's? | 离这儿最近的（夜营）药店在哪儿？ | lí zhèr zuì jìn de (yè-yíng) yào-diàn zài nǎr |
| What time does the chemist's open/close? | 药店几点开门/关门？ | yào-diàn jǐ diǎn kāi mén/guān mén |

### 1 — Pharmaceutical 药品

| I want something for (a) ... | 我要一些治…的药。 | wǒ yào yì-xiē zhì ... de yào |
| cold/cough | 感冒/咳嗽 | gǎn-mào/ké-sou |
| hay fever | 枯草热 | kū-cǎo-rè |
| insect bites | 虫咬伤 | chóng-yǎo-shāng |
| sunburn | 晒伤 | shài-shāng |
| travel sickness | 晕车 | yūn-chē |
| upset stomach | 反胃 | fǎn wèi |

DOCTOR, see page 138

采购指南

108

|  |  |  |
|---|---|---|
| I'd like Western medicine. | 我想要西药。 | wǒ xiǎng-yào xī-yào |
| Can I get it without a prescription? | 没有处方能买这药吗？ | méi-yǒu chǔ-fāng néng mǎi zhè yào ma |
| Can you make up this prescription for me? | 请按这个处方配药。 | qǐng àn zhè-ge chǔ-fāng pèi yào |
| Shall I wait? | 我得等吗？ | wǒ děi děng ma |
| Can I have a/an/some …? | 请给我拿一些… | qǐng gěi wǒ ná yì-xiē |
| analgesic | 止疼药 | zhǐ-téng-yào |
| aspirin | 阿司匹林 | ā-sī-pǐ-lín |
| bandage | 绷带 | bēng-dài |
| elastic bandage | 弹性绷带 | tán-xìng bēng-dài |
| Band-Aids | 带药垫橡皮膏 | dài yào-diàn xiàng-pí-gāo |
| chlorine tablets | 氯片 | lǜ-piàn |
| contraceptives | 避孕药 | bì-yùn-yào |
| corn plasters | 鸡眼膏 | jī-yǎn-gāo |
| cotton wool (absorbent cotton) | 脱脂棉 | tuō-zhī-mián |
| cough syrup | 止咳糖浆 | zhǐ ké táng-jiāng |
| disinfectant | 消毒剂 | xiāo-dú-jì |
| ear drops | 滴耳药水 | dī ěr yào-shuǐ |
| Elastoplast | 带药垫橡皮膏 | dài yào-diàn xiàng-pí-gāo |
| eye drops | 眼药水 | yǎn-yào-shuǐ |
| gauze | 纱布 | shā-bù |
| insect repellent | 除虫剂 | chú-chóng-jì |
| insect spray | 除虫喷雾剂 | chú-chóng pēn-wù-jì |
| iodine | 碘酒 | diǎn-jiǔ |
| laxative | 缓泻剂 | huǎn-xiè jì |
| mouthwash | 漱口药水 | shù kǒu yào-shuǐ |
| nose drops | 滴鼻药 | dī-bí-yào |
| quinine tablets | 奎宁片 | kuí-nǐng piàn |
| sanitary towels (napkins) | 妇女卫生巾 | fù-nü wèi-shēng-jīn |
| suppositories | 栓剂 | shuān-jì |
| … tablets | …片 | … piàn |
| thermometer | 体温表 | tǐ-wēn-biǎo |
| throat lozenges | 喉咙含片 | hóu-lóng hán-piàn |

| | |
|---|---|
| 只可外用<br>zhǐ kě wài yòng<br>FOR EXTERNAL USE ONLY | 有毒<br>yǒu dú<br>POISON |

## 2 — Toiletry 盥洗卫生用品及化妆品

Friendship Stores now carry a much wider range of Western goods, and the best selection will be found in the main cities. However, there are certain things that are still quite difficult to find, and it is worth taking a supply of them along with you. These things include shampoo, Western cosmetics and suntanning preparations.

| I'd like a/an/some … | 我想要… | wǒ xiǎng-yào |
|---|---|---|
| after-shave lotion* | 一瓶修面后香水 | yì-píng xiū miàn hòu xiāng-shuǐ |
| bath essence | 一瓶洗澡液 | yì-píng xǐ-zǎo-yè |
| bath salts | 一袋洗澡粉 | yí-dài xǐ-zǎo-fěn |
| blusher | 一盒胭脂 | yì-hé yān-zhī |
| cream | 一瓶雪花膏 | yì-píng xuě-huā-gāo |
|   cleansing cream | 一瓶下妆面霜 | yì-píng xià-zhuāng miàn-shuāng |
|   foundation cream | 一瓶底层面霜 | yì-píng dǐ-céng miàn-shuāng |
|   moisturizing cream | 一瓶润肤霜 | yì-píng rùn-fū-shuāng |
| cuticle remover | 一瓶除皮屑剂 | yì-píng chú pí-xiè jì |
| deodorant | 一瓶除体臭液 | yì-píng chú tǐ-xiù yè |
| emery board | 一打锉指甲砂纸 | yì-dá cuò zhī-jia shā-zhǐ |
| eye liner | 一支眼线笔 | yì-zhī yǎn-xiàn-bǐ |
| eyebrow pencil | 一支画眉笔 | yì-zhī huà-méi-bǐ |
| eye shadow | 一管眼影膏 | yì-guǎn yǎn-yǐng gāo |
| face powder | 一盒脸粉 | yì-hé liǎn-fěn |
| hand cream | 一瓶润手霜 | yì-píng rùn-shǒu-shuāng |
| lipsalve | 一盒防唇裂油膏 | yì-hé fáng chún liè yóu-gāo |
| lipstick | 一管口红 | yì-guǎn kǒu-hóng |
| make-up remover pads | 一袋下妆棉球 | yí-dài xià-zhuāng mián-qiú |
| mascara | 一瓶染睫毛油 | yì-píng rǎn jié-máo yóu |
| mirror | 一面镜子 | yí-miàn jìng-zi |
| nail brush | 一把指甲油刷子 | yì-bǎ zhī-jia-yóu shuā-zi |
| nail clippers | 一把指甲刀 | yì-bǎ zhī-jia-dāo |
| nail file | 一把指甲锉 | yì-bǎ zhī-jia-cuò |

* Where in English we use the word "some", the Chinese is more specific when necessary, using the translation "a bottle of …".

| nail polish | 一瓶指甲油 | yì-píng zhī-jia-yóu |
| nail polish remover | 一瓶退指甲油水 | yì-píng tuì zhī-jia-yóu shui |
| nail scissors | 一把指甲剪刀 | yì-bǎ zhī-jia-jiǎn-dāo |
| perfume | 一瓶香水 | yì-píng xiāng-shuǐ |
| powder puff | 一个粉扑 | yí-ge fěn-pū |
| razor | 一把剃须刀 | yì-bǎ tì-xū-dāo |
| razor blades | 一盒剃须刀片 | yì-hé tì-xū-dāo-piàn |
| safety pins | 一盒别针 | yì-hé bié-zhēn |
| shaving brush | 一把剃须肥皂刷 | yì-bǎ tì-xū féi-zào-shuā |
| shaving soap | 一瓶剃须皂液 | yì-píng tì-xū zào-yè |
| soap | 一块肥皂 | yí-kuài féi-zào |
| sponge | 一块海绵 | yí-kuài hǎi-mián |
| sun-tan cream | 一盒晒黑膏 | yì-hé shài-hēi-gāo |
| sun-tan oil | 一瓶晒黑油 | yì-píng shài-hēi-yóu |
| talcum powder | 一盒爽身粉 | yì-hé shuǎng-shēn-fěn |
| tissues | 一包纸手绢儿 | yì-bāo zhǐ shǒu-juànr |
| toilet paper | 一卷卫生纸 | yì-juǎn wèi-shēng-zhǐ |
| toilet water | 一瓶爽身香水 | yì-píng shuǎng-shēn xiāng-shuǐ |
| toothbrush | 一把牙刷 | yì-bǎ yá-shuā |
| (tube of) toothpaste | (一筒) 牙膏 | (yì-tǒng) yá-gāo |
| towel | 一条毛巾 | yì-tiáo máo-jīn |
| tweezers | 一把镊子 | yì-bǎ niè-zi |

## For your hair 洗发用品

| bobby pins | 几个卡子 | jǐ-ge qiǎ-zi |
| colour shampoo | 一瓶染发洗发膏 | yì-píng rǎn-fà xǐ-fà-gāo |
| comb | 一把梳子 | yì-bǎ shū-zi |
| curlers | 几个卷发夹子 | jǐ-ge juǎn-fà jiā-zi |
| dry shampoo | 一袋干性洗发剂 | yí-dài gān-xìng xǐ-fà-jì |
| dye | 一瓶染发剂 | yì-píng rǎn-fà-jì |
| hairbrush | 一把发刷 | yì-bǎ fà-shuā |
| hairgrips | 几个卡子 | jǐ-ge qiǎ-zi |
| hair lotion | 一瓶护发液 | yì-píng hù-fà-yè |
| hair spray | 一瓶喷雾发浆 | yì-píng pēn-wù fà-jiāng |
| setting lotion | 一瓶冷烫水 | yì-píng lěng-tàng-shuǐ |
| shampoo | 一瓶…洗发剂 | yì-píng … xǐ-fà-jì |
| for dry hair | 抗干发 | kàng gān fà |
| greasy (oily) hair | 抗多油发 | kàng duō yóu fà |
| wig | 一副假发 | yí-fù jiǎ-fà |

## For the baby 婴儿用品

| baby food | 婴儿食品 | yīng-ér shí-pǐn |
| dummy (pacifier) | 橡皮奶嘴儿 | xiàng-pí nǎi-zuǐr |
| feeding bottle | 奶瓶 | nǎi-píng |
| nappies (diapers) | 纸尿布 | zhǐ niào-bù |

### Clothing 衣服

If you want to buy something specific, prepare yourself in advance. Look at the list of clothing on page 116. Get some idea of the colour, material and size you want. They are all listed in the next few pages.

Provided you have brought a pattern along with you, you can have a shirt, blouse or simple silk dress made up in about 48 hours. Men's suits made to measure take a little longer. The tailoring is generally high quality and extremely reasonable in price. See phrases on page 114.

### General 一般询问

| | | |
|---|---|---|
| I'd like … | 我想要… | wǒ xiǎng-yào |
| I want something for a … | 我要买给…穿的衣服 | wǒ yào mǎi gěi … chuān de yī-fu |
| boy/girl<br>man/woman | 男孩儿/女孩儿<br>男人/女人 | nán-háir/nǚ-háir<br>nán-rén/nǚ-rén |
| I like the one in the window. | 我喜欢橱窗里的那个。 | wǒ xǐ-huan chú-chuāng li de nà-ge |
| Could you show me another one? | 可以再给我看一个别的吗 | kě-yǐ zài gěi wǒ kàn yí-ge bié de ma |
| I want something like this. | 我要一件像这个样子的。 | wǒ yào yí-jiàn xiàng zhè-ge yàng-zi de |

| | | | |
|---|---|---|---|
| 1 centimetre (cm.) | = 0.39 in. | 1 inch | = 2.54 cm. |
| 1 metre (m.) | = 39.37 in. | 1 foot | = 30.5 cm. |
| 10 metres | = 32.81 ft. | 1 yard | = 0.91 m. |

Although the metric system has been adopted in China, part of the population continues to use the following units for length measurement:

| | | |
|---|---|---|
| 1 市尺 (shì-chǐ) | = 0.33 m. | = 1.094 ft. |
| 3 市尺 (shì-chǐ) | = 1 m. | = 3.281 ft. |

## Colour 颜色

| | | |
|---|---|---|
| I want something in … | 我想要…的。 | wǒ xiǎng-yào … de |
| I want a … shade. | 我想要颜色…的。 | wǒ xiǎng-yào yán-sè … de |
| darker | 深些 | shēn xiē |
| lighter | 浅些 | qiǎn xiē |
| I want something to match this. | 我想要和这个相配的。 | wǒ xiǎng-yào hé zhè-ge xiāng pèi de |
| I don't like the colour. | 我不喜欢这种颜色。 | wǒ bù xǐ-huan zhè-zhǒng yán-sè |
| Is it colour-fast? | 这料子退色吗？ | zhè liào-zi tuì sè ma |

| | | |
|---|---|---|
| beige | 浅咖啡色 | qiǎn kā-fēi-sè |
| black | 黑色 | hēi-sè |
| blue | 蓝色 | lán-sè |
| brown | 褐色 | hè-sè |
| fawn | 浅黄褐色 | qiǎn huáng-hè-sè |
| golden | 金黄色 | jīn-huáng-sè |
| green | 绿色 | lǜ-sè |
| grey | 灰色 | huī-sè |
| mauve | 紫红色 | zǐ-hóng-sè |
| orange | 桔红色 | jú-hóng-sè |
| pink | 粉红色 | fěn-hóng-sè |
| purple | 紫色 | zǐ-sè |
| red | 红色 | hóng-sè |
| scarlet | 鲜红色 | xiān-hóng-sè |
| silver | 银灰色 | yín-huī-sè |
| turquoise | 青绿色 | qīng-lǜ-sè |
| white | 白色 | bái-sè |
| yellow | 黄色 | huáng-sè |
| light | 浅色 | qiǎn-sè |
| dark | 深色 | shēn-sè |

| | | | | |
|---|---|---|---|---|
| 一色 | 直条纹 | 小圆点 | 方格 | 图案 |
| (yī-sè) | (zhí-tiáo-wén) | (xiǎo yuán-diǎn) | (fāng-gé) | (tú-àn) |

## Material 布料

| Do you have anything in …? | 你这儿有…的吗？ | nǐ zhèr yǒu … de ma |
| Is it …? | 这是…的吗？ | zhè shì … de ma |
| colour fast | 不退色 | bú tuì sè |
| crease resistant | 抗皱 | kàng zhòu |
| pure cotton/silk | 纯棉/真丝 | chún mián/zhēn sī |
| synthetic | 人造纤维 | rén-zào xiān-wéi |
| hand-made | 手工制 | shǒu-gōng zhì |
| imported | 进口 | jìn-kǒu |
| made here | 本地生产 | běn-dì shēng-chǎn |
| Will it shrink? | 这料子缩水吗？ | zhè liào-zi suō-shuǐ ma |
| I'd like something … | 我想要…的料子。 | wǒ xiǎng-yào … de liào-zi |
| thicker/thinner | 厚些/薄些 | hòu xiē/báo xiē |
| Do you have any better quality? | 你这儿有质量好些的吗？ | nǐ zhèr yǒu zhí-liàng hǎo xiē de ma |
| What is it made of? | 这是什么料子？ | zhè shì shén-me liào-zi |
| How much is it per metre? | 一公尺多少钱？ | yì gōng-chǐ duō-shao qián |

| brocade | 织锦缎 | zhī-jǐn -duàn |
| corduroy | 灯芯绒 | dēng-xīn-róng |
| cotton | 棉布 | mián-bù |
| crepe | 绉绸 | zhòu-chóu |
| denim | 劳动布 | láo-dòng-bù |
| felt | 毡 | zhān |
| flannel | 法兰绒 | fǎ-lán-róng |
| gabardine | 华达呢 | huá-dá-ní |
| lace | 约织布料 | gōu-zhī bù-liào |
| leather | 皮子 | pí-zi |
| linen | 亚麻布 | yà-má-bù |
| poplin | 府绸 | fǔ-chóu |
| satin | 缎子 | duàn-zi |
| silk | 丝绸 | sī-chóu |
| raw silk | 生丝 | shēng-sī |
| suede | 翻毛皮 | fān-máo-pí |
| towelling | 毛巾布 | máo-jīn-bù |
| velvet | 天鹅绒 | tiān-é-róng |
| wool | 纯毛 | chún-máo |

## Tailor's — Dressmaker's 裁缝店

| I'd like a ... made to measure. | 我想订做… | wǒ xiǎng dìng zuò |
|---|---|---|
| blouse | 女衬衫 | nǚ chèn-shān |
| dress | 连衣裙 | lián-yī-qún |
| jacket | 上衣 | shàng-yī |
| shirt | 衬衫 | chèn-shān |
| skirt | 裙子 | qún-zi |
| Do you have any material samples? | 你有料子的样品吗？ | nǐ yǒu liào-zi de yàng-pǐn ma |
| How much material do I need for a ...? | 我做一件…要用多少布料？ | wǒ zuò yí-jiàn ... yào yòng duō-shao bù-liào |
| Can you copy this? | 你能照这个样子做吗？ | nǐ néng zhào zhè-ge yàng-zi zuò ma |
| I have some material. | 我有一些布料。 | wǒ yǒu yì-xiē bù-liào |
| I have a pattern. | 我有样子。 | wǒ yǒu yàng-zi |
| Please make up ... (quantity) to the same pattern. | 请照这个样子做…件。 | qǐng zhào zhè-ge yàng-zi zuò ... jiàn |
| How long will the job take? | 多长时间能做好？ | duō cháng shí-jiān néng zuò hǎo |
| How many fittings will be necessary? | 要试几次样子？ | yào shì jǐ cì yàng-zi |
| When must I come back? | 我什么时间再来？ | wǒ shén-me shí-jiān zài lái |

| button | 钮扣 | niǔ-kòu |
|---|---|---|
| collar | 衣领 | yī-lǐng |
| cuff | 袖口 | xiù-kǒu |
| elastic | 松紧带 | sōng-jǐn-dài |
| hem | 衣边 | yī-biān |
| lapel | 翻领 | fān-lǐng |
| lining | 衬里 | chèn-lǐ |
| ribbon | 彩带 | cǎi-dài |
| seam | 接缝 | jiē-fèng |
| sleeve | 袖子 | xiù-zi |
| waist | 腰 | yāo |
| longer | 长些 | cháng xiē |
| shorter | 短些 | duǎn siē |

FOR A GOOD FIT, see page 115

采购指南

**Sizes** 尺寸

Clothing sizes in China are still being standardized, and do not correspond to those in the West. In Friendship Stores, where clothes are made for export, you'll find three sizes — small, medium and large. As a general rule, though, clothes are designed for smaller people than in the West and are also cut more generously.

If you want to buy clothes in a department store you will find that the sizes are based on a combination of two measurements — one of which is usually height. For example, a jacket may be sized 165-88. This means it should fit someone who is 1 metre 65cm. tall, and has an 88cm. chest. Trousers will be sized according to height and waist.

When buying shoes the best bet is to try a few pairs on, if you can find any large enough (39/UK 6/US 7 ½ is considered large).

| | | |
|---|---|---|
| I don't know the Chinese sizes. | 我不知道中国尺寸。 | wǒ bù zhī-dao zhōng-guó chǐ-cùn |
| Could you measure me? | 请你给我量量好吗？ | qǐng nǐ gěi wǒ liáng-liang hǎo ma |

| 小<br>xiǎo<br>SMALL | 中<br>zhōng<br>MEDIUM | 大<br>dà<br>LARGE |
|---|---|---|

**A good fit?** 合适吗？

| | | |
|---|---|---|
| Can I try it on? | 我可以试穿一下儿吗？ | wǒ kě-yǐ shì-chuān yí xiàr ma |
| Where's the changing room? | 试衣室在哪儿？ | shì-yī-shì zài nǎr |
| Is there a mirror? | 这儿有镜子吗？ | zhèr yǒu jìng-zi ma |
| It fits very well. | 这很合适。 | zhè hěn hé-shì |
| It doesn't fit. | 这不合适。 | zhè bù hé-shì |

NUMBERS, see page 149

采购指南

| It's too … | 这太… | zhè tài |
| tight/loose | 紧/肥 | jǐn/féi |
| short/long | 短/长 | duǎn/féi |
| How long will it take to alter? | 改一下需要多长时间？ | gǎi yí-xià xū-yào duō cháng shí-jiān |

## Clothes and accessories 服装及有关用品

| I'd like a/an/some … | 我想要… | wǒ xiǎng-yào |
| anorak | 一件登山服 | yí-jiàn dēng-shān-fú |
| bathrobe | 一件浴衣 | yí-jiàn yù-yī |
| bathing cap | 一顶游泳帽 | yì-dǐng yóu-yǒng-mào |
| bathing suit | 一件游泳衣 | yí-jiàn yóu-yǒng-yī |
| blouse | 一件女衬衫 | yí-jiàn nǚ chèn-shān |
| bra | 一副乳罩 | yí-fù rǔ-zhào |
| braces (Br.) | 一副背带 | yí-fù bēi-dài |
| briefs | 一条内裤 | yì-tiáo nèi-kù |
| cap | 一顶帽子 | yì-dǐng mào-zi |
| cardigan | 一件开身毛衣 | yí-jiàn kāi shēn máo-yī |
| cheongsam | 一件旗袍 | yí-jiàn qí-páo |
| coat | 一件大衣 | yí-jiàn dà-yī |
| dress | 一件连衣裙 | yí-jiàn lián-yī-qún |
| dressing gown | 一件浴衣 | yí-jiàn yù-yī |
| evening dress (woman's) | 一件女晚礼服 | yí-jiàn nǚ wǎn-lǐ-fú |
| girdle | 一条健美内裤 | yì-tiáo jiàn-měi nèi-kù |
| gloves | 一副手套 | yí-fù shǒu-tào |
| handbag | 一个手提包 | yí-ge shǒu-tí-bāo |
| handkerchief | 一条手绢儿 | yì-tiáo shǒu-juànr |
| hat | 一顶礼帽 | yì-dǐng lǐ-mào |
| jacket | 一件上衣 | yí-jiàn shàng-yī |
| silk-padded jacket | 一件丝棉袄 | yí-jiàn sī mián-ǎo |
| cotton-padded jacket | 一件棉袄 | yí-jiàn mián-ǎo |
| jeans | 一条牛仔裤 | yì-tiáo niú-zǎi-kù |
| kimono | 一件和服 | yí-jiàn hé-fú |
| leotard | 一件体操服 | yí-jiàn tǐ-cāo-fú |
| nightdress | 一件长睡衣 | yí-jiàn cháng shuì-yī |
| overalls | 一条工装裤 | yì-tiáo gōng-zhuāng-kù |
| pair of … | 一双… | yì-shuāng |
| panties | 一条内裤 | yì-tiáo nèi-kù |
| pants (Am.) | 一条长裤 | yì-tiáo cháng kù |
| panty hose | 一条裤袜 | yì-tiáo kù-wà |
| parka | 一件登山服 | yí-jiàn dēng-shān-fú |
| pullover | 一件…毛衣 | yí-jiàn … máo-yī |
| polo-neck (turtle-neck) | 高领 | gāo lǐng |

| | | |
|---|---|---|
| round neck | 圆领 | yuán lǐng |
| V-neck | 鸡心领 | jī-xīn lǐng |
| with long/short sleeves | 长袖/短袖 | cháng xiù/duǎn xiù |
| sleeveless pullover | 一件毛背心 | yí-jiàn máo bèi-xīn |
| pyjamas | 一套睡衣 | yí-tào shuì-yī |
| raincoat | 一件雨衣 | yí-jiàn yǔ-yī |
| scarf | 一条围巾 | yì-tiáo wéi-jīn |
| shirt | 一件衬衫 | yí-jiàn chèn-shān |
| shorts | 一条短裤 | yì-tiáo duǎn-kù |
| skirt | 一条裙子 | yì-tiáo qún-zi |
| slip | 一条衬裙 | yì-tiáo chèn-qún |
| socks (a pair of) | 一双袜子 | yì-shuāng wà-zi |
| sports jacket | 一件运动衫 | yí-jiàn yùn-dòng-shān |
| stockings (a pair of) | 一双长袜 | yì-shuāng cháng wà |
| suit (men) | 一套男西服 | yí-tào nán xī-fú |
| suit (women) | 一套女西服 | yí-tào nǚ xī-fú |
| suspenders (Am.) | 一副背带 | yí-fù bēi-dài |
| sweater | 一件毛衣 | yí-jiàn máo-yī |
| sweatshirt | 一件长袖运动衫 | yí-jiàn cháng xiù yùn-dòng-shān |
| swimming trunks | 一条游泳裤 | yì-tiáo yóu-yǒng-kù |
| swimsuit | 一件游泳衣 | yí-jiàn yóu-yǒng-yī |
| T-shirt | 一件针织衬衫 | yí-jiàn zhēn-zhī chèn-shān |
| tie | 一条领带 | yì-tiáo lǐng-dài |
| tights | 一条裤袜 | yì-tiáo kù-wà |
| tracksuit | 一套运动衫 | yí-tào yùn-dòng-shān |
| trousers | 一条长裤 | yì-tiáo cháng kù |
| umbrella | 一把雨伞 | yì-bǎ yǔ-sǎn |
| underpants | 一条男内裤 | yì-tiáo nán nèi-kù |
| undershirt | 一件背心 | yí-jiàn bèi-xīn |
| vest (Am.) | 一件西服坎肩 | yí-jiàn xī-fú kǎn-jiān |
| vest (Br.) | 一件背心 | yí-jiàn bèi-xīn |
| waistcoat | 一件西服坎肩 | yí-jiàn xī-fú kǎn-jiān |

| | | |
|---|---|---|
| belt | 腰带 | yāo-dài |
| buckle | 带扣 | dài-kòu |
| button | 钮扣 | niǔ-kòu |
| pocket | 衣袋 | yī-dài |
| press stud (snap fastener) | 按扣 | àn-kòu |
| zip (zipper) | 拉锁 | lā-suǒ |

采购指南

## Shoes 鞋

| I'd like a pair of … | 我想买一双… | wǒ xiǎng mǎi yì-shuāng |
| --- | --- | --- |
| boots | 靴子 | xuē-zi |
| plimsolls (sneakers) | 球鞋 | qiú-xié |
| sandals | 凉鞋 | liáng-xié |
| shoes | …鞋 | … xié |
|   flat | 平底 | píng-dǐ |
|   with a heel | 有跟的 | yǒu gēn de |
| slippers | 拖鞋 | tuō-xié |
| These are too … | 这些都太… | zhè xiē dōu tài |
| narrow/wide | 紧/肥 | jǐn/féi |
| big/small | 大/小 | dà/xiǎo |
| Do you have a larger/smaller size? | 有你大些/小些的吗？ | nǐ yǒu dà-xiē/xiǎo-xiē de ma |
| Do you have the same in black? | 你们这儿有这种式样的黑颜色的吗？ | nǐ-men zhèr yǒu zhèi zhǒng shì-yàng de hēi yán-sè de ma |
| cloth | 布料 | bù-liào |
| leather | 皮子 | pí-zi |
| rubber | 橡胶 | xiàng-jiāo |
| suede | 翻毛皮 | fān-máo-pí |
| Is it genuine leather? | 这是真皮子的吗？ | zhè shì zhēn pí-zi de ma |
| I'd like some shoe polish. | 我想买一筒鞋油。 | wǒ xiǎng mǎi yì-tǒng xié-yóu |
| I'd like some shoelaces. | 我要买鞋带。 | wǒ yào mǎi xié-dài |

Shoes worn out? Here's the key to getting them fixed again:

| Can you repair these shoes? | 你能修这些鞋子吗？ | nǐ néng xiū zhè-xiē xié-zi ma |
| --- | --- | --- |
| Can you stitch this? | 你能缝补这个吗？ | nǐ néng féng-bǔ zhè-ge ma |
| I want new soles and heels. | 我要换新鞋底和鞋跟。 | wǒ yào huàn xīn xié-dǐ hé xié-gēn |
| When will they be ready? | 什么时候能修好？ | shén-me shí-hou néng xiū hǎo |

COLOURS, see page 112

**Electrical appliances** 电器

Electrical current is 220 volts, 50 cycles. It is advisable to take your own appliances with you as well as a plug adaptor — plug sizes vary throughout China. The electric current supply is not always stable, so be prepared for occasional power fluctuations.

| | | |
|---|---|---|
| Do you have a battery for this? | 你这儿有适用于这个…的电池吗？ | nǐ zhèr yǒu shì-yòng yú zhè-ge … de diàn-chí ma |
| Do you have a plug for this? | 你这儿有适用于这个…的插头吗？ | nǐ zhèr yǒu shì-yòng yú zhè-ge … de chā-tóu ma |
| This is broken. Can you repair it? | 这个坏了。你这儿能修吗？ | zhè-ge huài le. nǐ zhèr néng xiū ma |
| Can you show me how it works? | 能教我怎么用吗？ | néng jiāo wǒ zěn-me yòng ma |
| I'd like to hire a video cassette/video recorder. | 我想租一盘录像带/一台录像机 | wǒ xiǎng zū yì-pán lù-xiàng-dài/yì-tái lù-xiàng-jī |
| I'd like a/an/some … | 我想要… | wǒ xiǎng-yào |
| adaptor | 一个多路插座 | yí-ge duō-lù chā-zuò |
| amplifier | 一台扩音机 | yì-tái kuò-yīn-jī |
| battery | 几节电池 | jǐ-jié diàn-chí |
| bulb | 一个灯泡 | yí-ge dēng-pào |
| clock | 一座钟 | yí-zuò zhōng |
| extension lead (cord) | 一根接长电线 | yì-gēn jiē-cháng diàn-xiàn |
| hair dryer | 一个电吹发器 | yí-ge diàn chuī-fà-qì |
| headphones | 一副耳机 | yí-fù ěr-jī |
| iron | 一个熨斗 | yí-ge yùn-dǒu |
| lamp | 一盏灯 | yì-zhǎn dēng |
| plug | 一个插头 | yí-ge chā-tóu |
| portable … | 袖珍… | xiù-zhēn |
| radio | 一台收音机 | yì-tái shōu-yīn-jī |
| record player | 一台留声机 | yì-tái liú-shēng-jī |
| shaver | 一个电动剃须刀 | yí-ge diàn-dòng tì-xū-dāo |
| speakers | 一个扬声器 | yí-ge yáng-shēng-qì |
| (cassette) tape recorder | 一台（盒式）磁带录音机 | yì-tái (hé-shì) cí-dài lù-yīn-jī |
| (colour) television | 一台（彩色）电视机 | yì-tái (cǎi-sè) diàn-shì-jī |
| transformer | 一个变压器 | yí-ge biàn-yā-qì |
| video recorder | 一台录像机 | yì-tái lù-xiàng-jī |

### Grocery 副食店

Here are a few phrases to help you out when buying food for a picnic or journey.

| | | |
|---|---|---|
| I'd like a loaf of bread, please. | 我想要一个面包。 | wǒ xiǎng-yào yí-ge miàn-bāo |
| I'll have one of those, please. | 我要一块那种的。 | wǒ yào yí-kuài nèi-zhǒng de |
| May I help myself? | 我能自己拿吗？ | wǒ néng zì-jǐ ná ma |
| I'd like ... | 我想要… | wǒ xiǎng-yào |
| a kilo of eggs | 一公斤鸡蛋 | yì gōng-jīn jī-dàn |
| half a kilo of tomatoes | 半公斤西红柿 | bàn gōng-jīn xī-hóng-shì |
| 100 grams of butter | 一百克黄油 | 100 kè huáng-yóu |
| a bottle of milk | 一瓶牛奶 | yì-píng niú-nǎi |
| half a dozen apples | 六个苹果 | 6 ge píng-guǒ |
| 4 slices of ham | 四片火腿 | 4 piàn huǒ-tuǐ |
| a packet of tea | 一包茶叶 | yì-bāo chá-yè |
| a jar of jam | 一瓶果酱 | yì-píng guǒ-jiàng |
| a tin (can) of peaches | 一筒桃子罐头 | yì-tǒng táo-zi guàn-tou |
| a box of chocolates | 一盒巧克力 | yì-hé qiǎo-kè-lì |

### Household 日用品

These everyday items could come in handy on your trip.

| | | |
|---|---|---|
| I'd like a... | 我想要… | wǒ xiǎng-yào |
| bottle opener | 一个开瓶器 | yí-ge kāi-píng-qì |
| can opener | 一个开罐器 | yí-ge kāi-guàn-qì |
| chopsticks | 几双筷子 | jǐ shuāng kuài-zi |
| corkscrew | 一把拔塞钻 | yì-bǎ bá-sāi-zuàn |
| crockery | 一件陶瓷餐具 | yí-jiàn táo-cí cān-jù |
| cutlery | 一套刀叉餐具 | yí-tào dāo-chā cān-jù |
| first-aid kit | 一个急救箱 | yí-ge jí-jiù-xiāng |
| flashlight | 一只手电筒 | yì-zhī shǒu-diàn-tǒng |
| lamp | 一盏灯 | yì-zhǎn dēng |
| mosquito net | 一幅蚊帐 | yì-fú wén-zhàng |
| paper napkins | 一打纸餐巾 | yì-dá zhǐ-cān-jīn |
| penknife | 一把小刀 | yì-bǎ xiǎo-dāo |
| rucksack | 一个帆布背包 | yí-ge fān-bù bēi-bāo |
| scissors | 一把剪刀 | yì-bǎ jiǎn-dāo |
| screwdriver | 一把改锥 | yì-bǎ gǎi-zhuī |
| tin opener | 一个开罐器 | yí-ge kāi-guàn-qì |
| torch | 一只手电筒 | yì-zhī shǒu-diàn-tǒng |
| vacuum flask | 一个暖水瓶 | yí-ge nuǎn-shuǐ-píng |
| water flask | 一个水壶 | yí-ge shuǐ-hú |

FOOD, see also page 63

## Jeweller's — Watchmaker's 首饰店-钟表店

Jewellery is sold in antique shops. Look out for jade objects — the Chinese excel in the art of jade carving. If buying ivory check that it is the real thing and not a substitute — they are virtually indistinguishable.

| | | |
|---|---|---|
| Could I see that, please? | 我可以看看那个吗？ | wǒ kě-yǐ kàn-kan nèi-ge ma |
| Do you have anything in gold? | 你这儿有金制品吗？ | nǐ zhèr yǒu jīn-zhì-pǐn ma |
| How many carats is this? | 这是几开金的？ | zhè shì jǐ kāi jīn de |
| Is this real silver? | 这是银的吗？ | zhè shì yín de ma |
| Can you repair this watch? | 你这儿能修这块表吗？ | nǐ zhèr néng xiū zhè-kuài biǎo ma |
| I'd like a/an/some ... | 我想要… | wǒ xiǎng-yào |
| alarm clock | 一个闹钟 | yí-ge nào-zhōng |
| bangle | 一副手镯 | yí-fù shǒu-zhuó |
| battery | 几节电池 | jǐ-jié diàn-chí |
| bracelet | 一副手镯 | yí-fù shǒu-zhuó |
| chain bracelet | 链手镯 | liàn-shǒu-zhuó |
| charm bracelet | 带饰物链手镯 | dài shì-wù liàn-shǒu-zhuó |
| brooch | 一枚胸针 | yì-méi xiōng-zhēn |
| chop (uncarved Chinese seal) | 一块印章石料 | yí-kuài yìn-zhāng shí-liào |
| chop (carved) | 一枚印章 | yì-méi yìn-zhāng |
| cigarette case | 一个烟盒 | yí-ge yān-hé |
| cigarette lighter | 一个打火机 | yí-ge dǎ-huǒ-jī |
| clip | 一个夹子 | yí-ge jiā-zi |
| clock | 一座钟 | yí-zuò zhōng |
| cuff links | 一枚袖口链扣 | yì-méi xiù-kǒu liàn-kòu |
| cutlery | 一套刀叉餐具 | yí-tào dāo-chā cān-jù |
| earrings | 一副耳环 | yí-fù ěr-huán |
| gem | 一枚宝石 | yì-méi bǎo-shí |
| jewel box | 一个首饰箱 | yí-ge shǒu-shì-xiāng |
| mechanical pencil | 一支自动铅笔 | yì-zhī zì-dòng qiān-bǐ |
| music box | 一个八音盒 | yí-ge bā-yīn-hé |
| necklace | 一副项链 | yí-fù xiàng-liàn |
| pendant | 一些悬饰物 | yì-xiē xuán-shì-wù |
| pin | 一个别针 | yí-ge bié-zhēn |
| pocket watch | 一块怀表 | yí-kuài huái-biǎo |
| powder compact | 一个小粉盒 | yí-ge xiǎo fěn-hé |
| propelling pencil | 一枝自动铅笔 | yì-zhī zì-dòng qiān-bǐ |

| ring | 一枚戒指 | yì-méi jiè-zhi |
| engagement ring | 定婚戒指 | dìng-hūn jiè-zhi |
| wedding ring | 结婚戒指 | jié-hūn jiè-zhi |
| silverware | 一件银器 | yí-jiàn yín-qì |
| tie clip | 一枚领带夹子 | yì-méi lǐng-dài jiā-zi |
| tie pin | 一枚领带别针 | yì-méi lǐng-dài bié-zhēn |
| watch | 一块（…）表 | yí-kuài (…) biǎo |
| automatic | 自动 | zì-dòng |
| digital | 电子显示 | diàn-zǐ xiǎn-shì |
| quartz | 石英 | shí-yīng |
| with a secondhand | 带秒针的 | dài miǎo-zhēn de |
| watchstrap | 一条表带 | yì-tiáo biǎo-dài |
| wristwatch | 一块手表 | yí-kuài shǒu-biǎo |

| amber | 琥珀 | hǔ-pò |
| amethyst | 紫水晶 | zǐ-shuǐ-jīng |
| chromium | 铬 | luò |
| copper | 铜 | tóng |
| coral | 珊瑚 | shān-hú |
| crystal | 水晶 | shuǐ-jīng |
| cut glass | 雕玻璃 | diāo bō-li |
| diamond | 金钢石 | jīn-gāng-shí |
| ebony | 乌木 | wū-mù |
| emerald | 绿刚玉 | lǜ-gāng-yù |
| enamel | 搪瓷 | táng-cí |
| gold | 金 | jīn |
| gold-plated | 镀金的 | dù-jīn de |
| ivory | 象牙 | xiàng-yá |
| jade | 玉 | yù |
| onyx | 缟玛瑙 | gǎo mǎ-nǎo |
| pearl | 珍珠 | zhēn-zhū |
| pewter | 锡镶器皿 | xī-là qì-mǐn |
| platinum | 白金 | bái-jīn |
| ruby | 红宝石 | hóng-bǎo-shí |
| sapphire | 蓝宝石 | lán-bǎo-shí |
| silver | 银 | yín |
| silver-plated | 镀银的 | dù-yín de |
| stainless steel | 不锈钢 | bú-xiù-gāng |
| topaz | 黄玉 | huáng-yù |
| turquoise | 绿松石 | lǜ-sōng-shí |

## Optician's 眼镜店

| I've broken my glasses. | 我的眼镜坏了。 | wǒ de yǎn-jìng huài le |
| Can you repair them for me? | 你这儿能修吗？ | nǐ zhèr néng xiū ma |
| I need them in a hurry. | 我想尽快能用上。 | wǒ xiǎng jìn kuài néng yòng shang |
| When will they be ready? | 什么时候能修好？ | shén-me shí-hou néng xiū hǎo |
| Can you change the lenses? | 你这儿能换镜片吗？ | nǐ zhèr néng huàn jìng-piàn ma |
| I want tinted lenses. | 我想要着色镜片。 | wǒ xiǎng-yào zhuó-sè jìng-piàn |
| The frame is broken. | 这个镜架坏了。 | zhè-ge jìng-jià huài le |
| I'd like a spectacle case. | 我要一个眼镜盒。 | wǒ yào yí-ge yǎn-jìng-hé |
| I'd like to have my eyesight checked. | 我想验光。 | wǒ xiǎng yàn guāng |
| I'm short-sighted/long-sighted. | 我是近视/远视。 | wǒ shì jìn-shi/yuǎn-shi |
| I want some contact lenses. | 我想要角膜接触镜。 | wǒ xiǎng-yào jiǎo-mó jiē-chù-jìng |
| I've lost one of my contact lenses. | 我的角膜接触镜丢了一片。 | wǒ de jiǎo-mó jiē-chù-jìng diū le yí-piàn |
| Could you give me another one? | 你能给我配一片吗？ | nǐ néng gěi wǒ pèi yí-piàn ma |
| I have hard/soft lenses. | 我的角膜接触镜是硬/软的。 | wǒ de jiǎo-mó jiē-chù-jìng shì yìng/ruǎn de |
| Do you have any contact-lens fluid? | 你这儿有角膜接触镜清洗液吗？ | nǐ zhèr yǒu jiǎo-mó jiē-chù-jìng qīng-xǐ-yè ma |
| I'd like to buy a pair of sunglasses. | 我想买一副墨镜。 | wǒ xiǎng mǎi yí-fù mò-jìng |
| May I look in a mirror? | 这儿有镜子吗？ | zhèr yǒu jìng-zi ma |
| I'd like to buy a pair of binoculars. | 我想买一架双筒望远镜。 | wǒ xiǎng mǎi yí-jià shuāng-tǒng wàng-yuǎn-jìng |

### Photography 摄影

Some international brands of film are now available in China and can be found in Friendship Stores. But it is better to take a good supply of the film that you are used to. It is forbidden to take pictures of soldiers, bridges and tunnels, and if you want to take a close-up photo of a Chinese person, ask permission first.

| May I take a photo of you, please? | 我可以给你照像吗？ | wǒ kě-yǐ gěi nǐ zhào-xiàng ma |

### In the shop 在商店

| I want a(n) ... camera. | 我想买一个…照像机。 | wǒ xiǎng mǎi yí-ge ... zhào-xiàng-jī |
| automatic | 自动的 | zì-dòng de |
| inexpensive | 便宜的 | pián-yi de |
| simple | 简单的 | jiǎn-dān de |
| Show me some ..., please. | 请让我看看… | qǐng ràng wǒ kàn-kan |
| cine (movie) cameras | 摄影机 | shè-yǐng-jī |
| video cameras | 摄像机 | shè-xiàng-jī |
| I'd like to have some passport photos taken. | 我想照几张护照像片。 | wǒ xiǎng zhào jǐ zhāng hù-zhào xiàng-piàn |

### Film 胶卷

| I'd like a film for this camera. | 我想要一卷适于这种照像机的胶卷。 | wǒ xiǎng-yào yì-juǎn shì-yú zhè-zhǒng zhào-xiàng-jī de jiāo-juǎn |
| black and white | 黑白的 | hēi-bái de |
| colour | 彩色的 | cǎi-sè de |
| colour negative | 彩色底片 | cǎi-sè dǐ-piàn |
| colour slide | 彩色幻灯片 | cǎi-sè huàn-dēng-piàn |
| video cassette | 录像带 | lù-xiàng-dài |
| 24/36 exposures | 二十四/三十六张的 | èr-shí-sì/sān-shí-liù zhāng de |
| this size | 这个型号的 | zhè-ge xíng-hào de |
| artificial light type | 灯光片 | dēng-guāng piàn |
| daylight type | 日光片 | rì-guāng piàn |
| fast (high-speed) | 快速的 | kuài-sù de |
| fine grain | 细颗粒的 | xì kē-lì de |

## Developing 冲洗

| How much do you charge for processing? | 冲洗这卷胶卷多少钱？ | chōng-xǐ zhè-juǎn jiāo-juǎn duō-shao qián |
|---|---|---|
| I'd like … prints of each negative. | 每张底片洗…张。 | měi-zhāng dǐ-piàn xǐ … zhāng |
| with a mat finish | 要纹面纸的 | yào wén-miàn-zhǐ de |
| with a glossy finish | 要光面纸的 | yào guāng-miàn-zhǐ de |
| Will you enlarge this, please? | 请把这张放大一下。 | qǐng bǎ zhè-zhāng fàng-dà yí-xià |
| When will the photos be ready? | 什么时候能取？ | shén-me shí-hou néng qǔ |

## Accessories and repairs 零配件和修理

| I'd like a/an/some … | 我想要… | wǒ xiǎng-yào |
|---|---|---|
| battery | 几节电池 | jǐ-jié diàn-chí |
| cable release | 一个连线快门 | yí-ge lián-xiàn kuài-mén |
| camera case | 一个像机盒 | yí-ge xiàng-jī-hé |
| (electronic) flash | 一个（电子）闪光灯 | yí-ge (diàn-zǐ) shǎn-guāng-dēng |
| filter | 一片滤色镜 | yí-piàn lù-sè-jìng |
| for black and white | 用于黑白底片的 | yòng yú hēi-bái dǐ-piàn de |
| for colour | 用于彩色底片的 | yòng yú cǎi-sè dǐ-piàn de |
| lens | 镜头 | jìng-tóu |
| telephoto lens | 望远镜头 | wàng-yuǎn jìng-tóu |
| wide angle lens | 广角镜头 | guǎng-jiǎo jìng-tóu |
| lens cap | 镜头盖 | jìng-tóu-gài |
| Can you repair this camera? | 你这儿能修理这个像机吗？ | nǐ zhèr néng xiū zhè-ge xiàng-jī ma |
| The film is jammed. | 胶卷被卡住了。 | jiāo-juǎn bèi qiǎ zhù le |
| There's something wrong with the … | …有毛病。 | … yǒu máo-bìng |
| exposure counter | 胶片计数器 | jiāo-piàn jì-shù-qì |
| film winder | 缠绕胶卷柄 | chán-rào jiāo-juǎn bǐng |
| flash attachment | 闪光灯接口 | shǎn-guāng-dēng jiē-kǒu |
| lens | 镜头 | jìng-tóu |
| light meter | 测光表 | cè-guāng-biǎo |
| rangefinder | 测距器 | cè-jù-qì |
| shutter | 快门 | kuài-mén |

NUMBERS, see page 149

采购指南

### Smoker's supplies 香烟、烟草及烟具

There are no tobacconist's or kiosks specializing in cigarettes, instead you should go to a department store or a beer
and wine shop or ask at your hotel service desk. You will
find a wide variety of Chinese cigarettes as well as foreign
cigarettes made under licence. Pipe fans are advised to bring
along an adequate supply of their favourite blend, or buy it
Chinese style — by the leaf.

| | | |
|---|---|---|
| A packet of cigarettes, please. | 请拿一包香烟。 | qǐng ná yì-bāo xiāng-yān |
| Do you have any American/English cigarettes? | 你这儿有美国/英国香烟吗？ | nǐ zhèr yǒu měi-guó/yīng-guó xiāng-yān ma |
| I'd like a carton. | 我要一条。 | wǒ yào yì-tiáo |
| Give me a/some ..., please. | 请给我拿… | qǐng gěi wǒ ná |
| chewing tobacco | 一包口嚼烟草 | yì-bāo kǒu-jiáo yān-cǎo |
| cigarettes | 一包…香烟 | yì-bāo … xiāng-yān |
|   filter-tipped | 带过滤嘴的 | dài guò-lǜ-zuǐ de |
|   without filter | 不带过滤嘴的 | bú dài guò-lǜ-zuǐ de |
|   mild/strong | 柔和的/有劲的 | róu-hé de/yǒu jìn de |
|   king-size | 加长的 | jiā-cháng de |
| cigars | 一盒雪茄 | yì-hé xuě-jiā |
| lighter | 一个打火机 | yí-ge dǎ-huǒ-jī |
| lighter fluid | 打火机液体燃料 | dǎ-huǒ-jī yè-tǐ rán-liào |
| lighter gas | 打火机气体燃料 | dǎ-huǒ-jī qì-tǐ rán-liào |
| matches | 一盒火柴 | yì-hé huǒ-chái |
| pipe | 一个烟斗 | yí-ge yān-dǒu |
| pipe cleaners | 清洗烟斗的器具 | qīng-xǐ yān-dǒu de qì-jù |
| pipe tobacco | 一包烟斗烟草 | yì-bāo yān-dǒu yān-cǎo |
| pipe tool | 抽烟斗的用具 | chōu yān-dǒu de yòng-jù |
| snuff | 鼻烟 | bí-yān |
| wick | 灯芯 | dēng-xīn |

### Souvenirs 纪念品

Few countries can offer such a varied selection of souvenirs
as China. Here is a list of some of the most popular ones:

| | | |
|---|---|---|
| abacus | 算盘 | suàn-pan |
| acupuncture poster | 针灸经络穴位图 | zhēn-jiǔ jīng-luò xué-wèi tú |

| | | |
|---|---|---|
| bamboo products | 竹制品 | zhú zhì-pǐn |
| basketware | 藤编器具 | téng-biān qì-jù |
| bronzeware | 青铜制品 | qīng-tóng zhì-pǐn |
| carpet | 地毯 | dì-tǎn |
| cashmere | 开司米 | kāi-sī-mǐ |
| chinaware | 瓷器 | cí-qì |
| chop (carved seal) | 印章 | yìn-zhāng |
| chopsticks | 筷子 | kuài-zi |
| cloisonné-ware | 景泰兰 | jǐng-tài-lán |
| craft products | 工艺品 | gōng-yì-pǐn |
| fan | 扇子 | shàn-zi |
| folding screen | 折叠屏风 | zhé-dié píng-fēng |
| fur | 毛皮 | máo-pí |
| furniture | 家具 | jiā-jù |
| ginseng | 人参 | rén-shēn |
| hand embroidery | 手工刺绣 | shǒu-gōng cì-xiù |
| herbal remedies | 草药 | cǎo-yào |
| ink (Chinese) | 墨 | mò |
| ivory | 象牙制品 | xiàng-yá zhì-pǐn |
| jade | 玉石制品 | yù-shí zhì-pǐn |
| kimono | 和服 | hé-fú |
| kite | 风筝 | fēng-zheng |
| lacquerware | 漆器 | qī-qì |
|   carved lacquerware | 雕漆 | diāo-qī |
| lamp shade | 灯罩 | dēng-zhào |
| lantern | 安全风灯 | ān-quán fēng-dēng |
| linen | 亚麻布 | yà-má-bù |
| mahjong | 麻将 | má-jiàng |
| musical instrument | 乐器 | yuè-qì |
|   Chinese fiddle | 胡琴儿 | hú-qínr |
|   cymbals | 钹 | bó |
|   drum | 鼓 | gǔ |
|   flute | 笛子 | dí-zi |
|   gong | 锣 | luó |
|   guitar | 吉他 | jí-tā |
|   mouth organ | 口琴 | kǒu-qín |
|   seven-stringed lute | 古琴 | gǔ-qín |
| porcelain | 细瓷器 | xì cí-qì |
| pottery | 陶器 | táo-qì |
| prints | 版画儿 | bǎn-huàr |
| rubbings | 拓片 | tà-piàn |
| rug | 小地毯 | xiǎo dì-tǎn |
| scrolls | 卷轴 | juàn-zhóu |
| silk | 丝绸 | sī-chóu |
| spices | 作料 | zuò-liào |
| tea | 茶片 | chá-yè |
| teacup (with lid) | 茶杯（带盖的） | chá-bēi (dài gài de) |
| teapot | 茶壶 | chá-hú |
| toys | 玩具 | wán-jù |

## Miscellaneous 其他物品

### Records — Cassettes 唱片-盒式磁带

Records can be bought in record shops, musical instrument shops, and in the record department of bookshops.

| | | |
|---|---|---|
| Do you have any records by …? | 你这儿有…的唱片吗？ | nǐ zhèr yǒu … de chàng-piàn ma |
| Can I listen to this record? | 我可以试听这张唱片吗？ | wǒ kě-yǐ shì-tīng zhè-zhāng chàng-piàn ma |
| I'd like a cassette. | 我想要一盒盒式磁带。 | wǒ xiǎng-yào yì-hé hé-shì cí-dài |
| | | |
| chamber music | 室内乐 | shì-nèi-yuè |
| classical Chinese music | 中国古典音乐 | zhōng-guó gǔ-diǎn yīn-yuè |
| classical music | 古典音乐 | gǔ-diǎn yīn-yuè |
| folk music | 民间音乐 | mín-jiān yīn-yuè |
| instrumental music | 器乐演奏音乐 | qì-yuè yǎn-zòu yīn-yuè |
| jazz | 爵士乐 | jué-shì-yuè |
| light music | 轻音乐 | qīng yīn-yuè |
| orchestral music | 管弦乐 | guǎn-xián-yuè |

### Toys 玩具

Toys in China tend to be simpler than in the West. You can buy a hoop and stick for a bowling game, or a kind of shuttle-cock (毽子 *jiàn-zi*) made of three feathers stuck to a flat disc. The Chinese like to bounce this off the sides of their feet — rather like footballers controlling the ball.

| | | |
|---|---|---|
| I'd like a toy/game … | 我想要…的玩具/智力游戏。 | wǒ xiǎng-yào … de wán-jù/zhì-lì yóu-xì |
| for a boy | 给男孩儿玩儿的 | gěi nán-háir wánr de |
| for a 5-year-old girl | 给一个五岁女孩儿玩儿的 | gěi yí-ge wǔ-suì nǚ-háir wánr de |
| | | |
| ball | 球 | qiú |
| bucket and spade (pail and shovel) | 小桶和小铲子 | xiǎo tǒng hé xiǎo chǎn-zi |
| building blocks (bricks) | 积木 | jī-mù |
| chess set | 国际象棋 | guó-jì xiàng-qí |
| Chinese chequers | 中国象棋 | zhōng-guó xiàng-qí |
| doll | 娃娃 | wá-wa |
| hoop | 铁环 | tiě-huán |

# Your money: banks — currency

While foreign currency and traveller's cheques may be brought into the country in unlimited amounts, provided they are declared upon arrival, no local currency whatsoever (unless in foreign exchange certificates) may be either imported or exported. Money and traveller's cheques can only be exchanged at authorized currency exchange counters at main ports and airports, leading hotels, banks and Friendship Stores. Exchange rates are the same everywhere.

### Hours 营业时间

Exchange counters in Friendship Stores have the same opening hours as the shop itself, i.e.: 9 a.m. to 7 p.m. (8 p.m. in summer), seven days a week.

Banks in hotels open from 7.30 or 8 a.m. to around 7 p.m., with a break for lunch. (Generally, the larger the hotel, the later the foreign exchange facility stays open.) Money may also be changed on Sunday mornings.

### Currency 货币

China's two-tier currency system is almost bound to confuse you. The standard currency, called *renminbi* or people's money (RMB) is based on the *yuán* （元） divided into 10 *jiǎo* （角） or *máo* （毛） and 100 *fen* （分）.

However, foreign exchange bureaus also dispense a second currency called Foreign Exchange Certificates (FEC) in denominations of 1 and 5 jiao (=10 and 50 fen) and 1, 5, 10, 50 and 100 yuan.

Friendship Stores and other establishments catering primarily to foreigners accept only FEC, not RMB. In some small towns, merchants may not accept FEC, simply because they have never heard of them. FEC may be taken out of China, but RMB may not.

## Currency exchange 兑换外汇

Foreign currency and traveller's cheques may be exchanged for FEC in hotels and Friendship Stores. You'll have to show your passport. Keep the receipt as proof of the amount changed. You'll also need it if you want to convert excess Chinese money to a foreign currency when leaving the country.

## Credit cards — Traveller's cheques 信用卡-旅行支票

Credit cards are accepted more and more in tourist areas. (Note: a 4% commission is charged to users of credit cards.) In some major cities personal cheques are accepted on presentation of certain credit cards, though it may entail a trip to the bank. Traveller's cheques are recognized at the money-exchange counters of hotels and shops almost everywhere in China.

## General 一般询问

| | | |
|---|---|---|
| Is there a currency exchange office in the hotel? | 旅馆里有外汇兑换处吗？ | lǚ-guǎn li yǒu wài-huì duì-huàn-chù ma |
| Where's the nearest bank? | 离这儿最近的银行在哪儿？ | lí zhèr zuì jìn de yín-háng zài nǎr |
| At what time does it open/close? | 什么时候开门/关门？ | shén-me shí-hou kāi mén/guān mén |

## At the bank 在银行

| | | |
|---|---|---|
| I want to change some ... | 我想用…兑换。 | wǒ xiǎng yòng ... duì-huàn |
| U.S. dollars | 美元 | měi-yuán |
| Hongkong dollars | 港币 | gǎng-bì |
| Japanese yen | 日元 | rì-yuán |
| pounds sterling | 英镑 | yīng-bàng |
| I want to cash a traveller's cheque. | 我想兑现一张旅行支票。 | wǒ xiǎng duì-xiàn yì-zhāng lǚ-xíng-zhī-piào |

NUMBERS, see page 149

银行

| Here's my currency declaration form. | 这是我的外汇申报单。 | zhè shì wǒ de wài-huì shēn-bào-dān |
| What's the exchange rate? | 兑换率是多少？ | duì-huàn-lǜ shì duō-shao |
| How much commission do you charge? | 要付多少手续费？ | yào fù duō-shao shǒu-xù-fèi |
| Can you cash a personal cheque? | 这儿能兑现私人支票吗？ | zhèr néng duì-xiàn sī-rén zhī-piào ma |
| How long will it take to clear? | 兑现要等多少时间？ | duì-xiàn yào děng duō-shao shí-jiān |
| Can you telex my bank in …? | 你能给我在…的银行发个电传吗？ | nǐ néng gěi wǒ zài … de yín-háng fā ge diàn-chuán ma |
| I have a/an … | 我有… | wǒ yǒu |
| credit card | 一张信用卡 | yì-zhāng xìn-yòng-kǎ |
| introduction from … | 一封…的介绍信 | yì-fēng … de jiè-shào-xìn |
| letter of credit | 一封银行存款证明信 | yì-fēng yín-háng cún-kuǎn zhèng-míng-xìn |
| I'm expecting some money from … | 我在等从…汇来的一笔钱。 | wǒ zài děng cóng … huì lái de yì-bǐ qián |
| Has it arrived yet? | 已经到了吗？ | yǐ-jīng dào le ma |
| Could you please check that again? | 能再查对一次吗？ | néng zài chá-duì yí-cì ma |
| Please give me … | 请给我… | qǐng gěi wǒ |
| large/small notes (bills) | 面值大的/小的钞票 | miàn-zhí dà de/ xiǎo de chāo-piào |
| small change | 零钱 | líng-qián |
| coins | 硬币 | yìng-bì |

## Deposits — Withdrawals 存、取

| I'd like to … | 我想… | wǒ xiǎng |
| open an account | 开个帐户 | kāi ge zhàng-hù |
| withdraw … (yuan/ U.S. dollars) | 取…（元/美元） | qǔ (yuán/ měi-yuán) |
| I want to pay this into my account. | 我想把这笔钱存入我的帐户。 | wǒ xiǎng bǎ zhè bǐ qián cún-rù wǒ-de zhàng-hù |
| Where should I sign? | 我该在哪儿签名？ | wǒ gāi zài nǎr qiān-míng |

NUMBERS, see page 149

## Business and banking terms 贸易及银行术语

| | | |
|---|---|---|
| amount | 数额 | shù-é |
| balance | 结余 | jié-yú |
| bond | 公债券 | gōng-zhài-quàn |
| (to) borrow | 借 | jiè |
| (to) buy | 买 | mǎi |
| capital | 资本 | zī-běn |
| cheque (check) | 支票 | zhī-piào |
| contract | 合同 | hé-tong |
| discount | 折扣 | zhé-kòu |
| expenses | 开支 | kāi-zhī |
| export | 出口 | chū-kǒu |
| import | 进口 | jìn-kǒu |
| interest | 利息 | lì-xī |
| investment | 投资 | tóu-zī |
| invoice | 发票 | fā-piào |
| (to) lend | 借给 | jiè-gěi |
| loan | 贷款 | dài-kuǎn |
| loss | 亏损 | kuī-sǔn |
| mortgage | 抵押 | dǐ-yā |
| payment | 付款 | fù-kuǎn |
| percentage | 百分比 | bǎi-fēn-bǐ |
| price | 价钱 | jià-qián |
| profit | 利润 | lì-rùn |
| purchase | 买进的货品 | mǎi jìn de huò-pǐn |
| sale | 卖出的货品 | mài chū de huò-pǐn |
| (to) sell | 卖 | mài |
| share | 股份 | gǔ-fèn |
| transfer (of funds) | 转账 | zhuǎn-zhàng |
| value | 价值 | jià-zhí |

## Doing business 做生意

| | | |
|---|---|---|
| My name is ... | 我叫… | wǒ jiào |
| Here's my card. | 这是我的名片。 | zhè shì wǒ de míng-piàn |
| I represent ... | 我是…的代表。 | wǒ shì ... de dài-biǎo |
| I have an appointment with ... | 我和…约了个会谈。 | wǒ hé ... yuē le gè huì-tán |
| What's your name, please? | 您贵姓？ | nín guì xìng |
| Please write it down for me. | 请你写下这个。 | qǐng nǐ xiě xià zhè-ge |

| Can you provide me with a/an …? | 能为我找一位…吗？ | néng wèi wǒ zhǎo yí-wèi … ma |
|---|---|---|
| interpreter | 口译 | kǒu-yì |
| secretary | 秘书 | mì-shū |
| translator | 翻译 | fān-yì |

| I need an interpreter who specializes in … | 我需要一位专于…的口译。 | wǒ xū-yào yí-wèi zhuān-yú … de kǒu-yì |
|---|---|---|
| agriculture | 农业 | nóng-yè |
| chemistry | 化学 | huà-xué |
| electronics | 电子 | diàn-zǐ |
| engineering | 工程 | gōng-chéng |
| foodstuffs | 食品 | shí-pǐn |
| handicrafts | 手工艺 | shǒu-gōng-yì |
| machinery | 机械 | jī-xiè |
| mining | 矿业 | kuàng-yè |
| native produce | 土特产 | tǔ-tè-chǎn |
| textiles | 纺织 | fǎng-zhī |

| I'd like to see a sample of your latest collection. | 我想看你们最新产品的样品。 | wǒ xiǎng kàn nǐ-men zuì xīn chǎn-pǐn de yàng-pǐn |
|---|---|---|
| Do you have a photo of …? | 你有…的照片吗？ | nǐ yǒu … de zhào-piàn ma |
| Do you have any statistics? | 你们有有关的统计吗？ | nǐ-men yǒu yǒu-guān de tǒng-jì ma |
| Can you give me an estimate of the cost? | 能给个成本预算吗？ | néng gěi ge chéng-běn yù-suàn ma |

| goods | 货品 | huò-pǐn |
|---|---|---|
| joint venture | 合营 | hé-yíng |
| licence | 许可证 | xǔ-kě-zhèng |
| product | 产品 | chǎn-pǐn |
| (to) send (goods) | 发货 | fā-huò |
| (to) send back (goods) | 退货 | tuì-huò |
| shipment | 一批货 | yì-pī-huò |
| tax | 税 | shuì |

| Where can I make photocopies? | 哪儿能复印？ | nǎr néng fù-yìn |
|---|---|---|
| What's the rate of inflation? | 通货膨胀率是多少？ | tōng-huò péng-zhàng-lù shì duō-shao |

# At the post office

Hotels have branch post offices or postal service desks, open 7 days a week, selling stamps, writing paper, and post-cards. But you can also go to a post office, recognized by the sign 邮电局 *(yóu-diàn-jú)*. If you are sending a parcel, don't seal it until it has been checked at the post office.

The Chinese post office has no facilities for poste-restante (general delivery) mail. As confirmed hotel reservations are rare, this poses a problem. If you expect to receive mail while in China, ask correspondents to address letters c/o CITS in the various cities on your itinerary; if you're on a package tour, they should also write on the envelope your tour number, as well as the tour operator's name.

| | | |
|---|---|---|
| Where's the nearest post office? | 离这儿最近的邮局在哪儿？ | lí zhèr zuì-jìn de yóu-jú zài nǎr |
| What time does the post office … | 邮局几点… ？ | yóu-jú jǐ diǎn |
| open/close | 开门/关门 | kāi mén/guān mén |
| I want some stamps, please. | 我要几张邮票。 | wǒ yào jǐ zhāng yóu-piào |
| A stamp for this letter, please. | 请给一张寄这封信的邮票。 | qǐng gěi yì-zhāng jì zhè fēng xìn de yóu-piào |
| What's the postage for a postcard, please? | 一张明信片的邮费是多少？ | yì-zhāng míng-xìn-piàn de yóu-fèi shì duō-shao |
| Where's the letter box (mailbox)? | 邮筒在哪儿？ | yóu-tǒng zài nǎr |

| | |
|---|---|
| 邮票<br>yóu-piào<br>STAMPS | 包裹<br>bāo-guǒ<br>PARCELS |

| I'd like to send this parcel. | 我要寄这个包裹。 | wǒ yào jì zhèi-ge bāo-guǒ |
| I want to send this (by) … | 我想寄… | wǒ xiǎng jì |
| airmail | 航空 | háng-kōng |
| express (special delivery) | 快递 | kuài-dì |
| registered mail | 挂号 | guà-hào |
| surface mail | 平信 | píng-xìn |
| At which counter can I cash an international money order? | 哪个柜台可以兑现国际汇票？ | nǎ-ge guì-tái kě-yǐ duì-xiàn guó-jì huì-piào |

---

汇款
huì-kuǎn
MONEY ORDERS

---

## Telegrams — Telex 电报–电传

If your hotel does not have a service that deals with telegrams and telexes, you'll have to go to a post office. Only main post offices in the largest cities will have these facilities.

| Can I send a telex from here? | 我能在这儿发电传吗？ | wǒ néng zài zhèr fā diàn-chuán ma |
| I want to send a … | 我想拍发… | wǒ xiǎng pāi-fā |
| letter telegram (night letter) | 一封夜信电 | yì-fēng yè-xìn-diàn |
| phototelegram | 一封传真电报 | yì-fēng chuán-zhēn diàn-bào |
| telegram | 一封电报 | yì-fēng diàn-bào |
| telex | 一封电传 | yì-fēng diàn-chuán |
| May I have a form, please? | 可以给我一张电报纸吗？ | kě-yǐ gěi wǒ yì-zhāng diàn-bào-zhǐ ma |
| What's the basic charge? | 基价是多少？ | jī-jià shì duō-shao |
| How much is it per word? | 一个字多少钱？ | yí-ge zì duō-shao qián |
| Can I have the charges transferred? | 能请对方付费吗？ | néng qǐng duì-fāng fù-fèi ma |

## Telephoning 打电话

Through your hotel switchboard you will be able to phone inland subscribers and numbers abroad. Local calls are usually free of charge. To phone home, you should book your call well in advance. You can also book calls at the post office. There are few telephone booths, but you will see signs for public telephones. These are found in private houses, but are designated for public use.

| Where's the nearest public telephone? | 离这儿最近的公用电话在哪儿？ | lí zhèr zuì-jìn de gōng-yòng-diàn-huà zài-nǎr |
| May I use your phone? | 可以用你这儿的电话吗？ | kě-yǐ yòng nǐ zhèr de diàn-huà ma |
| Could you look up this company for me in the telephone directory? | 能帮我在电话簿上找到这个公司的名字吗？ | néng bāng wǒ zài diàn-huà-bù shang zhǎo-dào zhèi-ge gōng-sī de míng-zi ma |
| Can you help me get this number? | 请接这个号码。 | qǐng-jiē zhèi-ge hào-mǎ |
| I'd like to make a long-distance call. | 我想打长途电话。 | wǒ xiǎng dǎ cháng-tú-diàn-huà |
| I want to telephone to … | 我想给…打电话。 | wǒ xiǎng gěi … dǎ diàn-huà |

## Operator 总机

| Operator? | 喂，总机？ | wéi zǒng-jī |
| Could you get me this number …? | 请接… | qǐng jiē |
| What number must I dial …? | …我该拨什么号码？ | … wǒ gāi bō shén-me hào-mǎ |
| to get an outside line | 接外线 | jiē wài-xiàn |
| to call room no. … | 接…号房间 | jiē … hào fáng-jiān |

> **公用电话**
> gōng-yòng-diàn-huà
> PUBLIC TELEPHONE

NUMBERS, see page 149

电话

| Can I dial direct? | 能直拨吗？ | néng zhí bō ma |
| I want to reverse the charges (call collect). | 我想让对方付费。 | wǒ xiǎng ràng duì-fāng fù fèi |

## Speaking 通话

| Hello! This is … | 喂，我是… | wéi wǒ shì |
| I want to speak to … | 我想和…说话。 | wǒ xiǎng hé … shuō huà |
| I want extension … | 请转… | qǐng zhuǎn |
| Is that …? | 是…吗？ | shì … ma |
| Speak louder, please. | 请大点儿声。 | qǐng dà diǎnr shēng |
| Speak more slowly, please. | 请说慢点儿。 | qǐng shuō màn diǎnr |
| Would you please try again later? | 请过会儿再试试。 | qǐng guò huǐr zài shì-shi |
| You put me through to the wrong number. | 你接错号码了。 | nǐ jiē cuò hào-mǎ le |
| Operator, we've been cut off. | 总机，线断了。 | zǒng-jī xiàn duàn le |

## Not there 不在

| When will he/she be back? | 他/她什么时候能回来？ | tā/tā shén-me shí-hou néng huí-lai |
| Please tell him/her I called. My name is … | 请你告诉他/她，我来过电话。我叫… | qǐng nǐ gào-su tā/tā wǒ lái-guo diàn-huà. wǒ jiào |
| Please ask him/her to call me. | 麻烦你让他/她给我回电话。 | má-fan nǐ ràng tā/tā gěi wǒ huí diàn-huà |
| Would you take a message, please? | 你能转告他吗？ | nǐ néng zhuǎn-gào tā ma |

## Charges 费用

| What was the cost of that call? | 电话费是多少？ | diàn-huà-fèi shì duō-shao |
| I want to pay for the call. | 我要付电话费。 | wǒ yào fù diàn-huà-fèi |

# Doctor

Should you require medical care in China, your guide, hotel desk clerk or the local CITS office will call a doctor, or arrange for you to be taken to a hospital. Considering the language problem, it's a relief to have an interpreter on hand when discussing symptoms and treatment: there is no reason to expect that your doctor, however well-qualified in medicine, understands a single word of English.

Treatment may involve a combination of modern and traditional medicine — perhaps some tablets to swallow and some herbs to take in an infusion. You may also come across the traditional Chinese art of acupuncture.

*Warning:* In the extreme event of an emergency blood transfusion, those with Rhesus-negative blood should be warned that the Chinese are virtually all Rhesus-positive.

### General 一般询问

| | | |
|---|---|---|
| Can you get me a doctor? | 请找一位大夫。 | qǐng zhǎo yí-wèi dài-fu |
| Is there a doctor here? | 这儿有大夫吗？ | zhèr yǒu dài-fu ma |
| I need a doctor, quickly. | 我得马上见大夫。 | wǒ děi mǎ-shàng jiàn dài-fu |
| Where can I find a doctor who speaks English? | 这儿有会说英语的大夫吗？ | zhèr yǒu huì shuō yīng-yǔ de dài-fu ma |
| Where's the surgery (doctor's office)? | 外科门诊在哪儿？ | wài-kē mén-zhěn zài nǎr |
| What are the surgery (office) hours? | 外科门诊几点开门？ | wài-kē mén-zhěn jǐ-diǎn kāi mén |
| Could the doctor come to see me here? | 大夫能来这儿吗？ | dài-fu néng lái zhèr ma |
| What time can the doctor come? | 大夫什么时间到？ | dài-fu shén-me shí-jiān dào |

CHEMIST'S, see page 107

| Can you recommend a/an ...? | 请推荐一位… | qǐng tuī-jiàn yí-wèi |
|---|---|---|
| general practitioner | 门诊大夫 | mén-zhěn dài-fu |
| children's doctor | 儿科大夫 | ér-kē dài-fu |
| eye specialist | 眼科大夫 | yǎn-kē dài-fu |
| gynaecologist | 妇科大夫 | fù-kē dài-fu |
| I'd like to get in touch with a doctor who uses acupuncture. | 我想见会扎针灸的大夫。 | wǒ xiǎng jiàn huì zhā zhēn-jiǔ de dài-fu |
| I've been referred to Dr. ... This is his address. | 有人介绍我见…大夫，这是他的地址。 | yǒu rén jiè-shào wǒ jiàn ... dài-fu. zhè shì tā de dì-zhǐ |
| Can you contact him for me? | 能和他联系一下吗？ | néng hé tā lián-xì yí-xià ma |
| Can I have an appointment as soon as possible? | 能约个尽早的看病时间吗？ | néng yuē ge jìn-zǎo de kàn-bìng shí-jiān ma |

## Parts of the body 身体各部名称

| abdomen | 腹部 | fù-bù |
|---|---|---|
| ankle | 脚腕 | jiǎo-wàn |
| appendix | 阑尾 | lán-wěi |
| arm | 胳膊 | gē-bo |
| artery | 动脉 | dòng-mài |
| back | 背 | bèi |
| bladder | 膀胱 | páng-guāng |
| blood | 血 | xuè |
| bone | 骨 | gǔ |
| bowel | 大肠 | dà-cháng |
| brain | 脑 | nǎo |
| breast | 乳房 | rǔ-fáng |
| chest | 胸部 | xiōng-bù |
| coccyx | 尾骨 | wěi-gǔ |
| collar-bone | 锁骨 | suǒ-gǔ |
| ear | 耳朵 | ěr-duo |
| elbow | 肘 | zhǒu |
| eye | 眼 | yǎn |
| face | 脸 | liǎn |
| finger | 手指 | shǒu-zhǐ |
| foot | 脚 | jiǎo |
| forehead | 前额 | qián-é |
| gall-bladder | 胆囊 | dǎn-náng |
| genitals | 生殖器 | shēng-zhí-qì |
| gland | 分泌腺 | fēn-mì-xiàn |
| hand | 手 | shǒu |

大夫

| | | |
|---|---|---|
| head | 头 | tóu |
| heart | 心脏 | xīn-zàng |
| heel | 脚后跟 | jiǎo-hòu-gēn |
| hip | 屁股 | pì-gu |
| intestines | 肠 | cháng |
| jaw | 下巴 | xià-ba |
| joint | 关节 | guān-jié |
| kidney | 肾 | shèn |
| knee | 膝盖 | xī-gài |
| knee-cap | 膝盖骨 | xī-gài-gǔ |
| leg | 腿 | tuǐ |
| ligament | 韧带 | rèn-dài |
| lip | 嘴唇 | zuǐ-chún |
| liver | 肝 | gān |
| lung | 肺 | fèi |
| mouth | 嘴 | zuǐ |
| muscle | 肌肉 | jī-ròu |
| nail | 指甲 | zhǐ-jia |
| nape | 后颈 | hòu-jǐng |
| neck | 脖子 | bó-zi |
| nerve | 神经 | shén-jīng |
| nervous system | 神经系统 | shén-jīng-xì-tǒng |
| nose | 鼻子 | bí-zi |
| rib | 肋骨 | lèi-gǔ |
| scalp | 头皮 | tóu-pí |
| shoulder | 肩膀 | jiān-bǎng |
| shoulder blade | 肩胛骨 | jiān-jiá-gǔ |
| skin | 皮肤 | pí-fū |
| spine | 脊椎 | jǐ-zhuī |
| spleen | 脾 | pí |
| stomach | 胃 | wèi |
| tendon | 肌腱 | jī-jiàn |
| thigh | 大腿 | dà-tuǐ |
| throat | 嗓子 | sǎng-zi |
| thumb | 拇指 | mǔ-zhǐ |
| toe | 脚趾 | jiǎo-zhǐ |
| tongue | 舌头 | shé-tou |
| tonsils | 扁桃腺 | biǎn-táo-xiàn |
| vein | 静脉 | jìng-mài |
| wrist | 手腕 | shǒu-wàn |

| 左<br>zuǒ<br>LEFT | 右<br>yòu<br>RIGHT |
|---|---|

大夫

## Accident — Injury 事故-受伤

| | | |
|---|---|---|
| There's been an accident. | 出事了。 | chū shì le |
| My child has had a fall. | 我的孩子摔倒了。 | wǒ de hái-zi shuāi-dǎo le |
| He/She has hurt his/her head. | 他/她的头碰伤了。 | tā/tā de tóu pèng shāng le |
| He's/She's unconscious. | 他/她昏过去了。 | tā/tā hūn-guo-qu le |
| He's/She's bleeding. | 他/她在流血。 | tā/tā zài liú xuě |
| He's/She's injured. | 他/她受伤了。 | tā/tā shòu shāng le |
| It's serious. | 伤得很重。 | shāng de hěn zhòng |
| His/Her arm is broken. | 他/她的胳膊断了。 | tā/tā de gē-bo duàn le |
| His/Her ankle is swollen. | 他/她的脚腕子肿了。 | tā/tā de jiǎo-wàn-zi zhǒng le |
| I've been stung. | 我被蜇伤了。 | wǒ bèi zhē shāng le |
| I've been bitten by something. | 我被什么虫子咬了。 | wǒ bèi shén-me chōng-zi yǎo le |
| I've got something in my eye. | 我眼睛进东西了。 | wǒ yǎn-jīng jìn dōng-xi le |
| I've got a ... | 我有… | wǒ yǒu |
| blister | 一个水疱 | yí-ge shuǐ-pào |
| boil | 一个疖子 | yí-ge jiē-zi |
| bruise | 一块青紫 | yí-kuài qīng-zǐ |
| lump | 一个肿块 | yí-ge zhǒng-kuài |
| rash | 一片疹子 | yí-piàn zhěn-zi |
| swelling | 一块红肿 | yí-kuài hóng-zhǒng |
| wound | 一个伤口 | yí-ge shāng-kǒu |
| I've ... myself. | 我被… | wǒ bèi |
| scalded | 烫伤了 | tàng shāng le |
| burned | 烧伤了 | shāo shāng le |
| cut | 割破了 | gē pò le |
| grazed | 擦破了 | cā pò le |
| Could you have a look at it? | 请诊治一下。 | qǐng zhěn-zhì yí-xià |
| I can't move my ... | 我…动不了啦。 | wǒ ... dòng-bu-liǎo la |
| It hurts. | 这儿疼。 | zhèr téng |

| | |
|---|---|
| 哪儿疼？ | Where does it hurt? |
| 哪种疼？ | What kind of pain is it? |
| 纯疼 | dull |
| 刺疼 | sharp |
| 一跳一跳的疼 | throbbing |
| 持续的疼 | constant |
| 一阵阵的疼 | on and off |
| 这儿… | It's … |
| 断了 | broken |
| 脱臼了 | dislocated |
| 扭伤了 | sprained |
| 撕裂了 | torn |
| 需要去照张 X 光片子。 | I want you to have an X-ray. |
| 需要用石膏固定。 | You'll have to have a plaster. |
| 感染了。 | It's infected. |
| 你注射过预防破伤风的疫苗吗？ | Have you been vaccinated against tetanus? |
| 我会给你开止痛药的。 | I'll give you a painkiller. |

## Illness 生病

| | | |
|---|---|---|
| I'm not feeling well. | 我不舒服。 | wǒ bù shū-fu |
| I'm ill. | 我病了。 | wǒ bìng le |
| I feel … | 我觉得… | wǒ jué-de |
| dizzy | 头晕 | tóu-yūn |
| nauseous | 恶心 | ě-xīn |
| shivery | 发冷 | fā-lěng |
| I've got a fever. | 我在发烧。 | wǒ zài fā-shāo |
| My temperature is 38 degrees. | 我的体温是摄氏 38°。 | wǒ de tǐ-wēn shì shè-shì 38 dù |
| I've been vomiting. | 我一直在呕吐。 | wǒ yì-zhí zài ǒu-tù |
| I'm constipated/ I've got diarrhoea. | 我便秘/ 我腹泻。 | wǒ biàn-bì/ wǒ fù-xiè |
| My … hurt(s). | 我的…疼。 | wǒ de … téng |
| I've got (a/an) … | 我… | wǒ |

| asthma | 哮喘 | xiào-chuǎn |
| backache | 腰疼 | yāo-téng |
| cough | 咳嗽 | ké-sou |
| cramps | 肚子绞痛 | dù-zi jiǎo-tòng |
| earache | 耳朵疼痛 | ěr-duo téng |
| headache | 头疼 | tóu téng |
| indigestion | 消化不良 | xiāo-huà bù liáng |
| nosebleed | 流鼻血 | liú bí-xuě |
| palpitations | 心悸 | xīn-jì |
| sore throat | 嗓子疼 | sǎng-zi téng |
| stiff neck | 脖子发硬 | bó-zi fā yìng |
| stomach ache | 胃疼 | wèi téng |
| sunstroke | 中暑了 | zhòng-shǔ le |
| I've got (an) ... | 我有... | wǒ yǒu |
| arthritis | 关节炎 | guān-jié-yán |
| hay fever | 枯草热 | kū-cǎo-rè |
| haemorrhoids | 痔疮 | zhì-chuāng |
| rheumatism | 风湿 | fēng-shī |
| ulcer | 胃溃疡 | wèi-kuì-yáng |
| I have difficulties breathing. | 我呼吸困难。 | wǒ hū-xī kùn-nan |
| I have a pain in my chest. | 我胸部疼。 | wǒ xiōng-bù téng |
| I had a heart attack ... years ago. | 我...年以前曾有过一次心肌梗塞。 | wǒ ... nián yǐ-qián céng yǒu guo yí-cì xīn-jī gěng-sè |
| My blood pressure is too high/too low. | 我的血压过高/过低。 | wǒ de xuě-yā guò gāo/ guò dī |
| I'm allergic to ... | 我对...过敏。 | wǒ duì ... guò-mǐn |
| I've got diabetes. | 我有糖尿病。 | wǒ yǒu táng-niào-bìng |

## Women's section 妇产科

| I have period pains. | 我有痛经。 | wǒ yǒu tòng-jīng |
| I have a vaginal infection. | 我阴道发炎了。 | wǒ yīn-dào fā-yán le |
| I'm on the pill. | 我一直服避孕药。 | wǒ yì-zhí fú bì-yùn-yào |
| I haven't had my period for 3 months. | 我停经有三个月了。 | wǒ tíng-jīng yǒu sān-ge yuè le |
| I'm (3 months) pregnant. | 我怀孕（有三个月）了。 | wǒ huái-yùn (yǒu sān-ge yuè) le |
| I have morning sickness. | 我早晨恶心呕吐。 | wǒ zǎo-chen ě-xin ǒu-tù |

| | |
|---|---|
| 你这么不舒服有多长时间了？ | How long have you been feeling like this? |
| 这是你第一次有这种症状吗？ | Is this the first time you've had this? |
| 我给你测一下体温。 | I'll take your temperature. |
| 我给你量一下血压。 | I'll take your blood pressure. |
| 请卷起衣袖。 | Roll up your sleeve, please. |
| 请脱掉衣服。 | Please undress. |
| 请躺在这儿。 | Please lie down over here. |
| 张开嘴。 | Open your mouth. |
| 深呼吸。 | Breathe deeply. |
| 咳嗽一下。 | Cough, please. |
| 哪儿疼？ | Where does it hurt? |
| 你得了… | You've got (a/an) … |
| …发炎 | inflammation of … |
| 肺炎 | pneumonia |
| 黄疸 | jaundice |
| 阑尾炎 | appendicitis |
| 流感 | flu |
| 麻疹 | measles |
| 膀胱炎 | cystitis |
| 食物中毒 | food poisoning |
| 胃炎 | gastritis |
| 性病 | venereal disease |
| 这病（不）传染。 | It's (not) contagious. |
| 需要打针。 | I'll give you an injection. |
| 你得去取血化验。 | I want a specimen of your blood. |
| 你得去留大便/尿化验。 | I want a specimen of your stools/urine. |
| 你必须卧床休息…天。 | You must stay in bed for … days |
| 我得把你转到…科去。 | I want you to see a … specialist. |
| 你需要到医院做一个全面查体。 | I want you to go to hospital for a general checkup. |

## Prescription — Treatment 处方-治疗

| | | |
|---|---|---|
| This is my usual medicine. | 这是我常用的药。 | zhè shì wǒ cháng-yòng de yào |
| Can you give me a prescription for this? | 能给我开这种药吗？ | néng gěi wǒ kāi zhè zhǒng yào ma |
| Can you prescribe a/an/some ...? | 请给我开一些…？ | qǐng gěi wǒ kāi yì-xiē |
| antidepressant | 抗抑郁药 | kàng yì-yù yào |
| sleeping pills | 安眠药 | ān-mián yào |
| tranquillizer | 镇静药 | zhèn-jìng yào |
| I'm allergic to ... | 我对…过敏。 | wǒ duì ... guò-mǐn |
| antibiotics | 抗菌素 | kàng-jūn-sù |
| aspirin | 阿司匹林 | ā-sī-pǐ-lín |
| penicillin | 青霉素 | qīng-méi-sù |
| I don't want anything too strong. | 我不要太厉害的药。 | wǒ bú yào tài lì-hai de yào |
| How many times a day should I take it? | 一天吃几次？ | yì-tiān chī jǐ-cì |
| Must I swallow them whole? | 我必须吞服吗？ | wǒ bì-xū tūn-fú ma |

| | |
|---|---|
| 你目前在进行哪些治疗？ | What treatment are you having? |
| 你正在服用什么药？ | What medicine are you taking? |
| 是注射还是口服？ | By injection or orally? |
| 这种药每服…汤匙。 | Take ... teaspoons of this medicine. |
| 每服一片… | Take one pill ... |
| 每隔…小时一服 | every ... hours |
| 每日…次 | ... times a day |
| 饭前/饭后 | before/after each meal |
| 晨服/睡前服 | in the morning/at night |
| 痛时服 | if there is any pain |
| 连续服…天 | for ... days |

CHEMIST'S, see page 107

大夫

## Fee 医药费

| How much do I owe you? | 我该付多少钱？ | wǒ gāi fù duō-shao qián |
| May I have a receipt? | 请开张收据。 | qǐng kāi zhāng shōu-jù |
| Can I have a medical certificate? | 请开张医生证明。 | qǐng kāi zhāng yī-shēng zhèng-míng |
| Would you fill in this health insurance form, please? | 请填写这张健康保险单。 | qǐng tián-xiě zhè zhāng jiàn-kāng bǎo-xiǎn-dān |

## Hospital 医院

| Please notify my family. | 请通知我的家属。 | qǐng tōng-zhī wǒ de jiā-shǔ |
| What are the visiting hours? | 什么时间能探视？ | shén-me shí-jiān néng tàn-shì |
| When can I get up? | 我什么时候可以下床活动？ | wǒ shén-me shí-hou kě-yǐ xià chuáng huó-dòng |
| When will the doctor come? | 大夫什么时候来？ | dài-fu shén-me shí-hou lái |
| I'm in pain. | 我很疼。 | wǒ hěn téng |
| I can't eat. | 我吃不下。 | wǒ chī-bu-xià |
| I can't sleep. | 我睡不着 | wǒ shuì-bu-zháo |
| Where is the bell? | 铃在哪儿？ | líng zài nǎr |

| nurse | 护士 | hù-shì |
| patient | 病人 | bìng-rén |
| anaesthetic | 麻药 | má-yào |
| blood transfusion | 输血 | shū-xuě |
| injection | 注射 | zhù-shè |
| operation | 手术 | shǒu-shù |
| bed | 床 | chuáng |
| bedpan | 便盆儿 | biàn-pénr |
| thermometer | 体温表 | tǐ-wēn-biǎo |

大夫

## Dentist 牙科大夫

| | | |
|---|---|---|
| Can you recommend a good dentist? | 你能推荐一位好牙科大夫吗？ | nǐ néng tuī-jiàn yí-wèi hǎo yá-kē dài-fu ma |
| Can I make an (urgent) appointment? | 我能约个（急诊）看牙的时间吗？ | wǒ néng yuē ge (jí-zhěn) kàn yá de shí-jiān ma |
| Couldn't you make it earlier than that? | 能早点儿吗？ | néng zǎo diǎnr ma |
| I have a broken tooth. | 我的牙碰断了。 | wǒ de yá pèng duàn le |
| I have a toothache. | 我牙疼。 | wǒ yá téng |
| I have an abscess. | 我的牙化脓了。 | wǒ de yá huà-nóng le |
| This tooth hurts. | 这颗牙很疼。 | zhè kē yá hěn téng |
| at the top | 在上边 | zài shàng-bian |
| at the bottom | 在下边 | zài xià-bian |
| in the front | 在前边 | zài qián-bian |
| at the back | 在后边 | zài hòu-bian |
| Can you fix it temporarily? | 你能暂时把它治疗一下吗？ | nǐ néng zàn-shí bǎ tā zhì-liáo yí xià ma |
| I don't want it extracted. | 请不要拔这颗牙。 | qǐng bú yào bá zhè kē yá |
| Could you give me an anaesthetic? | 请给我打麻药。 | qǐng gěi wǒ dǎ má-yào |
| I've lost a filling. | 我牙里的镶补物丢了。 | wǒ yá-li de xiāng-bǔ-wù diū le |
| The gum is very sore. | 牙龈很疼。 | yá-yín hěn téng |
| The gum is bleeding. | 牙龈流血 | yá-yín liú xuě |
| I've broken this denture. | 我把这副假牙弄坏了。 | wǒ bǎ zhè fù jiǎ-yá nòng huài le |
| Can you repair this denture? | 你能修这副假牙吗？ | nǐ néng xiū zhè fù jiǎ-yá ma |
| When will it be ready? | 什么时候能修好？ | shén-me shí-hou néng xiū hǎo |

# Reference section

**Where do you come from?** 你是从哪儿来的？

| | | |
|---|---|---|
| Africa | 非洲 | fēi-zhōu |
| Asia | 亚洲 | yà-zhōu |
| Australia | 澳大利亚 | ào-dà-lì-yà |
| Europe | 欧洲 | ōu-zhōu |
| North America | 北美洲 | běi-měi-zhōu |
| South America | 南美洲 | nán-měi-zhōu |
| Afghanistan | 阿富汗 | ā-fù-hàn |
| Bangladesh | 孟加拉 | mèng-jiā-lā |
| Belgium | 比利时 | bǐ-lì-shí |
| Bhutan | 不丹 | bù-dān |
| Burma | 缅甸 | miǎn-diàn |
| Canada | 加拿大 | jiā-ná-dà |
| China | 中国 | zhōng-guó |
| England | 英格兰 | yīng-gé-lán |
| France | 法国 | fǎ-guó |
| Germany | 德国 | dé-guó |
| Great Britain | 英国 | yīng-guó |
| Hong Kong | 香港 | xiāng-gǎng |
| India | 印度 | yìn-dù |
| Indonesia | 印度尼西亚 | yìn-dù-ní-xī-yà |
| Ireland | 爱尔兰 | ài-ěr-lán |
| Israel | 以色列 | yǐ-sè-liè |
| Italy | 意大利 | yì-dà-lì |
| Japan | 日本 | rì-běn |
| Korea | 朝鲜 | cháo-xiǎn |
| Laos | 老挝 | lǎo-wō |
| Mongolia | 蒙古 | měng-gǔ |
| Nepal | 尼泊尔 | ní-bó-ěr |
| Netherlands | 荷兰 | hé-lán |
| New Zealand | 新西兰 | xīn-xī-lán |
| Pakistan | 巴基斯坦 | bā-jī-sī-tǎn |
| Philippines | 菲律宾 | fēi-lù-bīn |
| Scotland | 苏格兰 | sū-gé-lán |
| Singapore | 新加坡 | xīn-jiā-pō |
| South Africa | 南非 | nán-fēi |
| Soviet Union | 苏联 | sū-lián |
| Spain | 西班牙 | xī-bān-yá |
| Taiwan | 台湾 | tái-wān |
| Thailand | 泰国 | tài-guó |
| United States | 美国 | měi-guó |
| Vietnam | 越南 | yuè-nán |
| Wales | 威尔士 | wēi-ěr-shì |

## Numbers 数字

In Chinese, counting is based on the decimal system. From eleven to nineteen, numbers are formed by addition. E.g.: 11 is 10 plus 1,19 is 10 plus 9; 20 to 90 are formed by multiplication. E.g.: 30 is expressed as "3 times 10". The numerals between the tens are expressed in multiples of ten plus the remainder. E.g. 33 is "3 times ten plus 3".

Alongside their traditional system of numerals, the Chinese are also familiar with Western figure notation, which facilitates communication where money, the telephone and room location, etc., are concerned.

| 0 | 零 | líng |
| 1 | 一 | yī |
| 2 | 二 | èr |
| 3 | 三 | sān |
| 4 | 四 | sì |
| 5 | 五 | wǔ |
| 6 | 六 | liù |
| 7 | 七 | qī |
| 8 | 八 | bā |
| 9 | 九 | jiǔ |
| 10 | 十 | shí |
| 11 | 十一 | shí-yī |
| 12 | 十二 | shí-èr |
| 13 | 十三 | shí-sān |
| 14 | 十四 | shí-sì |
| 15 | 十五 | shí-wǔ |
| 16 | 十六 | shí-liù |
| 17 | 十七 | shí-qī |
| 18 | 十八 | shí-bā |
| 19 | 十九 | shí-jiǔ |
| 20 | 二十 | èr-shí |
| 21 | 二十一 | èr-shí yī |
| 22 | 二十二 | èr-shí èr |
| 23 | 二十三 | èr-shí sān |
| 24 | 二十四 | èr-shí sì |
| 25 | 二十五 | èr-shí wǔ |
| 26 | 二十六 | èr-shí liù |
| 27 | 二十七 | èr-shí qī |
| 28 | 二十八 | èr-shí bā |
| 29 | 二十九 | èr-shí jiǔ |
| 30 | 三十 | sān-shí |
| 31 | 三十一 | sān-shí yī |
| 32 | 三十二 | sān-shí èr |

| 33 | 三十三 | sān-shí sān |
| 40 | 四十 | sì-shí |
| 41 | 四十一 | sì-shí yī |
| 42 | 四十二 | sì-shí èr |
| 43 | 四十三 | sì-shí sān |
| 50 | 五十 | wǔ-shí |
| 51 | 五十一 | wǔ-shí yī |
| 52 | 五十二 | wǔ-shí èr |
| 53 | 五十三 | wǔ-shí sān |
| 60 | 六十 | liù-shí |
| 61 | 六十一 | liù-shí yī |
| 62 | 六十二 | liù-shí èr |
| 63 | 六十三 | liù-shí sān |
| 70 | 七十 | qī-shí |
| 71 | 七十一 | qī-shí yī |
| 72 | 七十二 | qī-shí èr |
| 73 | 七十三 | qī-shí sān |
| 80 | 八十 | bā-shí |
| 81 | 八十一 | bā-shí yī |
| 82 | 八十二 | bā-shí èr |
| 83 | 八十三 | bā-shí sān |
| 90 | 九十 | jiǔ-shí |
| 91 | 九十一 | jiǔ-shí yī |
| 92 | 九十二 | jiǔ-shí èr |
| 93 | 九十三 | jiǔ-shí sān |
| 100 | 一百 | yì-bǎi |
| 101 | 一百零一 | yì-bǎi líng-yī |
| 102 | 一百零二 | yì-bǎi líng-èr |
| 110 | 一百一十 | yì-bǎi yī-shí |
| 120 | 一百二十 | yì-bǎi èr-shí |
| 130 | 一百三十 | yì-bǎi sān-shí |
| 140 | 一百四十 | yì-bǎi sì-shí |
| 150 | 一百五十 | yì-bǎi wǔ-shí |
| 160 | 一百六十 | yì-bǎi liù-shí |
| 170 | 一百七十 | yì-bǎi qī-shí |
| 180 | 一百八十 | yì-bǎi bā-shí |
| 190 | 一百九十 | yì-bǎi jiǔ-shí |
| 200 | 二百 | èr-bǎi |
| 300 | 三百 | sān-bǎi |
| 400 | 四百 | sì-bǎi |
| 500 | 五百 | wǔ-bǎi |
| 600 | 六百 | liù-bǎi |
| 700 | 七百 | qī-bǎi |
| 800 | 八百 | bā-bǎi |
| 900 | 九百 | jiǔ-bǎi |
| 1,000 | 一千 | yì-qiān |
| 1,100 | 一千一百 | yì-qiān yì-bǎi |
| 1,200 | 一千二百 | yì-qiān èr-bǎi |
| 2,000 | 二千 | èr-qiān |

| | | |
|---|---|---|
| 5,000 | 五千 | wǔ-qiān |
| 10,000 | 一万 | yí-wàn |
| 50,000 | 五万 | wǔ-wàn |
| 100,000 | 十万 | shí-wàn |
| 1,000,000 | 一百万 | yì-bǎi-wàn |
| 1,000,000,000 | 十亿 | shí-yì |
| first | 第一 | dì-yī |
| second | 第二 | dì-èr |
| third | 第三 | dì-sān |
| fourth | 第四 | dì-sì |
| fifth | 第五 | dì-wǔ |
| sixth | 第六 | dì-liù |
| seventh | 第七 | dì-qī |
| eighth | 第八 | dì-bā |
| ninth | 第九 | dì-jiǔ |
| tenth | 第十 | dì-shí |
| once | 一次 | yí-cì |
| twice | 两次 | liǎng-cì |
| three times | 三次 | sān-cì |
| a half/half a … | 一半/半… | yí-bàn/bàn |
| half of …/half (adj.) | …的一半/半 | … de yí-bàn/bàn |
| a quarter | 四分之一 | sì-fēn-zhī-yī |
| a third | 三分之一 | sān-fēn-zhī-yī |
| a pair of | 一双 | yì-shuāng |
| a dozen | 一打 | yì-dá |
| one per cent | 百分之一 | bǎi-fēn-zhī-yī |
| 3.4% | 百分之三点四 | bǎi-fēn zhī sān-diǎn-sì |
| 1981 | 一九八一 | yī jiǔ bā yī |
| 1992 | 一九九二 | yī jiǔ jiǔ èr |
| 2003 | 二零零三 | èr líng líng sān |

## Year and age 年份和岁数

| | | |
|---|---|---|
| year | 年 | nián |
| leap year | 闰年 | rùn-nián |
| decade | 十年 | shí nián |
| century | 世纪 | shì-jì |
| this year | 今年 | jīn-nián |
| last year | 去年 | qù-nián |
| next year | 明年 | míng-nián |
| every year | 每年 | měi nián |
| 2 years ago | 两年前 | liǎng nián qián |
| in one year | 一年后 | yì nián hòu |

| in the eighties | 在八十年代 | zài bā-shí nián-dài |
| the 16th century | 十六世纪 | shí-liù shì-jì |
| in the 20th century | 在二十世纪 | zài èr-shí shì-jì |
| How old are you? | 你今年多大岁数？ | nǐ jīn-nián duō dà suì-shu |
| I'm 30 years old. | 我今年三十岁。 | wǒ jīn-nián sān-shí suì |
| He/She was born in 1960. | 他/她是一九六零年出生的。 | tā/tā shì yì jiǔ liù líng nián chū-shēng de |
| What is his/her age? | 他/她今年多大岁数？ | tā/tā jīn-nián duō dà suì-shu |

## Seasons 季节

| spring/summer | 春/夏 | chūn/xià |
| autumn/winter | 秋/冬 | qiū/dōng |
| in spring | 在春天 | zài chūn-tiān |
| during the summer | 在夏天的时候 | zài xià-tiān de shí-hou |
| in autumn | 在秋天 | zài qiū-tiān |
| during the winter | 在冬天的时候 | zài dōng-tiān de shí-hou |
| high season | 旺季 | wàng-jì |
| low season | 淡季 | dàn-jì |

## Months 月份

China adopted the Gregorian calendar at the beginning of this century. However, the traditional lunar calendar still holds sway in matters of local customs and festivals. The lunar calendar divides the year into 24 parts, each of which has agricultural significance.

| January | 一月 | yī-yuè |
| February | 二月 | èr-yuè |
| March | 三月 | sān-yuè |
| April | 四月 | sì-yuè |
| May | 五月 | wǔ-yuè |
| June | 六月 | liù-yuè |
| July | 七月 | qī-yuè |
| August | 八月 | bā-yuè |
| September | 九月 | jiǔ-yuè |
| October | 十月 | shí-yuè |
| November | 十一月 | shí-yī yuè |
| December | 十二月 | shí-èr yuè |

| | | |
|---|---|---|
| since June | 六月以来 | liù-yuè yǐ-lái |
| during August | 在八月份里 | zài bā-yuè-fèn li |
| last month | 上个月 | shàng-ge yuè |
| next month | 下个月 | xià-ge yuè |

## Days and date 日期

| | | |
|---|---|---|
| What day is it today? | 今天星期几？ | jīn-tiān xīng-qī jǐ |
| Sunday | 星期天/星期日 | xīng-qī-tiān/xīng-qī-rì |
| Monday | 星期一 | xīng-qī-yī |
| Tuesday | 星期二 | xīng-qī-èr |
| Wednesday | 星期三 | xīng-qī-sān |
| Thursday | 星期四 | xīng-qī-sì |
| Friday | 星期五 | xīng-qī-wǔ |
| Saturday | 星期六 | xīng-qī-liù |
| It's … | 今天… | jīn-tiān |
| March 1 | 三月一号 | sān-yuè yī-hào |
| December 7 | 十二月七号 | shí-èr-yuè qī-hào |
| in the morning | 在上午 | zài shàng-wǔ |
| during the day | 在白天 | zài bái-tiān |
| in the afternoon | 在下午 | zài xià-wǔ |
| in the evening | 在晚上 | zài wǎn-shang |
| at night | 在夜里 | zài yè-li |
| the day before yesterday | 前天 | qián-tiān |
| yesterday | 昨天 | zuó-tiān |
| today | 今天 | jīn-tiān |
| tomorrow | 明天 | míng-tiān |
| the day after tomorrow | 后天 | hòu-tiān |
| the day before | 前一天 | qián yì-tiān |
| the next day | 第二天 | dì-èr tiān |
| two days ago | 两天前 | liǎng tiān qián |
| in three days' time | 三天后 | sān tiān hòu |
| last week | 上个星期 | shàng-ge xīng-qī |
| next week | 下个星期 | xià-ge xīng-qī |
| for a fortnight (two weeks) | 两个星期 | liǎng-ge xīng-qī |
| birthday | 生日 | shēng-rì |
| day off | 休息日 | xiū-xi-rì |
| (public) holiday | 假日 | jià-rì |
| holidays/vacation | 假期 | jià-qī |
| week | 星期 | xīng-qī |
| weekend | 周末 | zhōu-mò |
| working day | 工作日 | gōng-zuò-rì |

## Public holidays and festivals 节假日

### Lunar calendar holidays 农历节假日

Some Chinese holidays are fixed according to the lunar calendar, not our Gregorian calendar, so precise dates cannot be given. Here are the main festivals:

春节
(chūn-jié)

Spring Festival (Chinese New Year)/Lunar New Year (late January/early February). This is the biggest Chinese festival of them all. Lasting three days, it's predominantly a family celebration.

清明节
(qīng-míng-jié)

The festival of *Qing-ming*, in April, is a time for honouring ancestors. The sweeping of graves is a traditional family obligation.

端午节
(duān-wǔ-jié)

The Dragon Boat Festival at the end of May is celebrated in memory of the ancient poet and statesman *Qu Yuan* who drowned in Hunan Province. Sweet rice cakes containing dates or nuts are served.

中秋节
(zhōng-qiū-jié)

Autumn "Moon" Festival. Takes place in September or October, when everyone turns out to look at the full moon, hope for a good harvest, and eat moon-shaped cakes.

### Greetings and wishes 问候和祝愿

| | | |
|---|---|---|
| Merry Christmas! | 圣诞快乐！ | shèng-dàn kuài-lè |
| Happy New Year! | 新年快乐！ | xīn-nián kuài-lè |
| Happy birthday! | 生日快乐！ | shēng-rì kuài-lè |
| Best wishes! | 祝一切顺利！ | zhù yí-qiè shùn-lì |
| Congratulations! | 祝贺！ | zhù-hè |
| Good luck! | 祝你好运！ | zhù nǐ hǎo-yùn |
| Good trip! | 旅行愉快！ | lǚ-xíng yú-kuài |
| Good holiday! | 假日愉快！ | jià-rì yú-kuài |

参照部分

**What time is it?** 几点了？

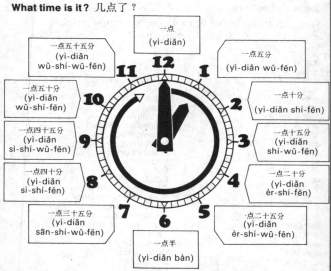

一点
(yì-diǎn)

一点五分
(yì-diǎn wǔ-fēn)

一点十分
(yì-diǎn shí-fēn)

一点十五分
(yì-diǎn shí-wǔ-fēn)

一点二十分
(yì-diǎn èr-shí-fēn)

一点二十五分
(yì-diǎn èr-shí-wǔ-fēn)

一点半
(yì-diǎn bàn)

一点三十五分
(yì-diǎn sān-shí-wǔ-fēn)

一点四十分
(yì-diǎn sì-shí-fēn)

一点四十五分
(yì-diǎn sì-shí-wǔ-fēn)

一点五十分
(yì-diǎn wǔ-shí-fēn)

一点五十五分
(yì-diǎn wǔ-shí-wǔ-fēn)

In everyday conversation, time is expressed as shown above (1 o'clock, 5 past 1, 10 past 1 etc.). However, airline and train timetables use a 24-hour clock, where the after noon hours are counted from 13 to 24.

| The train leaves at … | 列车…发车。 | liè-chē … fā chē |
|---|---|---|
| 13.04 (1.04 p.m.) | 十三点零四分 | shí-sān diǎn líng sì fēn |
| 0.40 (0.40 a.m.) | 零点四十分 | líng diǎn sì-shí fēn |
| in five minutes | 再过五分钟 | zài guò wǔ fēn-zhōng |
| in a quarter of an hour | 再过一刻钟 | zài guò yí-kè-zhōng |
| half an hour ago | 半小时以前 | bàn xiǎo-shí yǐ-qián |
| about two hours | 大约两小时 | dà-yuē liǎng xiǎo-shí |
| more than 10 minutes | 十多分钟 | shí duō fēn-zhōng |
| less than 30 seconds | 不到三十秒 | bú dào sān-shí miǎo |
| The clock is fast/slow. | 这个钟快/慢了 | zhè-ge zhōng kuài/màn le |

**Signs and notices** 招贴，指示标记和警告

Here are a number of signs you may see, unfortunately they are rarely accompanied by *pīn-yīn*.

| | |
|---|---|
| 出口 | Exit |
| 收款处 | Cash desk |
| 出售 | For sale |
| 出租 | To let, for hire |
| 大减价 | Sales |
| 电梯 | Lift (elevator) |
| 休息 | Closed |
| 禁止入内 | No admittance |
| 禁止摄影 | No photos allowed |
| 禁止吸烟 | No smoking |
| 禁止游泳 | No bathing |
| 客满 | Sold out (seats) |
| 无人 | Vacant |
| 拉 | Pull |
| 冷 | Cold |
| 男厕所 | Gentlemen (toilet) |
| 请随手关门 | Please close the door |
| 请勿打扰 | Do not disturb |
| 停电 | No electric power |
| 谢绝参观 | Visitors not allowed |
| 女厕所 | Ladies (toilet) |
| 请按铃 | Please ring |
| 请勿触摸 | Don't touch |
| 请勿靠近 | Keep away |
| 热 | Hot |
| 入口 | Entrance |
| 太平门 | Emergency exit |
| 停止 | Stop |
| 推 | Push |
| 危险 | Danger |
| 问询处 | Information office |
| 闲人免进 | No entrance |
| 严禁… | … forbidden |
| 已预定 | Reserved |
| 有死亡危险 | Danger of death |
| 有人 | Occupied |
| 私人住宅 | Private (house) |
| 油漆未干 | Wet paint |
| 待检修 | Out of order |
| 免费入场 | Admission free |
| 非饮用水 | Non-potable water |
| 非工作人员请勿入内 | Employees only |
| 候车室 | Waiting room |
| 厕所 | Toilets |

## Emergency 紧急情况

By the time the emergency is upon you it's too late to look up the Chinese for "Help!". So have a look at this list beforehand — and, if you want to be on the safe side, learn the expressions shown in capitals.

| Call the police | 叫警察 | jiào jǐng-chá |
| DANGER | 危险 | wēi-xiǎn |
| FIRE | 火 | huǒ |
| GAS | 煤气 | méi-qì |
| Get a doctor | 请医生来 | qǐng yī-shēng lái |
| Go away | 走开 | zǒu-kāi |
| HELP | 救人啊 | jiù rén a |
| Get help quickly | 快找人来 | kuài zhǎo rén lái |
| I'm ill | 我病了 | wǒ bìng le |
| I'm lost | 我迷路了 | wǒ mí lù le |
| Leave me alone | 别管我 | bié guǎn wǒ |
| LOOK OUT | 留神 | liú shén |
| POLICE | 警察 | jǐng-chá |
| Quick | 快 | kuài |
| STOP | 站住 | zhàn zhù |
| Stop that man/ woman | 拦住那人/女人 | lán zhù nà rén/nǚ-rén |
| STOP THIEF | 抓贼 | zhuā zéi |

## Lost 迷路了

| Where's the ...? | …在哪儿？ | ... zài nǎr |
| consulate | 领事馆 | lǐng-shì-guǎn |
| embassy | 大使馆 | dà-shǐ-guǎn |
| lost property (lost and found) office | 失物招领处 | shī-wù zhāo-lǐng-chù |
| police station | 公安局 | gōng-ān-jú |
| I want to report a theft. | 我要报一偷窃案。 | wǒ yào bào yì tōu-qiè-àn |
| My ... has been stolen. | 我的…被偷了。 | wǒ de ... bèi tōu le |
| handbag | 手提包 | shǒu-tí-bāo |
| passport | 护照 | hù-zhào |
| wallet | 钱包 | qián-bāo |

CAR ACCIDENTS, see page 75

参照部分

REFERENCE SECTION

参照部分

### Kilometres into miles

1 kilometre (km.) = 0.62 miles

| km. | 10 | 20 | 30 | 40 | 50 | 60 | 70 | 80 | 90 | 100 | 110 | 120 | 130 |
|-----|----|----|----|----|----|----|----|----|----|-----|-----|-----|-----|
| miles | 6 | 12 | 19 | 25 | 31 | 37 | 44 | 50 | 56 | 62 | 68 | 75 | 81 |

### Miles into kilometres

1 mile = 1.609 kilometres (km.)

| miles | 10 | 20 | 30 | 40 | 50 | 60 | 70 | 80 | 90 | 100 |
|-------|----|----|----|----|----|----|----|----|----|-----|
| km. | 16 | 32 | 48 | 64 | 80 | 97 | 113 | 129 | 145 | 161 |

### Fluid measures

1 litre (l.) = 0.88 imp. quarts = 1.06 U.S. quarts

| 1 imp. quart = 1.14 l. | 1 U.S. quart = 0.95 l. |
|---|---|
| 1 imp. gallon = 4.55 l. | 1 U.S. gallon = 3.8 l. |

| l. | 5 | 10 | 15 | 20 | 25 | 30 | 35 | 40 | 45 | 50 |
|----|---|----|----|----|----|----|----|----|----|----|
| imp. gal. | 1.1 | 2.2 | 3.3 | 4.4 | 5.5 | 6.6 | 7.7 | 8.8 | 9.9 | 11.0 |
| U.S. gal. | 1.3 | 2.6 | 3.9 | 5.2 | 6.5 | 7.8 | 9.1 | 10.4 | 11.7 | 13.0 |

### Weights and measures

1 kilogram or kilo (kg.) = 1000 grams (g.)

| 100 g. = 3.5 oz. | ½ kg. = 1.1 lb. |
|---|---|
| 200 g. = 7.0 oz. | 1 kg. = 2.2 lb. |

1 oz. = 28.35 g.
1 lb. = 453.60 g.

CLOTHING SIZES, see page 115/YARDS AND INCHES, see page 111

## Conversion tables

### Centimetres and inches

To change centimetres into inches, multiply by .39.

To change inches into centimetres, multiply by 2.54.

|       | in.   | feet  | yards |
|-------|-------|-------|-------|
| 1 mm  | 0.039 | 0.003 | 0.001 |
| 1 cm  | 0.39  | 0.03  | 0.01  |
| 1 dm  | 3.94  | 0.32  | 0.10  |
| 1 m   | 39.40 | 3.28  | 1.09  |

|       | mm    | cm    | m     |
|-------|-------|-------|-------|
| 1 in. | 25.4  | 2.54  | 0.025 |
| 1 ft. | 304.8 | 30.48 | 0.304 |
| 1 yd. | 914.4 | 91.44 | 0.914 |

(32 metres = 35 yards)

### Temperature

To convert Centigrade into degrees Fahrenheit, multiply Centigrade by 1.8 and add 32.

To convert degrees Fahrenheit into Centigrade, subtract 32 from Fahrenheit and divide by 1.8.

# A very basic grammar

Explaining the basic principles of such an intricate and subtle language as Chinese is not an easy matter. The difference between English and Chinese is nothing like the difference between, say, French and English. The pattern we are used to, that of differences in conjugations and declensions, vocabulary and idioms, is one that is limited to our group of Western languages. As soon as one sets out to compare English and an Oriental language, the difference is much more profound.

Generally speaking, a foreign language not only implies different words and sentence constructions, but also a different way of thinking and reasoning. This is all the more true for China. The country, the people, their customs and above all their language have been almost totally isolated for the whole of their history. The result is an entirely different way of experiencing life.

Most of us consider Chinese to be a forbiddingly difficult language to learn and are usually astonished to meet someone who has made the effort to master this tongue. For the traveller to China, it is not necessary to be fluent, but it will certainly be appreciated by your hosts if you take the time to familiarize yourself with some basic everyday phrases you're likely to need or hear during your visit. For your own appreciation of the new sights and sounds around you, you'll be glad to have acquired at least an inkling of Chinese. And remember, you'll be learning a language spoken by more people than any other, including English.

Mandarin Chinese is spoken by the majority of the people and is the official language of the country. There are nine groups of dialects, six of which are not mutually intelligible, including Cantonese and Hakka. Northern, southern and southwestern Mandarin speakers, however, are able to communicate with one another and their language is the official *pǔ tōng huà* (national language); it is this which you'll find featured in this book. Although the dialects differ a great deal in pronunciation, less so in vocabulary, and very little in grammar, written Chinese is always the same.

### Nouns and adjectives

There is no definite article (the), singular or plural in Chinese. Thus, the word 书 (*shū*) may mean book, the book, books or the books, depending on the context. Adjectives are generally preceded by the adverb 很 (*hěn* — very) in its positive form. When used predicatively, the verb "to be" (*shì*) can be dropped:

| 我很高兴。 | wǒ hěn gāo-xìng | I am happy. |

### Word order

The word order in Chinese sentences is always:

> subject — verb — object

which is also the usual order in English sentences. For example:

| 我 | 学 | 汉语 |
| wǒ | xué | hàn-yǔ |
| I | learn | Chinese. |

### Verbs

Chinese verb forms are even more invariable than English ones, with no differences between the singular and plural verb forms at all.

| 我学 | wǒ xué | I learn |
| 你学 | nǐ xué | you learn |
| 他/她/它学 | tā xué | he/she/it learns |
| 我们学 | wǒ-men xué | we learn |
| 你们学 | nǐ-men xué | you learn |
| 他们学 | tā-men xué | they learn |

Although written differently, the characters 他 (tā — he), 她 (tā — she), 它 (tā — it) are all pronounced the same. Note that the form of tā meaning "it" is never used at the beginning of a sentence. Personal pronouns (I/me, you, he/him, she/her, etc.) have the same form whether used as subject or object.

## Past tense

The suffix 了 (le) is placed after the verb to show that the action has been completed:

| | | |
|---|---|---|
| 我喝茶。 | wǒ hē chá | I drink tea. |
| 我喝了茶。 | wǒ hē le chá | I drank (have drunk) tea. |

The suffix 过 (guò) after a verb indicates the indefinite past, i.e. whether something has or has not happened but without a specific notion of point in time:

| | | |
|---|---|---|
| 他去过中国。 | tā qù-guo zhōng-guó | He has been to China. |
| 他没去过中国。 | tā méi qù-guo zhōng-guó | He hasn't been to China. |

## Future

The future tense has exactly the same form as the present. To indicate the future nature of the action, an adverb or adverbial phrase must be added:

| | | |
|---|---|---|
| 我学汉语。 | wǒ xué hàn-yǔ | I learn Chinese. |
| 我明年学汉语。 | wǒ míng-nián xué hàn-yǔ | I shall learn Chinese next year. |

## Questions

Word order in interrogative sentences is the same as in statements, but the word 吗 (mā) is added at the end of the sentence:

| | | |
|---|---|---|
| 你学汉语。 | nǐ xué hàn-yǔ | You learn Chinese. |
| 你学汉语吗? | nǐ xué hàn-yǔ ma | Do you learn Chinese? |

A question may feature an interrogative pronoun (e.g.: *shén–me* = what, *shuí* = who, etc.). In this case, the particle *(mā)* 吗 is not added at the end of the sentence:

| 你喝什么？ | nǐ hē shén-me | What do you drink? |
| 谁喝茶？ | shuí hē chá | Who drinks tea? |

A question can also be formed by presenting a choice between a positive and a negative. The particle 不 *(bù)* is inserted between the two propositions:

| 你喝不喝茶？ | nǐ hē bù hē chá | Do you drink tea or not? |

In a question involving a choice between two possibilities, the words 还是 *(hái-shì)* are placed between the two alternatives:

| 你喝茶还是喝咖啡？ | nǐ hē chá hái-shì hē kā-fēi | Do you drink tea or coffee? |

### Negatives

不 *(bù)* is placed in front of a verb to indicate negation:

| 我不学汉语。 | wǒ bù xué hàn-yǔ | I do not study Chinese. |

The negative form of 有 *(yǒu — to have)* is 没有 *(méi yǒu)*. *Méi* is also used before the verb to indicate negation in the past tense:

| 我没学汉语。 | wǒ méi xué hàn-yǔ | I didn't learn Chinese. |

### Yes and No

There are no specific words in Chinese for yes and no. You simply repeat the verb which was used in the question:

| 你学汉语吗？ | nǐ xué hàn-yǔ ma | Do you learn Chinese? |
| 我学。 | wǒ xué | Yes. (I.e.: "I learn".) |
| 我不学。 | wǒ bù xué | No. (I.e.: "I don't learn".) |

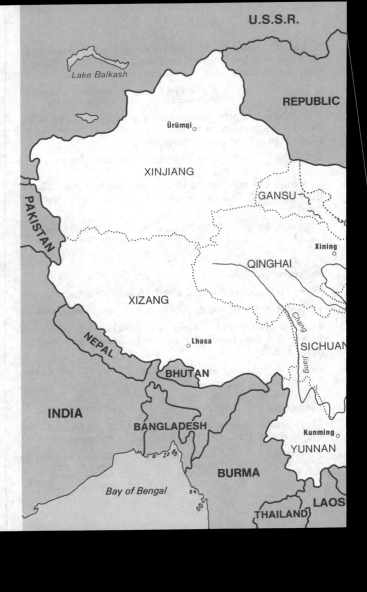

# Dictionary
and alphabetical index

## English – Chinese

*n* noun

**abacus** *n* suàn-pan 算盘 105, 126
**abdomen** *n* fù-bù 腹部 139
**about** *(approximately)* dà-yuē 大约 155
**above** zài...zhī shàng 在...之上 16
**abscess** *n* huà nóng 化脓 147
**absorbent cotton** *n* tuō-zhī-mián 脱脂棉 108
**accept, to** *(payment)* shōu 收 62, 103
**accessories** *(mechanical)* *n* líng-pèi-jiàn 零配件 125
**accident** *n* shì-gù 事故 75, 141
**account** *n* zhàng-hù 帐户 131
**ache** *n* téng 疼 143
**acupuncture** *n* (zhā) zhēn-jiǔ (扎) 针灸 81, 139
**adaptor** *n* duō-lù chā-zuò 多路插座 28, 119
**address** *n* dì-zhǐ 地址 21, 32, 75, 77, 102
**address book** *n* tōng-xùn-bù 通讯簿 105
**adhesive tape** *n* jiāo-tiáo 胶条 105
**admission** *n* rù chǎng 入场 79, 156
**after** *(time)* hòu 后 16; *(place)* guò le...zhī hòu 过了...之后 77
**afternoon** *n* xià-wǔ 下午 153
**after-shave lotion** *n* xiū miàn hòu xiāng-shuǐ 修面后香水 109
**age** *n* suì-shu 岁数 151, 152
**ago** qián 前 151
**agriculture** *n* nóng-yè 农业 133
**air conditioner/conditioning** *n* kōng-tiáo 空调 24, 29
**airmail** *n* háng-kōng (yóu -dì) 航空 (邮递) 135
**air mattress** *n* qì-rù-zi 气褥子 91
**airplane** *n* fēi-jī 飞机 65

**airport** *n* fēi-jī-chǎng 飞机场 20, 21, 65, 73
**airport bus** *n* jī-chǎng bān-chē 机场班车 20, 65
**alarm clock** *n* nào-zhōng 闹钟 121
**alcohol** *n* jiǔ 酒 58
**allergic to...** duì...guò-mǐn 对...过敏 143, 145
**almond** *n* xìng-rénr 杏仁儿 57
**also** yě 也 16
**alter, to** gǎi 改 116
**amber** *n* hǔ-pò 琥珀 122
**amethyst** *n* zǐ-shuǐ-jīng 紫水晶 122
**amount** *n* shù-é 数额 132
**amplifier** *n* kuò-yīn-jī 扩音机 119
**anaesthetic** *n* má-yào 麻药 146, 147
**analgesic** *n* zhǐ-téng-yào 止疼药 108
**and** hé 和 16
**animal** *n* dòng-wù 动物 84
**ankle** *n* jiǎo-wàn-zi 脚腕子 139, 141
**anorak** *n* dēng-shān-fú 登山服 116
**antibiotic** *n* kàng-jūn-sù 抗菌素 145
**antidepressant** *n* kàng yì-yù yào 抗抑郁药 145
**antiques** *n* gǔ-dǒng 古董 81, 104
**antique shop** *n* gǔ-dǒng-diàn 古董店 98
**appendicitis** *n* lán-wěi-yán 阑尾炎 144
**appendix** *n* lán-wěi 阑尾 139
**apple** *n* píng-guǒ 苹果 56, 64, 120
**appliance** *n* diàn-qì 电器 119
**appointment** *(to make)* yuē...shí-jiān 约...时间 31, 139, 147; *(business)* yuē...huì-tán 约...会谈 132
**apricot** *n* xìng 杏 56
**April** *n* sì-yuè 四月 152
**aquarium** *n* shuǐ-zú-guǎn 水族馆 79
**archaeology** *n* kǎo-gǔ-xué 考古学 81

**architect** n jiàn-zhù-shī 建筑师 82
**architecture** n jiàn-zhù-xué 建筑学 81
**arm** n gē-bo 胳膊 139, 141
**arrival** n dào-dá 到达 65
**arrive, to** dào 到 65, 68, 131
**art** n yì-shù 艺术 81
**art gallery** n huà-diàn 画店 79
**arthritis** n guān-jié-yán 关节炎 143
**artist** n yì-shù-jiā 艺术家 82
**ashtray** n yān-huī-gāng 烟灰缸 28, 37
**ask, to** wèn 问 77
**ask for, to** yào 要 26, 61
**aspirin** n ā-sī-pǐ-lín 阿司匹林 108, 145
**asthma** n xiào-chuǎn 哮喘 143
**at** zài 在 16
**at least** zuì shǎo 最少 25
**attendant** n fú-wù-yuán 服务员 27
**August** n bā-yuè 八月 152
**automatic** zì-dòng-de 自动的 122, 124
**autumn** n qiū-tiān 秋天 152

## B

**baby** n yīng-ér 婴儿 25, 110
**baby food** n yīng-ér shí-pǐn 婴儿食品 110
**babysitter** n lín-shí bǎo-mǔ 临时保姆 28
**back** (body) bèi 背 139; (lower part) yāo 腰 143
**back** (rear) hòu-biān 后边 87
**backache** n yāo-téng 腰疼 143
**bacon** n xián-ròu 咸肉 39
**bad** huài (de) 坏(的) 14
**badminton** n yǔ-máo-qiú 羽毛球 89
**bag** n dài (zi) 袋(子) 19, 103
**baggage** n xíng-li 行李 19, 65, 110
**baggage cart** n shǒu-tuī-chē 手推车 19, 71
**baggage check** n xíng-li jì-cún-chù 行李寄存处 19, 67, 71
**balance** (account) n jié-yú 结余 132
**balcony** n yáng-tái 阳台 24
**ball** n qiú 球 128
**ballet** n bā-léi-wǔ 芭蕾舞 88
**ballpoint pen** n yuán-zhū-bǐ 圆珠笔 105
**bamboo** zhú (zi de) 竹(子的) 126
**banana** n xiāng-jiāo 香蕉 56, 64
**bandage** n bēng-dài 绷带 108
**Band-Aid** n dài yào-diàn xiàng-pí-gāo 带药垫橡皮膏 108
**bangle** n shǒu-zhuó 手镯 121

**bank** (finance) n yín-háng 银行 98, 130, 131
**banknote** n chāo-piào 钞票 131
**banquet** n yàn-huì 宴会 34
**bar** n jiǔ-bā 酒吧 96
**barber's** n lǐ-fà-diàn 理发店 31, 98; (in hotel) lǐ-fà-shì 理发室 31
**basketball** n lán-qiú 篮球 89
**basketware** n téng-biān qì-jù 藤编器具 127
**bath** n zǎo-pén 澡盆 24, 26
**bathing cap** n yóu-yǒng-mào 游泳帽 116
**bathing suit** n yóu-yǒng-yī 游泳衣 91, 116
**bathrobe** n yù-yī 浴衣 116
**bathroom** n yù-shì 浴室 27, 28
**bath essence** n xǐ-zǎo-yè 洗澡液 109
**bath salts** n xǐ-zǎo-fěn 洗澡粉 109
**bath towel** n yù-jīn 浴巾 28
**battery** n diàn-chí 电池 119, 121, 125
**be, to** shì 是 11; (location) zài 在 12
**beach** n shā-tān 沙滩 91
**bean** n dòu 豆 51
**bean curd** n dòu-fu 豆腐 51, 52
**bean sprout** n dòu-yár 豆芽儿 51
**beard** n xià-hū-zi 下胡子 32
**beautiful** hǎo kàn (de) 好看(的) 15
**beauty salon** n měi-róng-shì 美容室 31, 98
**bed** n chuáng (wèi) 床(位) 20, 25, 144, 146
**bedpan** n biàn-pénr 便盆儿 146
**beef** n niú-ròu 牛肉 47, 48
**beer** n pí-jiǔ 啤酒 59
**before** (place) zài...qián-miàn 在...前面 16; (time) qián 前 16
**begin, to** (film, play) kāi yǎn 开演 87, 88
**behind** zài...hòu-miàn 在...后面 16, 77
**beige** qiǎn kā-fēi-sè (de) 浅咖啡色(的) 112
**bell** n líng 铃 146
**below** zài...xià 在...下 16
**belt** n yāo-dài 腰带 117
**berth** n wò-pù 卧铺 69, 70
**better** hǎo xiē (de) 好些(的) 15, 26, 101
**between** zài...zhōng-jiān 在...中间 16
**bicycle** n zì-xíng-chē 自行车 76
**bicycle hire/rental** n (chū) zū zì-xíng-chē (出)租自行车 76

DICTIONARY

**big** dà (de) 大(的) 15, 101
**bill** n zhàng-dān 帐单 32, 62, 102;
  (banknote) chāo-piào 钞票 131
**billion** (Am.) n shí yì 十亿 151
**binoculars** n shuāng-tǒng wàng-
  yuǎn-jìng 双筒望远镜 123
**bird** n niǎor 鸟儿 84
**birthday** n shēng-rì 生日 153, 154
**biscuit** (Br.) n bǐng-gān 饼干 64
**bitter** kǔ (de) 苦(的) 61
**black** hēi-sè (de) 黑色(的) 106, 112
**bladder** n páng-guāng 膀胱 139
**blade** n dāo-piàn 刀片 110
**blanket** n tǎn-zi 毯子 28
**bleed, to** liú xuè 流血 141, 142
**blind** (window) n bǎi-yè-chuāng 百叶
  窗 30
**blister** n shuǐ-pào 水疱 141
**block, to** dǔ (le) 堵(了) 29
**blood** n xuè 血 139, 144
**blood pressure** n xuè-yā 血压 144
**blood transfusion** n shū-xuè 输血 146
**blouse** n nǚ chèn-shān 女衬衫 31
**blow-dry** n chuī gān dìng xíng 吹干定
  型 31
**blue** lán-sè (de) 蓝色(的) 106, 112
**blusher** n yān-zhi 胭脂 109
**boat** n chuán 船 74
**bobby pin** n qiǎ-zi 卡子 110
**body** n shēn-tǐ 身体 139
**boil** n jiē-zi 疖子 141
**boiled** zhǔ (de) 煮(的) 39
**boiled water** n kāi-shuǐ 开水 28
**bond** (finance) n gōng-zhài-quàn 公
  债卷 131
**bone** n gǔ 骨 139
**book** n shū 书 13, 105
**book, to** yù-dìng 预订 20, 37
**bookshop** n shū-diàn 书店 98, 105
**boot** n xuē-zi 靴子 118
**borrow, to** jiè 借 132
**botanical gardens** n zhí-wù-yuán 植
  物园 79
**botany** n zhí-wù-xué 植物学 81
**bottle** n píng (zi) 瓶(子) 18, 59, 64
**bottle opener** n kāi-píng-qì 开瓶器
  64, 120
**bowel** n dà-cháng 大肠 139
**box** n hé (zi) 盒(子) 64, 120
**boxing** n quán-jī 拳击 89
**boy** n nán-háir 男孩儿 111, 128
**boyfriend** n nán-péng-you 男朋友
  93, 95
**bra** n rǔ-zhào 乳罩 116

**bracelet** n shǒu-zhuó 手镯 121
**braces** (suspenders) n bēi-dài 背带
  116
**brain** n nǎo 脑 139
**braised** gān-shāo 干烧 41
**brandy** n bái-lán-dì 白兰地 58
**bread** n miàn-bāo 面包 38, 120
**break, to** nòng huài 弄坏 30, 119,
  123, 147; zhé duàn 折断 141, 142
**breakfast** n zǎo-fàn 早饭 25, 28, 36,
  39
**breast** n rǔ-fáng 乳房 139
**breathe, to** hū-xī 呼吸 143, 144
**bridge** n qiáo 桥 79, 84
**bring, to** ná 拿 14, 59; dài 带 95
**brocade** n zhī-jǐn-duàn 织锦缎 113
**broken** huài le 坏了 30, 119; duàn le
  断了 141, 142
**bronzeware** n qīng-tóng zhì-pǐn 青铜
  制品 104, 127
**brooch** n xiōng-zhēn 胸针 121
**brother** (older) n gē-ge 哥哥 93;
  (younger) dì-di 弟弟 93
**brown** hè-sè (de) 褐色(的) 112
**bruise** n qīng-zǐ 青紫 141
**brush** n shuā (zi) 刷(子) 110
**bucket** n (xiǎo) tǒng 小桶 128
**buckle** n dài-kòu 带扣 117
**Buddhist temple** n fó-sì 佛寺 81
**build, to** jiàn 建 82
**building** n jiàn-zhù 建筑 79, 82
**building blocks/bricks** n jī-mù 积木
  128
**bulb** n dēng-pào 灯泡 29, 30, 119
**burn** n shāo-shāng 烧伤 141
**burn out, to** (bulb) shāo huài (le) 烧坏
  (了) 29
**bus** n gōng-gòng qì-chē 公共汽车
  20, 72, 73; (airport) jī-chǎng bān-
  chē 机场班车 20, 65
**business** n mào-yì 贸易 132
**business district** n shāng-yè-qū 商业
  区 80
**business trip** (to be on) chū chāi 出差
  93
**bus stop** n gōng-gòng qì-chē-zhàn
  公共汽车站 72, 73
**busy** máng 忙 96
**but** dàn-shì 但是 16
**butcher's** n ròu-diàn 肉店 98
**butter** n huáng-yóu 黄油 38, 120
**button** n niǔ-kòu 纽扣 30, 114, 117
**buy, to** mǎi 买 12, 68, 105, 132

词汇表

# C

**cabin** *(ship)* n kè-cāng 客舱 74
**cable release** n lián-xiàn kuài-mén 连线快门 125
**cable** *(telegram)* n diàn-bào 电报 135
**cake** n dàn-gāo 蛋糕 64
**cake shop** n gāo-diǎn-diàn 糕点店 98
**calculator** n jì-suàn-qì 计算器 106
**calendar** n rì-lì 日历 105
**call** *(phone)* n diàn-huà 电话 137
**call, to** *(give name)* jiào 叫 12;
  *(summon)* jiào 叫 75, 157;
  *(phone)* dǎ diàn-huà 打电话 137
**calligraphy** n shū-fǎ 书法 81, 104
**calm** píng-jìng 平静 91
**camel** n luò-tuo 骆驼 104
**camera** n zhào-xiàng-jī 照像机 18, 124, 125
**camera case** n xiàng-jī-hé 像机盒 125
**camera shop** n zhào-xiàng qì-cái shāng-diàn 照像器材商店 98
**can** *(of peaches)* n guàn-tou 罐头 120
**can** *(to be able)* néng 能 13, 14
**canal** n yùn-hé 运河 84
**cancel, to** qǔ-xiāo 取消 65
**can opener** n kāi-guàn-qì 开罐器 64, 120
**cap** n mào-zi 帽子 116
**capital** *(finance)* n zī-běn 资本 132
**car** n (xiǎo-qì) chē (小汽)车 20, 75
**carat** n kāi 开 121
**carbon paper** n fù-xiě-zhǐ 复写纸 106
**card** *(business)* n míng-piàn 名片 132; *(playing)* pái 牌 93
**cardigan** n kāi-shēn máo-yī 开身毛衣 116
**car hire** n zū bāo-chē 租包车 22, 75
**carpet** n dì-tǎn 地毯 104, 127
**car rental** n zū bāo-chē 租包车 22
**carry, to** tí 提 71
**cart** *(trolley)* n shǒu-tuī-chē 手推车 19, 71
**carton** *(of cigarettes)* n tiáo 条 126
**carving** n diāo-kè-pǐn 雕刻品 81
**case** *(camera, etc)* n hé 盒 121, 125
**cash, to** duì-xiàn 兑现 131, 135
**cash desk** n shōu-kuǎn-chù 收款处 103, 156
**cashmere** n kāi-sī-mǐ 开司米 127
**cassette** n hé-shì cí-dài 盒式磁带 128; *(video)* lù-xiàng-dài 录像带 119, 124

**cassette recorder** n hé-shì cí-dài lù-yīn-jī 盒式磁带录音机 119
**catalogue** n jiǎn-jiè 简介 79
**cathedral** n dà-jiào-táng 大教堂 80
**Catholic** tiān-zhǔ-jiào (de) 天主教(的) 82
**cave** n dòng-xué 洞穴 80
**celery** n qín-cài 芹菜 51
**cemetery** n gōng-mù 公墓 80
**centre** n zhōng-xīn 中心 21, 80
**century** n shì-jì 世纪 151
**certificate** n zhèng (míng) 证(明) 17, 146
**chain** *(jewellery)* n liàn 链 121
**chain bracelet** n liàn-shǒu-zhuó 链手镯 121
**change** *(money)* n líng-qián 零钱 131
**change, to** huàn 换 61; *(train)* huàn chē 换车 68, 69, 73, 123; *(money)* duì-huàn 兑换 19, 20, 130; *(reservation)* gēng-huàn 更换 65
**charge** *(hire)* n zū-jīn 租金 89, 91; *(telephone)* fèi 费 135, 137
**charge, to** *(money)* yào (fù) qián yào (付)钱 25, 75, 131
**charm bracelet** n dài shì-wù liàn-shǒu-zhuó 带饰物链手镯 121
**cheap** pián-yi 便宜 15, 25, 26, 69, 101
**check** *(Am.)* n zhī-piào 支票 130, 131, 132; *(restaurant)* zhàng-dān 帐单 62
**check, to** chá-duì 查对 131; *(luggage)* tuō-yùn 托运 71
**check in, to** *(airport)* bàn dēng-jī shǒu-xù 办登机手续 65
**check out, to** jié-zhàng lí-kāi 结帐离开 32
**checkup** (jiǎn) chá (shēn) tǐ (检)查(身)体 144
**cheers!** gān-bēi 干杯 58
**chemist's** n yào-diàn 药店 98, 107
**chemistry** n huà-xué 化学 133
**cheque** n zhī-piào 支票 131, 132
**chess set** n guó-jì xiàng-qí 国际象棋 128
**chest** n xiōng-bù 胸部 139, 143
**chewing tobacco** n kǒu-jiáo yān-cǎo 口嚼烟草 126
**chicken** n jī 鸡 49, 50
**chicken breast** n jī-xiōng-pú 鸡胸脯 49
**child** n ér-tóng 儿童 25, 69, 79; hái-zi 孩子 61, 91, 93, 141

**children's doctor** *n* ér-kē dài-fu 儿科
大夫 139
**China** *n* zhōng-guó 中国 148
**chinaware** *n* cí-qì 瓷器 104, 127
**Chinese** *n* hàn-yǔ 汉语 13, 95
**Chinese** zhōng-shì (de) 中式 (的) 39
**chocolate** *n* qiǎo-ke-lì 巧克力 64, 120
**chop** *(carved)* *n* yìn-zhāng 印章
121, 127; *(uncarved Chinese seal)*
yìn-zhāng shí-liào 印章石料 121
**chopsticks** *n* kuài-zi 筷子 36, 61, 127
**Christmas** *n* shèng-dàn-jié 圣诞节
154
**chromium** *n* luò 铬 122
**church** *n* jiào-táng 教堂 80, 82
**cigar** *n* xuě-jiā 雪茄 126
**cigarette** *n* xiāng-yān 香烟 18, 95, 126
**cigarette case** *n* yān-hé 烟盒 121
**cigarette lighter** *n* dǎ-huǒ-jī 打火机
121
**cinema** *n* diàn-yǐng-yuàn 电影院
88, 96
**circle** *(theatre)* *n* lóu-shàng 楼上 87
**city** *n* chéng-shì 城市 80
**classical** gǔ-diǎn (de) 古典 (的) 128
**classical music** *n* gǔ-diǎn yīn-yuè 古
典音乐 128
**clean** gān-jìng 干净 61
**clean, to** nòng gān-jìng 弄干净 30
**cleansing cream** *n* xiǎ-zhuāng
miàn-shuāng 下妆霜 109
**clerk** *n* zhí-yuán 职员 27
**cliff** *n* shān-yá 山崖 84
**clinic** *n* mén-zhěn-bù 门诊部 98
**clip** *n* jiā-zi 夹子 121
**cloakroom** *n* yī-mào-jiān 衣帽间 87
**clock** *n* zhōng 钟 119, 121, 155
**cloisonné** *n* jǐng-tài-lán 景泰蓝 81,
104, 127
**close, to** guān xì 12, 79, 107, 130, 134
**closed** *(sign)* xiū-xi 休息 98
**cloth** *n* bù-liào 布料 118
**clothes** *n* yī-fu 衣服 30, 111
**cloud** *n* yún 云 94
**coach** *(bus)* *n* cháng-tú qì-chē 长途
汽车 72
**coat** *n* dà-yī 大衣 116
**coffee** *n* kā-fēi 咖啡 39, 60, 64
**coin** *n* yìng-bì 硬币 131
**cold** *adj* lěng 冷 15, 25, 39
**cold** *(illness)* *n* gǎn-mào 感冒 107
**cold cuts** *n* shóu-ròu 熟肉 64
**collar** *n* yī-lǐng 衣领 114
**collar-bone** *n* suǒ-gǔ 锁骨 139

**collect call** *n* ràng duì-fāng fù-fèi de
diàn-huà 让对方付费的电话 137
**colour** *n* yán-sè 颜色 103, 112; *(film)*
cǎi-sè (de) 彩色 (的) 124
**colour fast** bú tuì-sè (de) 不退色 (的)
113
**colour negative** *n* cǎi-sè dǐ-piàn 彩色
底片 124
**colour rinse** *n* zhuó sè xǐ fà 着色洗发
31
**colour shampoo** *n* rǎn-fà xǐ-fà-gāo
染发洗发膏 110
**colour slide** *n* cǎi-sè huàn-dēng-piàn
彩色幻灯片 124
**colouring pencil** *n* cǎi-sè qiān-bǐ 彩
色铅笔 106
**comb** *n* shū-zi 梳子 110
**come, to** lái *v* 来 92, 95, 138
**comedy** *n* xǐ-jù (de) 喜剧 (的) 88
**commission** *n* shǒu-xù-fèi 手续费 131
**commune** *n* gōng-shè 公社 80
**company** *n* gōng-sī 公司 136
**complain, to** yán *v* 言 61
**concert** *n* yīn-yuè-huì 音乐会 88
**concert hall** *n* yīn-yuè-tīng 音乐厅
80, 88
**conductor** *(orchestra)* *n* zhǐ-huī 指挥
88
**confirm, to** què-rèn 确认 65
**congratulations** *n* zhù-hè 祝贺 154
**connection** *(flight)* *n* lián-chéng
háng-bān 联程航班 65
**constipated** biàn-bì 便秘 142
**consulate** *n* lǐng-shì-guǎn 领事馆 157
**contact, to** lián-xì 联系 139
**contact lens** *n* jiǎo-mó jiē-chù-jìng
角膜接触镜 123
**contagious** chuán-rǎn (de) 传染 (的)
144
**contain, to** hán-yǒu 含有 38
**contraceptive** *n* bì-yùn-yào 避孕药
108, 143
**contract** *n* hé-tong 合同 132
**cookie** *(Am.)* *n* bǐng-gān 饼干 64
**copper** *n* tóng 铜 122
**coral** *n* shān-hú 珊瑚 122
**corduroy** *n* dēng-xīn-róng 灯芯绒
122
**coriander** *n* xiāng-cài 香菜 53
**corkscrew** *n* bá-sāi-zuàn 拔塞钻 120
**corn** *(Am.)* *n* tián-yù-mǐ 甜玉米 51;
*(foot)* jī-yǎn 鸡眼 108
**corner** *n* jiǎo 角 37; *(street)* lù-kǒu
路口 22, 77

**correct** duì 对 11
**cost** n fèi 费 137; *(business)* chéng-běn 成本 133
**cost, to** yào duō-shao qián 要多少钱 12
**cot** n xiǎo-chuáng 小床 25
**cotton** n mián-bù 棉布 113
**cotton wool** n tuō-zhī-mián 脱脂棉 108
**cough** n ké-sou 咳嗽 108
**cough, to** ké-sou 咳嗽 107, 143, 144
**cough syrup** n zhǐ-ké táng-jiāng 止咳糖浆 108
**counter** n guì-tái 柜台 135
**country** n guó-jiā 国家 93
**countryside** n nóng-cūn 农村 84
**courtyard** n tíng-yuàn 庭院 80
**crab** n páng-xiè 螃蟹 45
**cramp** n dù-zi jiǎo-tòng 肚子绞痛 143
**crayon** n là-bǐ 腊笔 106
**cream** n nǎi-yóu 奶油 60; *(cosmetic)* xuě-huā-gāo 雪花膏 109
**crease resistant** kàng zhòu (de) 抗皱(的) 113
**credit card** n xìn-yòng-kǎ 信用卡 32, 62, 102, 131
**crepe** n zhòu-chóu 皱绸 113
**crockery** n táo-cí cān-jù 陶瓷餐具 120
**crossroads** n shí-zì lù-kǒu 十字路口 77
**cruise** n zuò chuán yóu-lǎn 坐船游览 74
**crystal** n shuǐ-jīng 水晶 122
**cuff** n xiù-kǒu 袖口 114
**cuff link** n xiù-kǒu liàn-kòu 袖口链扣 121
**cup** n chá-bēi 茶杯 37
**curler** n juǎn-fà jiā-zi 卷发夹子 110
**currency** n huò-bì 货币 139
**currency exchange office** n wài-huì duì-huàn-chù 外汇兑换处 19, 130
**current** *(water)* n cháo-liú 潮流 91
**curtain** n chuāng-liánr 窗帘 29
**customs** n hǎi-guān 海关 17, 102
**cut, to** *(self)* gē pò 割破 141
**cut, to** jiǎn 剪 31
**cut glass** n diāo-bō-li 雕玻璃 122
**cuticle remover** n chú pí-xiè jì 除皮屑剂 109
**cutlery** n dāo-chā cān-jù 刀叉餐具 120, 121
**cycling** qí zì-xíng-chē 骑自行车 89
**cymbals** n bó 钹 127
**cystitis** n páng-guāng-yán 膀胱炎 144

**D**

**dairy** n nǎi-zhì-pǐn diàn 奶制品店 98
**dance, to** tiào wǔ 跳舞 88, 96
**danger** n wēi-xiǎn 危险 156, 157
**dangerous** wēi-xiǎn-de 危险的 91
**dark** àn (de) 暗(的) 25; *(colour)* shēn-sè (de) 深色(的) 101, 112, 113
**date** *(day)* n rì-qī 日期 26, 153; *(fruit)* zǎo 枣 56
**daughter** n nǚ-er 女儿 93
**day** n tiān 天 17, 22, 25, 75, 76, 78; rì-qī 日期 153
**day off** n xiū-xi-rì 休息日 153
**decade** n shí nián 十年 151
**decaffeinated** bú dài kā-fēi-yīn de 不带咖啡因的 39, 60
**December** n shí-èr yuè 十二月 152
**decision** n jué-dìng 决定 25, 102
**deck** *(ship)* n jiǎ-bǎn 甲板 74
**deck chair** n tǎng-yǐ 躺椅 91
**declare, to** *(customs)* bào guān 报关 18
**deep** shēn (de) 深(的) 91
**deep-fried** jiāo-zhá 焦炸 41
**degree** *(temperature)* n dù 度 142
**delay** *(transport)* n wǎn diǎn 晚点 69
**deliver, to** sòng 送 102
**delivery** n jì-sòng 寄送 102
**denim** n láo-dòng-bù 劳动布 113
**dental clinic** n yá-kē mén-zhěn-bù 牙科门诊部 98
**dentist** n yá-kē dài-fu 牙科大夫 147
**denture** n jiǎ-yá 假牙 147
**deodorant** n chú tǐ-xiù yè 除体臭液 109
**department** *(shop)* n bù 部 81, 100
**department store** n bǎi-huò shāng-diàn 百货商店 80, 98
**departure** n chū-fā 出发 65
**deposit** n yā-jīn 押金 22, 76
**deposit, to** *(bank)* cún 存 131
**dessert** n gāo-diǎn tián-shí 糕点甜食 57
**develop, to** *(film)* chōng-xǐ 冲洗 125
**diabetes** n táng-niào-bìng 糖尿病 143
**diabetic** táng-niào-bìng (de) 糖尿病(的) 38
**dial, to** bō 拨 136, 137
**diamond** n jīn-gāng-shí 金钢石 122
**diaper** n zhǐ-niào-bù 纸尿布 110
**diarrhoea** n fù-xiè 腹泻 142
**dictionary** n zì-diǎn 字典 106

DICTIONARY

**diet** *(to be on a)* zūn-shǒu tè-bié de shí-pǔ 遵守特别的食谱 38
**difficult** nán 难 15
**dining car** *n* cān-chē 餐车 68, 71
**dining room** *n* cān-tīng 餐厅 28
**dinner** *n* wǎn-fàn 晚饭 28, 36, 94
**direct, to** zhí 指 77
**direction** zhǐ lù 指路 77
**director** *(cinema)* *n* dǎo-yǎn 导演 88
**directory** *(phone)* *n* diàn-huà-bù 电话簿 136
**disabled** *n* cán-fèi-rén 残废人 79
**discotheque** *n* dí-sī-kē wǔ-huì 迪斯科舞会 88
**discount** *n* zhé-kòu 折扣 132
**dish** *n* cài 菜 37, 38, 47, 61
**disinfectant** *n* xiāo-dú-yào 消毒药 108
**dislocate, to** tuō-jiù 脱臼 142
**dissatisfied** bù mǎn-yì 不满意 103
**disturb, to** dǎ-rǎo 打扰 28, 156
**dizzy** tóu-yūn 头晕 142
**docks** *n* mǎ-tou 码头 80
**doctor** *n* dài-fu 大夫 75, 138, 146
**doctor's office** *n* mén-zhěn 门诊 138
**dog** *n* gǒu 狗 104
**doll** *n* wá-wa 娃娃 128
**dollar** *n* měi-yuán 美元 20, 130; *(Hong Kong)* gǎng-bì 港币 130
**door** *n* mén 门 156
**double bed** *n* shuāng-rén-chuáng 双人床 24
**double room** *n* shuāng-rén fáng-jiān 双人房间 20, 24
**downstairs** lóu xià 楼下 16
**downtown** *n* shì-zhōng-xīn 市中心 80
**dozen** *n* yì-dá 一打 151
**draught beer** *n* sǎn-zhuāng pí-jiǔ 散装啤酒 59
**drawing paper** *n* tú-huà-zhǐ 图画纸 106
**drawing pin** *n* tú-dīng 图钉 106
**dress** *n* lián-yī-qún 连衣裙 114, 116
**dressmaker's** *n* cái-feng-diàn 裁缝店 99
**dressing gown** *n* yù-yī 浴衣 116
**drink** *n* yǐn-liào 饮料 60, 61; *(alcoholic)* jiǔ 酒 58,
**drink, to** hē 喝 13, 58;
**drive, to** kāi *(chē)* 开 (车) 22
**driver** *n* sī-jī 司机 75
**drugstore** *n* yào-diàn 药店 99, 107
**drum** *n* gǔ 鼓 127
**dry** gān 干 31, 59
**drycleaner's** *n* gān-xǐ-diàn 干洗店 30

**dry shampoo** *n* gān-xìng xǐ-fà-jì 干性洗发剂 110
**duck** *n* yā 鸭 49
**duckling** *n* chú-yā 雏鸭 49
**dull** *(pain)* dùn *(de)* 钝 (的) 142
**dummy** *n* xiàng-pí nǎi-zuǐr 橡皮奶嘴儿 110
**during** zài...de shí-hou 在…的时候 16, 152
**duty** *(customs)* *n* shuì 税 18
**duty-free shop** *n* miǎn-shuì shāng-diàn 免税商店 20
**dye** *(hair)* rǎn-fà-jì 染发剂 110

**E**

**each** měi 每 125
**ear** *n* ěr-duo 耳朵 139
**earache** *n* ěr-duo-tòng 耳朵疼 143
**ear drops** *n* dī ěr yào-shuǐ 滴耳药水 108
**early** zǎo 早 15
**earring** *n* ěr-huán 耳环 121
**east** dōng 东 77
**easy** róng-yi 容易 15
**eat, to** chī 吃 38, 146
**ebony** *n* wū-mù 乌木 122
**eel** *n* màn-yú 鳗鱼 45
**egg** *n* jī-dàn 鸡蛋 39, 43, 64, 120
**eggplant** *n* qié-zi 茄子 51
**eight** bā 八 149
**eighteen** shí-bā 十八 149
**eighth** dì bā 第八 151
**eighties** *n* bā-shí nián-dài 八十年代 151
**eighty** bā-shí 八十 150
**elastic** *n* sōng-jǐn-dài 松紧带 114
**elastic bandage** *n* tán-xìng bēng-dài 弹性绷带 108
**Elastoplast** *n* dài yào-diàn xiàng-pí-gāo 带药垫橡皮膏 108
**elbow** *n* zhǒu 肘 139
**electric(al)** diàn *(de)* 电 (的) 119
**electrical appliance** *n* diàn qì 电器 119
**electrician's** *n* diàn-qì xiū-lǐ-bù 电器修理部 99
**electronic** diàn-zǐ *(de)* 电子 (的) 125
**electronics** *n* diàn-zǐ 电子 133
**eel** *n* màn-yú 鳗鱼 45
**elevator** *n* diàn-tī 电梯 28, 100
**eleven** shí-yī 十一 149
**embassy** *n* dà-shǐ-guǎn 大使馆 157
**embroidery** *n* cì-xiù 刺绣 127
**emerald** *n* lǜ-gāng-yù 绿刚玉 122
**emergency** *n* jǐn-jí qíng-kuàng 紧急情况 157

**emergency exit** n tài-píng-mén 太平门 28, 99, 156

**emery board** n cuò zhǐ-jia shā-zhǐ 锉指甲砂纸 109

**empty** kōng 空 15

**enamel** n táng-cí 搪瓷 122

**end** n mò (wěi) 末(尾) 153

**engineering** n gōng-chéng 工程 133

**England** n yīng-gé-lán 英格兰 148

**English** yīng-guó (de) 英国(的) 126

**English** n yīng-yǔ 英语 13, 106

**enjoyable** yú-kuài 愉快 32

**enlarge, to** fàng-dà 放大 125

**enough** zú-gòu (le) 足够(了) 15, 68

**entrance** n rù-kǒu 入口 67, 99, 156

**entrance fee** n mén-piào 门票 79

**envelope** n xìn-fēng 信封 28, 106

**equipment** n qì-cái 器材 18, 89

**eraser** n xiàng-pí 橡皮 106

**estimate** (cost) n yù-suàn 预算 133

**Europe** n ōu-zhōu 欧洲 148

**evening** n wǎn-shang 晚上 95, 153

**evening dress** n wǎn-lǐ-fú 晚礼服 88; (woman) nǚ wǎn-lǐ-fú 女晚礼服 116

**every** měi 每 151

**exchange, to** huàn 换 103

**exchange rate** n duì-huàn-lǜ 兑换率 19, 131

**excuse me** (sorry) duì bu qǐ 对不起 12, 70; (may I ask) qǐng-wèn 请问 12

**exercise book** n liàn-xí-běn 练习本 106

**exhibition** n zhǎn-lǎn-huì 展览会 80

**exit** n chū-kǒu 出口 67, 156

**expect, to** děng(dài) 等(待) 131

**expenses** n kāi-zhī 开支 132

**expensive** guì 贵 15, 25, 101

**export** n chū-kǒu 出口 132

**exposure counter** n jiāo-piàn jì-shù-qì 胶片计数器 125

**express** (train) tè-kuài (de) 特快(的) 66, 68; (mail) kuài-dì 快递 135

**extension lead/cord** n jiē cháng diàn-xiàn 接长电线 119

**external** wài(bù de) 外(部的) 108

**eye** n yǎn (-jīng) 眼(睛) 139, 141

**eyebrow pencil** n huà-méi-bǐ 画眉笔 109

**eye drops** n yǎn-yào-shuǐ 眼药水 108

**eye liner** n yǎn-xiàn-bǐ 眼线笔 109

**eye shadow** n yǎn-yǐng-gāo 眼影膏 109

**eye specialist** n yǎn-kē dài-fu 眼科大夫 139

## F

**face** n liǎn 脸 139

**face powder** n liǎn-fěn 脸粉 109

**factory** n gōng-chǎng 工厂 80, 81

**fall** (autumn) n qiū(tiān) 秋(天) 152

**fall, to** shuāi dǎo 摔倒 141

**family** n jiā(shǔ) 家(属) 93, 146

**fan** n shàn(zi) 扇(子) 28, 127

**far** yuǎn 远 15, 77, 100

**fare** n piào-jià 票价 67, 68, 73; (taxi) chē-fèi 车费 21

**farm** n nóng-chǎng 农场 84

**fast** kuài 快 66, 124, 155

**fat** n zhī-fáng 脂肪 38

**father** n fù-qin 父亲 93

**faucet** n shuǐ-lóng-tóu 水龙头 29

**fawn** dàn huáng-hè-sè (de) 淡黄褐色(的) 112

**February** n èr-yuè 二月 152

**fee** (doctor) n yī-yào-fèi 医药费 146

**feeding bottle** n nǎi-píng 奶瓶 110

**feel, to** (physical state) jué de 觉得 142

**felt** n zhān (-zi) 毡(子) 113

**felt-tip pen** n ruǎn-xīn-bǐ 软芯笔 106

**fever** n fā shāo 发烧 142

**few** hěn shǎo 很少 15; (a) yǒu jǐ-ge 有几个 15, 17

**field** n nóng-tián 农田 84

**fifteen** shí-wǔ 十五 149

**fifth** dì-wǔ 第五 151

**fifty** wǔ-shí 五十 150

**file** (nail) n cuò 锉 109

**fill in, to** tián-xiě 填写 26

**filling** (tooth) n yá-li de xiāng-bǔ-wù 牙里的镶补物 147

**film** (cinema) n diàn-yǐng 电影 88; (photography) jiāo-juǎn 胶卷 18, 124, 125

**film winder** n chán-rào jiāo-juǎn bǐng 缠绕胶卷柄 125

**filter** n lǜ-sè-jìng 滤色镜 125

**filter-tipped** dài guò-lǜ-zuǐ de 带过滤嘴的 126

**find, to** zhǎo 找 13, 28, 77

**fine** (OK) hěn hǎo 很好 11, 26

**fine grain** (film) xì-kē-lì de 细颗粒的 124

**finger** n shǒu-zhǐ 手指 139

**fire** n huǒ 火 157

**first** dì-yī 第一 77, 151

**first-aid kit** n jí-jiù-xiāng 急救箱 120

**first name** n míng 名 26

**fish** n yú 鱼 45

**fish, to** diào yú 钓鱼 90
**fishing** n diào-yú 钓鱼 90
**fishmonger's** n yú-diàn 鱼店 99
**fitting** (tailor) n shì yàng-zi 试样子 114
**fitting room** n shì-yī-shì 试衣室 115
**five** wǔ 五 149
**fizzy** dài qì de 带气的 60
**flannel** n fǎ-lán-róng 法兰绒 113
**flash** (photography) n shǎn-guāng-dēng 闪光灯 125
**flash attachment** n shǎn-guāng-dēng jiē-kǒu 闪光灯接口 125
**flashlight** n shǒu-diàn-tǒng 手电筒 120
**flat** píng (de) 平 (的) 118
**flight** n háng-bān 航班 65
**flight number** n háng-bān bān-cì 航班班次 65
**floor** n lóu-céng 楼层 27
**florist's** n huā-diàn 花店 99
**flounder** n píng-yú 鲆鱼 45
**flour** n miàn-fěn 面粉 38
**flower** n huār 花儿 84
**flu** n liú-gǎn 流感 144
**fluid** n yè 液 123
**flute** (Chinese) n dí-zi 笛子 127
**fog** n wù 雾 94
**folding screen** n zhé-dié píng-fēng 折叠屏风 104, 127
**folk music** n mín-jiān yīn-yuè 民间音乐 128
**food** n shí-wù 食物 38
**food poisoning** n shí-wù zhòng-dú 食物中毒 144
**foot** n jiǎo 脚 139
**football** n zú-qiú 足球 89
**footpath** n xiǎo-lù 小路 84
**for** wèi le 为了 78
**forbid, to** yán-jìn 严禁 156
**forecast** n yù-bào 预报 94
**forehead** n qián-é 前额 139
**foreign** wài (-guó de) 外 (国的) 105
**forest** n sēn-lín 森林 84
**forget, to** wàng 忘 61
**fork** n chā-zi 叉子 37, 61
**form** (document) n biǎo 表 26
**fortnight** n liǎng-ge xīng-qī 两个星期 153
**fortress** n yào-sài 要塞 80
**forty** sì-shí 四十 149
**foundation cream** n dǐ-céng miàn-shuāng 底层面霜 109
**fountain** n quán 泉 80

**fountain pen** n gāng-bǐ 钢笔 106
**four** sì 四 149
**fourteen** shí-sì 十四 149
**fourth** dì-sì 第四 151
**frame** (glasses) n jìng-jià 镜架 123
**free** (vacant) méi rén 没人 15; (time) yǒu kòng 有空 96
**French** fǎ-yǔ 法语 13
**French bean** n biǎn-dòu 扁豆 51
**fresh** xīn-xiān(de) 新鲜 (的) 56, 61
**Friday** xīng-qī-wǔ 星期五 30, 153
**fried** zhá (de) 炸 (的) 41
**fried egg** n jiān-jī-dàn 煎鸡蛋 39
**friend** n péng-you 朋友 95
**Friendship Store** n yǒu-yì shāng-diàn 友谊商店 99
**from** cóng 从 16
**frost** n shuāng 霜 94
**fruit** n shuǐ-guǒ 水果 56
**fruit salad** n shí-jǐn shuǐ-guǒ 什锦水果 56
**fruit juice** n guǒ-zhī 果汁 38, 39, 60
**full** mǎn 满 15
**fur** n máo-pí 毛皮 127
**furniture** n jiā-jù 家具 81, 127
**furrier's** n pí-huò-diàn 皮货店 99

## G

**gabardine** n huá-dá-ní 华达呢 113
**gallbladder** n dǎn-náng 胆囊 139
**game** n zhì-lì yóu-xì 智力游戏 128; (food) yě-wèi 野味 49
**garden** n huā-yuán 花园 84
**gardens** n yuán-lín 园林 80
**garlic** n suàn 蒜 51
**gas** n méi-qì 煤气 157
**gastritis** n wèi-yán 胃炎 144
**gauze** n shā-bù 纱布 108
**gem** n bǎo-shí 宝石 121
**general** quán-miàn(de) 全面 (的) 144
**general practitioner** n mén-zhěn dài-fu 门诊大夫 139
**genitals** n shēng-zhí-qì 生殖器 139
**genuine** zhēn de 真的 118
**geology** n dì-zhì-xué 地质学 81
**German** dé-yǔ 德语 13
**get, to** (find) zhǎo 找 11, 138; (call) jiào 叫 21, 32; (obtain) gǎo 搞 90; (go) qù 去 100
**get off, to** xià chē 下车 73
**gift** n lǐ-wù 礼物 18
**gin** n jīn-jiǔ 金酒 58
**gin and tonic** n jīn-jiǔ hé kuí-níng-shuǐ 金酒和奎宁水 58

ginger n jiāng 姜 51, 53
ginseng n rén-shēn 人参 127
girdle n jiàn-měi nèi-kù 健美内裤 16
girl n nǚ-háir 女孩儿 111, 128
girlfriend n nǚ-péng-you 女朋友 93, 95
give, to gěi 给 14, 123, 126
gland n fēn-mì-xiàn 分泌腺 139
glass n bēi-zi 杯子 37, 59, 61
glasses n yǎn-jìng 眼镜 123
glove n shǒu-tào 手套 116
glue n jiāo-shuǐ 胶水 106
go, to qù 去 96; (walk) zǒu 走 22, 77
go away, to zǒu kāi 走开 157
gold n jīn 金 18, 121, 122
golden jīn-huáng-sè (de) 金黄色 (的) 112
gold-plated dù-jīn (de) 镀金 (的) 122
gong n luó 锣 127
good hǎo (de) 好 (的) 15, 36, 101
goodbye zài-jiàn 再见 11
goods n huò-pǐn 货品 133
goose n é 鹅 49
go out, to (chū)qù wánr (出) 去玩儿 96
gram n kè 克 120
grape n pú-táo 葡萄 56
grapefruit juice n xī-yòu-zhī 西柚汁 39, 60
gray huī-sè (de) 灰色 (的) 112
graze, to (skin) cā pò 擦破 141
greasy duō yóu (de) 多油 (的) 110
Great Britain n yīng-guó 英国 148
Great Wall n cháng-chéng 长城 84
green lǜ-sè(de) 绿色 (的) 112
green bean n biǎn-dòu 扁豆 51
greengrocer's n shū-cài-diàn 蔬菜店 99
green tea n lǜ-chá 绿茶 38, 60
greeting n wèn-hòu 问候 11, 154
grey huī-sè(de) 灰色 (的) 112
grocery n fù-shí-diàn 副食店 99, 120
grotto n xiǎo yán-dòng 小岩洞 80
group n tuán-tǐ 团体 17, 79
guide n xiàng-dǎo 向导 18; (tourist) dǎo-yóu 导游 75, 78, 79
guidebook n lǚ-yóu zhǐ-nán 旅游指南 79, 106
guitar n jí-tā 吉他 127
gum (teeth) n yá-yín 牙龈 147
gymnastics n tǐ-cāo 体操 89, 90
gynaecologist n fù-kē dài-fu 妇科大夫 139

## H

haemorrhoids n zhì-chuāng 痔疮 143
hair n tóu-fa 头发 31, 110
hairbrush n fà-shuā 发刷 110
haircut n jiǎn fà 剪发 31
hairdresser's n lǐ-fà-diàn 理发店 99; (hotel) lǐ-fà-shì 理发室 28, 31
hair dryer n diàn chuī-fà-qì 电吹发器 119
hairgrip n qiǎ-zi 卡子 110
hair lotion n hù-fà-yè 护发液 110
hairpin n qiǎ-zi 卡子 110
hair spray n pēn-wù fà-jiāng 喷雾发浆 110
half bàn 半 59, 151
half n yí-bàn 一半 151
half an hour bàn xiǎo-shí 半小时 155
ham n huǒ-tuǐ 火腿 39, 64
hand n shǒu 手 139
handbag n shǒu-tí-bāo 手提包 116, 157
hand cream n rùn-shǒu-shuāng 润手霜 109
handicrafts n shǒu-gōng-yì (pǐn) 手工艺(品) 81, 133
handkerchief n shǒu-juànr 手绢儿 116
handmade shǒu-gōng zhì de 手工制的 113
hanger n guà-gōu 挂钩 28
harbour n gǎng-wān 港湾 74, 80
hard yìng (de) 硬 (的) 123
hard seating n (train) yìng-zhuò 硬座 69
hard sleeping n (train) yìng-wò 硬卧 69
hardware store n wǔ-jīn shāng-diàn 五金商店 99
hat n lǐ-mào 礼帽 116
hay fever n kū-cǎo-rè 枯草热 107, 143
he tā 他 161
head n tóu (bù) 头(部) 31, 140
headache n tóu-téng 头疼 143
headphones n ěr-jī 耳机 119
health n jiàn-kāng 健康 146
health insurance n jiàn-kāng bǎo-xiǎn 健康保险 146
health insurance form n jiàn-kāng bǎo-xiǎn-dān 健康保险单 146
heart n xīn-zàng 心脏 140
heart attack n xīn-jī gěng-sè 心肌梗塞 143

**heating** n nuǎn-qì 暖气 24, 29
**heavy** zhòng (de) 重(的) 15, 101
**heel** n jiǎo-hòu-gēn 脚后跟 140;
(shoe) gēn 跟 118
**helicopter** n zhí-shēng fēi-jī 直升飞机 152
**hello!** (phone) wéi 喂 137
**help!** jiù rén a 救人啊 157
**help, to** bāng-zhù 帮助 14, 22, 100
**hem** n yī-biān 衣边 114
**her** tā-de 她的 152
**herbal remedies** n cǎo-yào 草药 127
**here** zhèr 这儿 152
**high** gāo (de) 高(的) 26, 84, 143
**high season** n wàng-jì 旺季 152
**hike, to** tú-bù lǚ-xíng 徒步旅行 76
**hill** n xiǎo shān 小山 84
**hip** n pì-gǔ 屁股 140
**hire, to** zū (yòng) 租(用) 20, 22, 74, 76, 89, 90, 91, 119
**his** tā-de 他的 152
**history** n lì-shǐ 历史 81
**hitchhike, to** dā chē 搭车 76
**hole** n dòng 洞 31
**holiday** n jià-rì 假日 153, 154
**holidays** n jià (qī) 假(期) 17, 153
**home** n jiā 家 32, 96
**home address** n jiā-tíng zhù-zhǐ 家庭住址 26
**honey** n fēng-mì 蜂蜜 39
**hoop** (toy) n tiě-huán 铁环 128
**horse** n mǎ 马 104
**hospital** n yī-yuàn 医院 99, 144, 146
**hot** rè (de) 热(的) 15, 25, 39
**hotel** n lǚ-guǎn 旅馆 20, 21, 22, 27, 31
**hotel reservation** n yù-dìng fáng-jiān 预订房间 20
**hot water** n rè-shuǐ 热水 24, 29
**hot-water bottle** n nuǎn-shuǐ-dài 暖水袋 29
**hour** n xiǎo-shí 小时 74, 76, 91, 155
**house** n fáng-wū 房屋 84
**how** zěn-me 怎么 12
**how far** duō yuǎn 多远 12, 77, 84
**how long** duō cháng shí-jiān 多长时间 12, 25; duō-shao shí-jiān 多少时间 21, 77
**how many** duō-shao gè 多少个 12
**how much** duō-shao 多少 12
**hundred** yì-bǎi 一百 160
**hungry, to be** è le 饿了 14, 36
**hurry** (to be in a) hěn jí 很急 22
**hurt, to** téng 疼 141, 142, 144, 147
**husband** n zhàng-fu 丈夫 93

**I**

**I** wǒ 我 161
**ice** n bīng 冰 60, 94
**ice cream** n bīng-qí-lín 冰淇淋 64
**ice cube** n bīng-kuài 冰块 28
**iced tea** n bīng-chá 冰茶 60
**ill** bìng le 病了 142
**import** n jìn-kǒu 进口 132
**important** (hěn) zhòng-yào (很)重要 14
**imported** jìn-kǒu (de) 进口(的) 59, 113
**in** zài...lǐ 在...里 16
**include, to** bāo-kuò 包括 25, 62
**incorrect** bú-duì 不对 11
**indigestion** n xiāo-huà bù liáng 消化不良 143
**indoor** (swimming pool) shì-nèi de 室内的 90
**inexpensive** pián-yi de 便宜的 124
**infected** gǎn-rǎn 感染 142
**inflammation** n ...fā yán ...发炎 144
**inflation** n tōng-huò péng-zhàng 通货膨胀 133
**inflation rate** n tōng-huò péng-zhàng-lǜ 通货膨胀率 133
**influenza** n liú-gǎn 流感 144
**information office** n wèn-xùn-chù 问询处 20, 67, 156
**injection** n zhù-shè 注射 145, 146
**injured** shòu shāng le 受伤了 141
**ink** n mò-shuǐ 墨水 106;
(calligraphy) mò 墨 127
**inquiry** n wèn-xùn 问讯 68
**insect** n chóng-zi 虫子 30
**insect bite** n chóng-yǎo-shāng 虫咬伤 107
**insect repellent** n chú-chóng-jì 除虫剂 108
**insect spray** n chú-chóng pēn-wù-jì 除虫喷雾剂 108
**inside** lǐ-bianr 里边儿
**insurance** n bǎo-xiǎn 保险 146
**interest** (money) n lì-xī 利息 132
**interested, to be** gǎn xìng-qu 感兴趣 96
**interesting** yǒu qù (de) 有趣(的) 82
**international** guó-jì (de) 国际(的) 135
**interpreter** n kǒu-yì 口译 75, 133
**intersection** shí-zì lù-kǒu 十字路口 77
**intestine** n cháng 肠
**introduce, to** jiè-shào 介绍 92
**introduction** n jiè-shào 介绍 92, 131
**investment** n tóu-zī 投资 132
**invite, to** qǐng 请 94

DICTIONARY

**invoice** n fā-piào 发票 132
**iodine** n diǎn-jiǔ 碘酒 108
**Ireland** n ài-ěr-lán 爱尔兰 148
**Irish** ài-ěr-lán (de) 爱尔兰 (的) 93
**iron** *(laundry)* n yùn-dǒu 熨斗 119
**iron, to** yùn 熨 30
**ironmonger's** n wǔ-jīn shāng-diàn 五金商店 99
**Italy** n yì-dà-lì 意大利 148
**island** n dǎo 岛 80, 84
**ivory** n xiàng-yá 象牙 122; *(article)* xiàng-yá zhì-pǐn 象牙制品 81, 104, 127

## J

**jacket** n shàng-yī 上衣 114, 116
**jade** n yù 玉 122; *(article)* yù-shí zhì-pǐn 玉石制品 81, 104, 127
**jam** n guǒ-jiàng 果酱 39, 120
**jammed** qiǎ zhù 卡住 29, 125
**jasmine tea** n mò-lì huā-chá 茉莉花茶 38, 60
**January** n yī-yuè 一月 152
**Japan** n rì-běn 日本 148
**jar** n tǒng 筒 64
**jaundice** n huáng-dǎn 黄疸 144
**jaw** n xià-ba 下巴 140
**jazz** n jué-shì-yuè 爵士乐 128
**jeans** n niú-zǎi-kù 牛仔裤 116
**jewel** n zhū-bǎo shǒu-shì 珠宝首饰 104
**jewel box** n shǒu-shì-xiāng 首饰箱 121
**jeweller's** n zhū-bǎo shǒu-shì-diàn 珠宝首饰店 99, 121
**joint** n guān-jié 关节 140
**juice** n zhī 汁 39, 60
**July** n qī-yuè 七月 152
**June** n liù-yuè 六月 152

## K

**key** n yào-shi 钥匙 27
**kidney** n shèn 肾 140
**kilo (gram)** n gōng-jīn 公斤 120
**kimono** n hé-fú 和服 116, 127
**kind** *(type)* n zhǒng 种 142
**king-size** *(cigarette)* jiā cháng de 加长的 126
**kite** n fēng-zheng 风筝 127
**knee** n xī-gài 膝盖 140
**knee-cap** n xī-gài-gǔ 膝盖骨 140
**knife** n dāo-zi 刀子 37, 61
**know, to** rèn-shi 认识 21

## L

**label** n qiān-tiáo 签条 106
**lace** n gōu-zhī bù-liào 钩织布料 113
**lacquerware** n qī-qì qì-qì 漆器 81, 104, 127
**lake** n hú 湖 80, 84, 90
**lamb** n yáng-ròu 羊肉 48
**lamp** n (diàn) dēng (电) 灯 30, 119, 120
**lamp shade** n dēng-zhào 灯罩 127
**landscape** n fēng-jǐng 风景 92
**lantern** n ān-quán fēng-dēng 安全风灯 127
**lapel** n fān-lǐng 翻领 114
**large** n dà (de) 大 (的) 101, 115, 118
**last** zuì-hòu (de) 最后(的) 68; *(year)* qù 去 151; *(month, week)* shàng-ge 上个 153
**late** wǎn 晚 15
**laugh, to** xiào 笑 95
**laundry** *(place)* n xǐ-yī-diàn 洗衣店 30, 99; *(clothes)* gāi xǐ de yī-fu 该洗的衣服 31
**laundry service** n xǐ-yī fú-wù 洗衣服务 24
**laxative** n huǎn-xiè-jì 缓泻剂 108
**leap year** n rùn-nián 闰年 151
**learn, to** xué 学 161
**leather** n pí-zi 皮子 113, 118
**leave, to** zǒu 走 32, 95; *(train)* fā chē 发车 69; *(deposit)* jì-cún 寄存 27
**left** zuǒ (biān) 左 (边) 22, 69, 77, 140
**left-luggage office** n xíng-li jì-cún-chù 行李寄存处 19, 67, 71
**leg** n tuǐ 腿 140
**lemon** n níng-méng 柠檬 38, 39, 56, 60, 64
**lemonade** n níng-méng qì-shuǐ 柠檬汽水 60
**lemon juice** n níng-méng-zhī 柠檬汁 60
**lend, to** jiè 借 132
**lens** *(glasses)* n jìng-piàn 镜片 123; *(camera)* jìng-tóu 镜头 125
**lens cap** n jìng-tóu-gài 镜头盖 125
**leotard** n tǐ-cāo-fú 体操服 116
**less** shǎo xiē de 少些的 15
**letter** n xìn 信 29, 134
**letter box** n yóu-tǒng 邮筒 134
**letter of credit** n yín-háng cún-kuǎn zhèng-míng-xìn 银行存款证明信 131
**letter telegram** n yè-xìn-diàn 夜信电 135
**library** n tú-shū-guǎn 图书馆 99

词汇表

**licence** (business) n xǔ-kě-zhèng 许可证 133
**lid** n gài 盖 127
**lie down, to** tǎng xià 躺下 144
**life belt** n jiù-shēng-yī 救生衣 74
**life boat** n jiù-shēng-tǐng 救生艇 74
**lifeguard** n jiù-shēng-yuán 救生员 91
**lift** n diàn-tī 电梯 28, 100
**ligament** n rèn-dài 韧带 140
**light** qīng (de) 轻(的) 15, 101, 128; (colour) qiǎn-sè (de) 浅色(的) 101, 112
**light** n (electric) diàn-dēng 电灯 29; (cigarette) huǒr 火儿 95
**lighter** n dǎ-huǒ-jī 打火机 126
**lighter fluid** n dǎ-huǒ-jī yè-tǐ rán-liào 打火机液体燃料 126
**lighter gas** n dǎ-huǒ-jī qì-tǐ rán-liào 打火机汽体燃料 126
**light meter** n cè-guāng-biǎo 测光表 125
**lightning** n shǎn-diàn 闪电 94
**like, to** xǐ-huan 喜欢 25, 92, 102, 112; (want) xiǎng (yào) 想(要) 14, 24, 62, 96, 103, 113
**linen** n yà-má-bù 亚麻布 113, 127
**lining** n chèn-lǐ 衬里 114
**lip** n zuǐ-chún 嘴唇 140
**lipsalve** n fáng chún liè yóu-gāo 防唇裂油膏 109
**lipstick** n kǒu-hóng 口红 109
**listen, to** tīng 听 128
**litre** n shēng 升 59
**little** (a) yì-diǎnr 一点儿 13, 15, 31
**liver** n gān 肝 140
**loan** n dài-kuǎn 贷款 132
**lobster** n lóng-xiā 龙虾 45
**local** dì-fāng 地方 37
**long** cháng (de) 长(的) 12, 15, 61, 116, 117
**long-distance call** n cháng-tú diàn-huà 长途电话 136
**long-sighted** yuǎn-shì (de) 远视(的) 123
**look, to** kàn 看 100
**look for, to** zhǎo 找 14
**look out!** liú-shén 留神 157
**loose** (clothes) féi 肥 116
**lose, to** diū 丢 123
**loss** (business) n kuī-sǔn 亏损 132
**lost** (object) diū le 丢了 123, 147; (self) mí-lù le 迷路了 14
**lost and found office** n shī-wù zhāo-lǐng-chù 失物招领处 67, 157

**lost property office** n shī-wù zhāo-lǐng-chù 失物招领处 67, 157
**lot** n hěn duō 很多 15
**lotion** n yè yè 液 110
**lotus root** n ǒu 藕 56
**loud** dà-shēng (de) 大声(的) 137
**low** dī 低 26, 143
**lower** xià (céng de) 下(层的) 69, 70
**low season** n dàn-jì 淡季 152
**luck** n yùn-qi 运气 154
**luggage** n xíng-li 行李 19, 22, 27, 32, 71
**luggage trolley** n shǒu-tuī-chē 手推车 19, 71
**lump** n zhǒng-kuài 肿块 141
**lunch** n wǔ-fàn 午饭 28, 78, 94
**lung** n fèi 肺 140
**lychees** n lì-zhī 荔枝 56

## M

**machinery** n jī-xiè 机械 133
**mackerel** n qīng-yú 鲭鱼 45
**magazine** n zá-zhì 杂志 106
**mahjong** n má-jiàng (pái) 麻将(牌) 127
**mail, to** jì 寄 29
**mailbox** n yóu-tǒng 邮筒 134
**main** zhǔ-yào (de) 主要(的) 107
**make, to** zhì (zào) 制(造) 113
**make-up remover pad** n xià zhuāng mián-qiú 卸妆棉球 109
**man** n nán-rén 男人 111
**manager** n jīng-lǐ 经理 27, 61
**mango** n máng-guǒ 芒果 56
**manicure** n xiū shǒu zhī-jia 修手指甲 32
**many** hěn duō 很多 15
**map** n dì-tú 地图 77, 106
**March** n sān-yuè 三月 152
**marinaded** yān (de) 腌(的) 41
**market** n nóng-mào shì-chǎng 农贸市场 80, 99
**marmalade** n jú-zi-jiàng 桔子酱 39
**married** yǐ-jīng jié-hūn (de) 已经结婚(的) 93
**mascara** n rǎn jié-máo yóu 染睫毛油 109
**mass** (church) n mí-sā 弥撒 82
**massage** n àn-mó 按摩 31
**match** n huǒ-chái 火柴 64, 126; (sport) bǐ-sài 比赛 90
**match, to** xiāng-pèi 相配 112
**material** (cloth) n bù-liào 布料 114
**matinée** n zǎo-chǎng 早场 87

**mattress** n rù-zi 褥子 91
**mauve** zǐ-hóng-sè (de) 紫红色(的) 112
**May** n wǔ-yuè 五月 152
**may** (can) néng 能 13
**meadow** n cǎo-chǎng 草场 84
**meal** n fàn 饭 62, 145; huǒ-shí 伙食 25
**measles** n má-zhěn 麻疹 144
**measure, to** liáng 量 115
**meat** n ròu 肉 47, 61
**mechanical pencil** n zì-dòng qiān-bǐ 自动铅笔 106, 121
**medical certificate** n yī-shēng zhèng-míng 医生证明 146
**medicine** n yī-xué 医学 81; (drug) yào 药 108, 145
**medium** (size) zhōng 中 115
**meet, to** jiàn miàn 见面 96
**memorial** (museum) n jì-niàn-guǎn 纪念馆 80; (monument) jì-niàn-bēi 纪念碑 80
**mend, to** n bǔ 补 30
**menu** n cài-dān 菜单 37
**message** n liú-yán 留言 29
**method** n fāng-fǎ 方法 41
**metre** n gōng-chǐ 公尺 111, 113
**mezzanine** (theatre) n lóu-shàng 楼上 87
**middle** zhōng (-jiān de) 中(间的) 69, 87
**mild** (cigarette) róu-hé de 柔和的 126
**mileage** n lǐ-chéng (shù) 里程(数) 22
**milk** n niú-nǎi 牛奶 39, 60, 64, 120
**milliard** n shí-yì 十亿 151
**million** n bǎi-wàn 百万 151
**mineral water** n kuàng-quán-shuǐ 矿泉水 60
**mining** n kuàng-yè 矿业 133
**minister** (religion) n mù-shī 牧师 82
**minute** n fēn-zhōng 分钟 69, 155
**mirror** n jìng-zi 镜子 109, 115, 123
**Miss** n xiǎo-jiě 小姐 11
**missing** (to be) shǎo le 少了 19, 31, 61
**mistake** n cuò (-wù) 错(误) 32, 61, 62, 102
**moisturizing cream** n rùn-fū-shuāng 润肤霜 109
**Monday** n xīng-qī-yī 星期一 153
**money** n qián yuè 钱 12; (foreign currency) wài-huì 外汇 19, 131
**money order** n huì-piào 汇票 135

**monosodium glutamate** n wèi-jīng 味精 38, 53
**month** n yuè (fèn) 月(份) 17, 152
**monument** n jì-niàn-bēi 纪念碑 80
**moon** n yuè-liàng 月亮 94
**moped** n xiǎo mó-tuō-chē 小摩托车 76
**more** duō xiē 多些 15
**morning** n shàng-wǔ 上午 153; (early) zǎo-shàng 早上 32
**mortgage** n dǐ-yā 抵押 132
**mosque** n qīng-zhēn-sì 清真寺 80, 82
**mosquito net** n wén-chàng 蚊帐 28, 120; (window) shā-chuāng 沙窗 29
**mother** n mǔ-qīn 母亲 93
**motorbike** n mó-tuō-chē 摩托车 76
**motorboat** n qì-tǐng 汽艇 91
**mountain** n shān 山 84
**mountain pass** n shān-kǒu 山口 84
**moustache** n shàng hú-zi 上胡子 32
**mouth** n zuǐ 嘴 140
**mouth organ** n kǒu-qín 口琴 127
**mouthwash** n shù kǒu yào-shuǐ 漱口药水 108
**move, to** dòng 动 140
**movie** n diàn-yǐng 电影 88, 96
**movie camera** n shè-yǐng-jī 摄影机 124
**Mr.** n xiān-sheng 先生 11
**Mrs.** n fū-rén 夫人 11
**much** hěn duō 很多 15
**muscle** n jī-ròu 肌肉 140
**museum** n bó-wù-guǎn 博物馆 80
**mushroom** n mó-gu 蘑菇 51, 53
**music** n yīn-yuè 音乐 128
**musical instrument** n yuè-qì 乐器 81, 127
**music box** n bā-yīn-hé 八音盒 121
**must** (have to) bì-xū 必须 32; (mustn't) bù néng 不能 38
**mustard** n jiè-mo 芥末 64
**mutton** n yáng-ròu 羊肉 47
**my** wǒ de 我的 18, 20, 27

**N**

**nail** (human) n zhǐ-jiǎ 指甲 109, 140
**nail brush** n zhǐ-jiǎ-yóu shuā-zi 指甲油刷子 109
**nail clippers** n zhǐ-jiǎ-dāo 指甲刀 109
**nail file** n zhǐ-jiǎ-cuò 指甲锉 109
**nail polish** n zhǐ-jiǎ-yóu 指甲油 109
**nail polish remover** n tuì zhǐ-jiǎ-yóu shuǐ 退指甲油水 110

**nail scissors** n zhī-jia jiǎn-dāo 指甲剪刀 110

**name** n (surname) xìng 姓 26; (surname & first name) xìng-míng 姓名 26, 75; jiào 叫 24, 92, 132

**napkin** n cān-jīn 餐巾 37, 64

**nappy** n zhǐ niào-bù 纸尿布 110

**National Art Gallery** n zhōng-guó měi-shù-guǎn 中国美术馆 81

**nationality** n guó-jí 国籍 26

**natural** zì-rán de (的) 自然 (的) 81

**natural history** n zì-rán bó-wù 自然博物 81

**nauseous** ě-xīn (de) 恶心 (的) 142

**near** (zài...fù-) jìn (在...附) 近 16

**nearest** lí zhèr zuì jìn de 离这儿最近的 73, 98, 100

**neat** (drink) chún de 纯的 58

**neck** n bó-zi 脖子 31, 140

**necklace** n xiàng-liàn 项链 121

**need, to** xū-yào 需要 30, 90, 132

**needle** n zhēn 针 28

**negative** n dǐ-piàn 底片 124, 125

**nerve** n shén-jīng 神经 140

**nervous system** n shén-jīng xì-tǒng 神经系统 140

**never** cóng lái méi-yǒu 从来没有 16

**new** n xīn (de) 新 (的) 15, 18

**newspaper** n bào-zhǐ 报纸 105

**newsstand** n shòu-bào-tíng 售报亭 20, 67, 105

**next** xià... 下... 65, 68, 77, 153

**next to** zài...páng-biān-r 在...旁边儿 16, 77

**night** n yè (li) 夜(里) 25, 153

**nightclub** n yè-zǒng-huì 夜总会 88

**nightdress** n cháng shuì-yī 长睡衣 116

**night letter** n yè-xìn-diàn 夜信电 135

**nine** jiǔ 九 149

**nineteen** shí-jiǔ 十九 149

**ninety** jiǔ-shí 九十 150

**ninth** dì-jiǔ 第九 151

**no** bù (duì/shì) 不(对/是) 11

**noisy** chǎo 吵 25

**nonalcoholic drink** n yǐn-liào 饮料 60

**nonsmoking** jìn-zhǐ xī-yān de 禁止吸烟的 37

**noodle** n miàn-tiáo 面条; fěn-sī 粉丝 55

**noon** n zhōng-wǔ 中午 32

**normal** pǔ-tōng (de) 普通 (的) 31

**north** n běi 北 77

**nose** n bí-zi 鼻子 140

**nosebleed** n liú bí-xuè 流鼻血 143

**nose drops** n dī-bí-yào 滴鼻药 108

**not** bù 不 11, 16

**note** (banknote) n chāo-piào 钞票 131

**notebook** n bǐ-jì-běn 笔记本 106

**note paper** n xìn-zhǐ 信纸 106

**notice** n zhāo-tiē 招贴 156

**notify, to** tōng-zhī 通知 146

**November** n shí-yī yuè 十一月 152

**now** xiàn-zài 现在 16

**number** n hào (-mǎ) 号 (码) 27, 65, 136; (numeral) shù-zì 数字 149

**nurse** n hù-shi 护士 146

## O

**observatory** n tiān-wén-tái 天文台 80

**occupied** yǒu rén 有人 15, 156

**o'clock** diǎn 点 37, 70, 76, 155

**October** n shí yuè 十月 152

**oily** (hair) chū yóu de 出油 的 31; (food) yóu-nì (de) 油腻 (的) 61

**old** jiù (de) 旧 (的) 15; (person) nián lǎo 年老 15

**old town** n lǎo chéng 老城 80

**olive** n gǎn-lǎn 橄榄 56

**on** zài...shàng 在...上 16

**once** yí-cì 一次 151

**one** yī 一 149

**one-way ticket** n dān-chéng-piào 单程票 65

**on foot** zǒu lù 走路 77, 84

**only** zhǐ 只 13, 16, 108

**onyx** n gǎo mǎ-nǎo 缟玛瑙 122

**open** (sign) yíng-yè 营业 88

**open, to** kāi (mén) 开 (门) 12, 15, 108, 134

**open-air** shì-wài de 室外的 90

**opera** n gē-jù 歌剧 88

**opera house** n gē-jù-yuàn 歌剧院 80, 88; (Chinese) xì-yuàn 戏院 80

**operation** n shǒu-shù 手术 144

**operator** (telephone) n jiē-xiàn-yuán 接线员 137

**opposite** zài...duì-miàn 在...对面 77

**optician's** n yǎn-jìng-diàn 眼镜店 99, 123

**or** hái shì 还是 16

**orange** jú-hóng-sè (de) 桔红色 (的) 112

**orange** n gān-zi 柑子 56, 64

**orangeade** n jú-zi qì-shuǐ 桔子汽水 60

DICTIONARY

**orange juice** n jú-zi-zhī 桔子汁 39, 60

**orchestra** n (guǎn-xián) yuè-duì (管弦) 乐队 88; (seats) lóu-xià 楼下 87

**order, to** (goods) dìng-gòu 订购 102; (meal) diǎn cài 点菜 37, 61

**outlet** (electric) n chā-zuò 插座 27

**outside** wài-bianr 外边儿 16

**oval** tuǒ-yuán (de) 椭圆 (的) 101

**overalls** n gōng-zhuāng-kù 工装裤 116

**overdone** huǒ tài guò le 火太过了 61

**overnight** (stay) yì-yè 一夜 25

**owe, to** gāi fù qián 该付钱 146

**oyster** n háo 蚝 45

**P**

**pacifier** n xiàng-pí nǎi-zuǐr 橡皮奶嘴儿 110

**packet** n bāo 包 18, 64, 120, 126

**paddy field** n dào-tián 稻田 84

**pagoda** n bǎo-tǎ 宝塔 80

**pail** (toy) n xiǎo-tǒng 小桶 128

**pain(ful)** téng 疼 142, 143, 145, 146

**painkiller** n zhǐ-tòng-yào 止痛药 142

**paint** n yóu-qī 油漆 156

**paint, to** huà 画 80

**paintbox** n yóu-huà-xiāng 油画箱 106

**painter** n huà-jiā 画家 82

**painting** n huàr 画儿 81

**pair** n yì-shuāng 一双 116, 118, 151

**pajamas** n (yí-tào) shuì-yī (一套) 睡衣 117

**palace** n gōng-diàn 宫殿 80

**palpitation** n xīn-jì 心悸 143

**panties** n nèi-kù 内裤 116

**pants** (trousers) n cháng-kù 长裤 116

**panty hose** n kù-wà 裤袜 116

**paper** n zhǐ 纸 106

**paperback** n jiǎn-zhuāng-běn 简装本 106

**paperclip** n qū-bié-zhēn 曲别针 106

**paper napkin** n zhǐ cān-jīn 纸餐巾 64, 120

**parcel** n bāo-guǒ 包裹 134

**parents** n fù-mǔ 父母 93

**park** n gōng-yuán 公园 80

**parka** n dēng-shān-fú 登山服 116

**party** (social gathering) n wǎn-huì 晚会 95

**pass** (mountain) n shān-kǒu 山口 84

**passport** n hù-zhào 护照 17, 26, 157

**passport number** n hù-zhào hào-mǎ 护照号码 26

**passport photo** n hù-zhào xiàng-piàn 护照像片 124

**pastry shop** n gāo-diǎn-diàn 糕点店 99

**path** n xiǎo-lù 小路 84

**patient** n bìng-rén 病人 146

**pattern** n yàng-zi 样子 114

**pavilion** n tíng-zi 亭子 80

**pay, to** fù (qián) 付 (钱) 32, 62, 102, 137, 147

**payment** n (fù) kuǎn (付) 款 132

**pea** n wān-dòu 豌豆 51

**peach** n táo-zi 桃子 54

**peak** n shān-fēng 山峰 84

**pear** n lí 梨 56

**pearl** n zhēn-zhū 珍珠 104, 122

**pedalo** n jiǎo-tà yóu-tǐng 脚踏游艇 91

**pedicab** n sān-lún-chē 三轮车 75

**pedicure** n xiū jiǎo zhǐ-jia 修脚指甲 32

**pen** n gāng-bǐ 钢笔 106

**pencil** n qiān-bǐ 铅笔 106

**pencil sharpener** n zhuàn-bǐ-dāo 转笔刀 106

**pendant** n xuán-shì-wù 悬饰物 121

**penicillin** n qīng-méi-sù 青霉素 145

**penknife** n xiǎo-dāo 小刀 120

**pensioner** n tuì-xiū de (rén) 退休的 (人) 79

**pepper** n hú-jiāo 胡椒 38, 64

**per cent** n bǎi-fēn-zhī 百分之 151

**percentage** n bǎi-fēn-bǐ 百分比 132

**per day** yì tiān 一天 22, 89

**performance** n yǎn-chū 演出 88

**perfume** n xiāng-shuǐ 香水 110

**perhaps** yě-xǔ 也许 18

**period** n shí-qī 时期 104

**period** (monthly) n (yuè) jīng (月)经 143

**period pains** n tòng-jīng 痛经 143

**perm(anent wave)** n tàng fà 烫发 31

**permit** n xǔ-kě 许可 90

**per night** yí yè 一夜 25

**personal** sī-rén (de) 私人(的) 18

**per week** yì xīng-qī 一星期 25

**pewter** n xī-là qì-mǐn 锡镴器皿 122

**pheasant** n yě-jī 野鸡 49

**photo** n zhào-piàn 照片 133

**photocopy** fù-yìn 复印 133

**photographer's** n zhào-xiàng-guǎn 照像馆 99

词汇表

**Protestant** xīn-jiào (de) 新教(的) 82
**prune** n méi-zi 梅子 56
**public holiday** n jià-rì 假日 153
**pull, to** lā 拉 156
**pullover** n máo-yī 毛衣 116
**pumpkin** n nán-guā 南瓜 51
**purchase** n mǎi jìn de huò-pǐn 买进的货品 132
**pure** chún (de) 纯(的) 113
**purple** zǐ-sè (de) 紫色(的) 112
**push, to** tuī 推 156
**pyjamas** n (yí-tào) shuì-yī (一套) 睡衣 117

**Q**

**quail** n ān-chún 鹌鹑 49
**quality** n zhì-liàng 质量 101, 103, 113
**quantity** n shù-liàng 数量 15, 103
**quarter** n sì-fēn-zhī-yī 四分之一 151
**question** n wèn-huà 问话 12
**quick(ly)** kuài 快 75, 157; mǎ-shàng 马上 138
**quiet** ān-jìng (de) 安静(的) 24, 26
**quinine tablets** n kuí-níng-piàn 奎宁片 108

**R**

**racket** (sport) n qiú-pāi 球拍 89
**radio** (set) n shōu-yīn-jī 收音机 29, 119
**radish** (white) n bái luó-bo 白萝卜 51; (red) xiǎo luó-bo 小萝卜 51
**railway station** n huǒ-chē-zhàn 火车站 21, 67
**rain** n yǔ 雨 94
**rain, to** xià yǔ 下雨 94
**raincoat** n yǔ-yī 雨衣 117
**rangefinder** n cè-jù-qì 测距器 125
**rash** n zhěn-zi 疹子 141
**raspberry** n mù-méi 木莓 56
**raw** shēng (de) 生(的) 113
**razor** n tì-xū-dāo 剃须刀 110
**razor blade** n tì-xū dāo-piàn 剃须刀片 110
**reading-lamp** n tái-dēng 台灯 28
**ready** hǎo (le) 好(了) 30, 118, 123, 144
**receipt** n shōu-jù 收据 67, 102, 103, 146
**reception** (hotel) n jiē-dài (chù) 接待(处) 24
**receptionist** n jiē-dài-yuán 接待员 27
**recommend, to** tuī-jiàn 推荐 88, 139, 147; (food) jiè-shào 介绍 36, 37
**record** (disc) n chàng-piàn 唱片 128

**record player** n liú-shēng-jī 留声机 119
**rectangular** cháng-fāng (de) 长方(的) 101
**red** hóng-sè (de) 红色(的) 59, 106, 112
**reduction** n jiǎn jià 减价 25, 74
**refill** (cartridge) n gāng-bǐ-xīn 钢笔芯 106
**refund** n tuì kuǎn 退款 103
**register, to** (luggage) tuō-yùn 托运 71
**registered mail** n guà-hào 挂号 135
**registration** (hotel) n dēng-jì 登记 26
**registration form** (hotel) n dēng-jì-biǎo 登记表 26
**religious service** n (zuò) lǐ-bài (作) 礼拜 82
**rent, to** zū yòng 租(用) 20, 22, 74, 76, 89, 90, 91, 119
**repair, to** xiū-lǐ 修理 30, 118, 119, 121, 125, 147
**repeat, to** zài shuō yí-biàn 再说一遍 13
**report, to** bào (-gào) 报(告) 157
**represent, to** dài-biǎo 代表 132
**reservation** n yù-dìng 预订 20, 24, 65
**reserve, to** (yù) dìng (预)订 20, 37
**restaurant** n fàn-guǎn 饭馆 36, 67; (hotel) cān-tīng 餐厅 26
**return, to** (give back) huán 还 76
**return ticket** n wǎng-fǎn-piào 往返票 65
**reverse the charges, to** ràng duì-fāng fù-fèi 让对方付费 137
**rheumatism** n fēng-shī 风湿 143
**rib** n lèi-gǔ 肋骨 140
**ribbon** n cǎi-dài 彩带 114; (typewriter) dǎ-zì-jī sè-dài 打字机色带 106
**rice** n mǐ 米 51; (cooked) (mǐ) fàn (米)饭 52
**right** yòu (biān) 右(边) 22, 69, 77; (correct) duì 对 11, 15
**ring** (on finger) n jiè-zhi 戒指 122
**ring, to** (doorbell) àn-líng 按铃 156
**river** n hé 河 74, 80, 84, 90
**road** n lù 路 84
**rock** n (yán) shí (岩) 石 81
**roll** n xiǎo yuán-miàn-bāo 小圆面包 39, 64
**room** n fáng-jiān 房间 20, 24, 25, 26, 27, 28, 29
**room number** n fáng-jiān-hào 房间号 27

**DICTIONARY**

**room service** n qīng-sǎo zhěng-lǐ fú-wù 清扫整理服务 24
**round** yuán (de) 圆 (的) 101
**round neck** yuán-lǐng (de) 圆领(的) 116
**roundtrip ticket** n wǎng-fǎn-piào 往返票 65
**rowing boat** n yóu-chuán 游船 74, 91
**rubber** (material) n xiàng-jiāo 橡胶 118; (eraser) xiàng-pí 橡皮 106
**rubber band** n xiàng-pí-jīnr 橡皮筋儿 106
**rubbings** n tà-piàn 拓片 127
**ruby** n hóng-bǎo-shí 红宝石 122
**rucksack** n fān-bù bēi-bāo 帆布背包 84
**rug** n xiǎo dì-tǎn 小地毯 127
**ruin** n jiù-zhǐ 旧址 80
**ruler** (for measuring) n chǐ-zi 尺子 106
**running water** n zì-lái-shuǐ 自来水 24

**S**

**safe** (not dangerous) ān-quán 安全 91
**safe** n bǎo-xiǎn-xiāng 保险箱 27
**safety pin** n bié-zhēn 别针 110
**sailing boat** n fān-chuán 帆船 91
**sale** n mài chū de huò-pǐn 卖出的货品 132
**salt** n yán 盐 38, 39, 64
**salty** xián 咸 61
**sample** n yàng-pǐn 样品 114, 133
**sandal** n liáng-xié 凉鞋 118
**sandwich** n sān-míng-zhì 三明治 64
**sanitary towel/napkin** n fù-nǚ wèi-shēng-jīn 妇女卫生巾 108
**sapphire** n lán-bǎo-shí 蓝宝石 122
**satin** n duàn-zi 缎子 113
**Saturday** n xīng-qī-liù 星期六 153
**scald, to** tàng shāng 烫伤 141
**scalp** n tóu-pí 头皮 140
**scallop** n shàn-bèi 扇贝 45
**scarf** n wéi-jīn 围巾 117
**scarlet** xiān hóng-sè (de) 鲜红色(的) 112
**scenic route** n fēng-jǐng hǎo de lù 风景好的路 84
**scissors** n jiǎn-dāo 剪刀 120
**scrambled egg** n chǎo-jī-dàn 炒鸡蛋 39
**screwdriver** n gǎi-zhuī 改锥 120
**scroll** n juàn-zhóu 卷轴 104, 127
**sculptor** n diāo-sù-jiā 雕塑家 82

**sculpture** n diāo-sù 雕塑 81
**sea** n hǎi 海 24, 84, 91
**seafood** n hǎi-xiān 海鲜 45
**seam** n jiē-fèng 接缝 114
**season** n jì (jié) 季(节) 152
**seasoning** n tiáo-liào 调料 38, 53
**seat** n zuò-wèi 座位 69, 70, 87
**second** dì-èr 第二 77, 151
**second class** n èr-děng 二等 74
**second hand** n miǎo-zhēn 秒针 122
**second-hand** jiù (de) 旧(的) 105
**secretary** n mì-shū 秘书 28, 133
**see, to** kàn 看 13, 25, 81; (meet) jiàn-miàn 见面 96
**sell, to** mài 卖 100, 132
**send, to** (goods) fā huò 发货 133; (post) jì 寄 102, 103, 134, 135, 147
**sentence** n jù (zi) 句(子) 11
**September** n jiǔ-yuè 九月 152
**serious** (injury) (yán) zhòng (de) (严)重(的) 141
**service** n fú-wù 服务 100; (religion) (zuò) lǐ-bài (作)礼拜 82
**serviette** n cān-jīn 餐巾 37
**setting lotion** n lěng-tàng-shuǐ 冷烫水 110
**seven** qī 七 149
**seventeen** shí-qī 十七 149
**seventh** dì-qī 第七 151
**seventy** qī-shí 七十 150
**sew, to** féng 缝 30
**shade** (colour) n sè (diào) 色(调) 112
**shampoo** n xǐ-fà-jì 洗发剂 31, 110
**shampoo and set** n xǐ tóu hé zuò fà 洗头和做发 31
**shape** n yàng-zi 样子 103
**share** (finance) n gǔ-fèn 股份 132
**shave, to** guā liǎn 刮脸 32
**shaver** n diàn-dòng tì-xū-dāo 电动剃须刀 27, 119
**shaving brush** n tì xū féi-zào-shuā 剃须肥皂刷 110
**shaving soap** n tì xū zào-yè 剃须皂液 110
**she** tā 她 161
**ship** n lún-chuán 轮船 74
**shipment** n yì-pī huò 一批货 133
**shirt** n chèn-shān 衬衫 114, 117
**shivery** fā-lěng 发冷 142
**shoe** n xié 鞋 118
**shoelace** n xié-dài 鞋带 118
**shoemaker's** n bǔ-xié-diàn 补鞋店 99

**shoe polish** n xié-yóu 鞋油 118
**shoe shop** n xié-diàn 鞋店 99
**shop** n shāng-diàn 商店 98
**shopping area** n shāng-yè-qū 商业区 80, 100
**shopping centre** n shāng-chǎng 商场 99
**shop window** n chú-chuāng 橱窗 100
**short** duǎn 短 15, 31, 116, 117
**shorts** n duǎn-kù 短裤 117
**short-sighted** jìn-shì (yǎn de) 近视(眼的) 123
**shoulder** n jiān-bǎng 肩膀 140
**shoulder blade** n jiān-jiǎ-gǔ 肩胛骨 140
**shovel** (toy) n xiǎo chǎn-zi 小铲子 128
**show, to** ràng...kàn-kàn 让...看看 14, 124; gěi...kàn-kàn 给...看看 100, 101
**shower** n lín-yù 淋浴 24, 27
**shrimp** n xiā 虾 45, 53
**shrink, to** suō (xiǎo) 缩(小) 113
**shut** guān (de) 关(的) 15
**shutter** (camera) n kuài-mén 快门 125
**sideboards/burns** n liǎng-cè de hú-zi 两侧的胡子 32
**sightseeing** n yóu-lǎn 游览 78
**sign** (notice) n zhǐ-shì biāo-jì 指示标记 156
**sign, to** qiān míng 签名 26, 131
**signature** n qiān-míng 签名 26
**silk** n sī-chóu 丝绸 113, 127
**silk factory** n sī-chóu-chǎng 丝绸厂 81
**silk painting** n juàn-huà 绢画 81
**silver** (colour) yín-huī-sè (de) 银灰色(的) 112
**silver** n yín 银 121, 122
**silver-plated** dù-yín (de) 镀银(的) 122
**silverware** n yín-qì 银器 122
**simple** jiǎn-dān de 简单的 124
**since** cóng 从 16
**single** (not married) méi-yǒu jié-hūn (de) 没有结婚(的) 93
**single room** n dān-rén fáng-jiān 单人房间 20, 24
**single ticket** n dān-chéng-piào 单程票 65
**sister** (older) n jiě-jie 姐姐 93; (younger) n mèi-mei 妹妹 93
**sit, to** zuò 坐 95
**six** liù 六 149

**sixteen** shí-liù 十六 149
**sixth** dì-liù 第六 151
**sixty** liù-shí 六十 150
**size** (format) n xíng-hào 型号 124; (clothes) chǐ-cùn 尺寸 115
**skate** n bīng-xié 冰鞋 90
**skating** n huá bīng 滑冰 89
**skating rink** n huá-bīng-chǎng 滑冰场 90
**skin** n pí-fū 皮肤 140
**skin-diving** n qián-shuǐ 潜水 91
**skirt** n qún-zi 裙子 114, 117
**sky** n tiān-kōng 天空 94
**sleep, to** shuì 睡 146
**sleeping car** n wò-pù chē-xiāng 卧铺车厢 68, 69, 70
**sleeping pill** n ān-mián-yào 安眠药 145
**sleeve** n xiù-zi 袖子 114, 117, 144
**slice** n piàn 片 120
**slip** n chèn-qún 衬裙 117
**slipper** n tuō-xié 拖鞋 118
**slow** màn (de) 慢(的) 15, 155
**slowly** màn diānr (de) 慢点儿(的) 13, 22, 137
**small** xiǎo (de) 小 (的) 15, 25, 61, 101, 115, 118
**small change** n líng-qián 零钱 131
**smoke, to** xī yān 吸烟 67, 95
**snack** n xiǎo-chī 小吃 62
**snap fastener** n àn-kòu 按扣 117
**sneakers** n qiú-xié 球鞋 118
**snow** n xuě 雪 94
**snow, to** xià xuě 下雪 94
**snuff** n bí-yān 鼻烟 126
**snuff bottle** n bí-yān-hú 鼻烟壶 104
**soap** n féi-zào 肥皂 28, 110
**soccer** n zú-qiú 足球 89
**sock** n wà-zi 袜子 117
**socket** (outlet) n chā-zuò 插座 27
**soft** ruǎn de 软的 69, 123
**soft drink** n bú dài jiǔ-jīng de yǐn-liào 不带酒精的饮料 64
**soft-boiled** (egg) (zhǔ) nèn de (煮)嫩的 39
**soft seating** (train) n ruǎn-zuò 软座 69
**soft sleeping** (train) n ruǎn-wò 软卧 69
**sole** n xié-dǐ 鞋底 118; (fish) tǎ-yú 鳎鱼 45
**soloist** (musician) n dú-zòu yǎn-yuán 独奏演员 88
**some** n yì-xiē 一些 15

**son** n ér-zi 儿子 93

**soon** hěn kuài jiù 很快就 16

**sore throat** n sǎng-zi-téng 嗓子疼 143

**sorry!** duì-bu-qǐ 对不起 12

**sort** (kind) n zhǒng 种 87

**soup** n tāng 汤 44

**south** n nán 南 77

**souvenir** n jì-niàn-pǐn 纪念品 126

**souvenir shop** n lǚ-yóu jì-niàn-pǐn shāng-diàn 旅游纪念品商店 99

**soy sauce** n jiàng-yóu 酱油 38, 53, 64

**spade** (toy) n xiǎo chǎn-zi 小铲子 128

**sparkling** (wine) dài qì de 带汽的 59

**speak, to** shuō 说 13, 137

**speaker** (loudspeaker) n yáng-shēng-qì 扬声器 119

**special** tè-bié de 特别的 38

**special delivery** kuài-dì 快递 135

**spectacles** n yǎn-jìng 眼镜 123

**spectacle case** n yǎn-jìng-hé 眼镜盒 123

**spice** n zuó-liào 作料 53, 127

**spicy** hòu-wèir de 厚味儿的 38

**spinach** n bō-cài 菠菜 51

**spine** n jǐ-zhuī 脊椎 140

**spleen** n pí 脾 140

**sponge** n hǎi-mián 海绵 110

**spoon** n sháo-zi 勺子 37, 61

**sport** n tǐ-yù yùn-dòng 体育运动 89

**sporting goods shop** n tǐ-yù yòng-pǐn shāng-diàn 体育用品商店 99

**sports jacket** n yùn-dòng-shān 运动衫 117

**sprain, to** niǔ-shāng 扭伤 142

**spring** n chūn (tiān) 春(天) 152; (water) quán 泉 84

**spring onion** n cōng 葱 51, 53

**squab** n chú-gē 雏鸽 49

**square** fāng (de) 方(的) 101

**square** n guǎng-chǎng 广场 80

**squid** n yóu-yú 鱿鱼 45

**stadium** n tǐ-yù-chǎng 体育场 80

**stain** n wū-diǎn 污点 30

**stainless steel** n bú-xiù-gāng 不锈钢 122

**stalls** (theatre) n lóu-xià 楼下 87

**stamp** (postage) n yóu-piào 邮票 29, 134

**staple** n shū-dīng 书钉 106

**star** n xīng-xing 星星 94

**starter** (appetizer) n liáng-cài pīn-pánr 凉菜拼盘儿 42

**station** (rail) n (huǒ-chē) zhàn (火车)站 21, 67, 70, 73

**stationer's** n wén-jù-diàn 文具店 99, 105

**stationery** n wén-jù 文具 105

**statistics** n tǒng-jì (shù-zì) 统计(数字) 133

**statue** n diāo-xiàng 雕像 80

**stay, to** zhù 住 25, 93; tíng-liú 停留 17

**steal, to** tōu 偷 157

**steamed** qīng-zhēng (de) 清蒸(的) 41

**stiff neck** n bó-zi fā yìng 脖子发硬 143

**still** (mineral water) bú dài qì de 不带汽的 60

**sting, to** zhē 蜇 141

**stir-fried** chǎo-chāo (de) 爆炒(的) 41

**stitch, to** féng (bǔ) 缝(补) 30, 118

**stocking** n cháng-wà 长袜 117

**stomach** n wèi 胃 140

**stomach ache** n wèi téng 胃疼 143

**stools** n dà-biàn 大便 144

**stop!** zhàn zhù 站住 157

**stop, to** tíng (xià) 停(下) 22, 68, 70, 72

**stop thief!** zhuā zéi 抓贼 157

**store** (shop) n shāng-diàn 商店 98

**straight** (drink) chún de 纯的 58

**straight ahead** yì-zhí 一直 22, 77

**strange** qí-guài 奇怪 82

**strawberry** n cǎo-méi 草莓 56

**street** n jiē (dào) 街(道) 26, 77

**streetcar** n diàn-chē 电车 72

**street map** n jiāo-tōng-tú 交通图 21

**string** n shéng-zi 绳子 106

**strong** lì-hai (de) 厉害(的) 145; (cigarette) yǒu jìn de 有劲的 126

**student** n xué-sheng 学生 17, 20, 79, 93

**student hostel** n zhuān-mén jiē-dài xué-sheng de lǚ-guǎn 专门接待学生的旅馆 20

**study, to** xué (xí) 学(习) 93

**sturdy** jiē-shi (de) 结实(的) 101

**subway** (rail) n dì-tiě 地铁 73

**suede** n fān-máo-pí 翻毛皮 113, 118

**sugar** n táng 糖 38, 64

**sugar cane** n gān-zhe 甘蔗 56

**suit** n yí-tào xī-fú 一套西服 117

**suitcase** n xiāng-zi 箱子 19

**summer** n xià (tiān) 夏(天) 152

**Summer Palace** n yí-hé-yuán 颐和园 81

**sun** n tài-yáng 太阳 94

**sunburn** n shài-shāng 晒伤 107

**Sunday** n xīng-qī-tiān 星期天 79, 153; xīng-qī-rì 星期日 153

**sunglasses** n mò-jìng 墨镜 123

**sunshade** (beach) n zhē-yáng-sǎn 遮阳伞 91

**sunstroke** n zhòng-shǔ 中暑 143

**sun-tan cream** n shài-hēi-gāo 晒黑膏 110

**sun-tan oil** n shài-hēi-yóu 晒黑油 110

**supermarket** n zì-xuǎn shāng-chǎng 自选商场 99

**supervisor** n fù-zé-rén 负责人 27

**suppository** n shuān-jì 栓剂 108

**surgery** (consulting room) n wài-kē mén-zhěn 外科门诊 138

**suspenders** (Am.) n bēi-dài 背带 117

**swallow, to** tūn-fú 吞服 145

**swamp** n zhǎo-zé 沼泽 84

**sweater** n máo-yī 毛衣 117

**sweatshirt** n cháng-xiù yùn-dòng-shān 长袖运动衫 117

**sweet** (food) tián (de) 甜(的) 59, 61

**sweet pepper** n shì-zi-jiāo 柿子椒 51

**swell, to** zhǒng 肿 141

**swelling** n (hóng) zhǒng (红)肿 141

**swim, to** yóu-yǒng 游泳 90

**swimming** n yóu-yǒng 游泳 89, 91

**swimming pool** n yóu-yǒng-chí 游泳池 90

**swimming trunks** n yóu-yǒng-kù 游泳裤 117

**swimsuit** n yóu-yǒng-yī 游泳衣 117

**switch** n kāi-guān 开关 30

**switchboard operator** n jiē-xiàn-yuán 接线员 27

**swollen** zhǒng le 肿了 141

**synagogue** n yóu-tài jiào-táng 犹太教堂 82

**synthetic** rén-zào (de) 人造(的) 113

**system** n xì-tǒng 系统 140

**T**

**table** n zhuō-zi 桌子 37

**tablet** n piàn 片 108

**table-tennis** n bīng-bāng-qiú 乒乓球 89, 90

**tailor's** n cái-feng-diàn 裁缝店 99

**take, to** (carry) bān 搬 19

**take away, to** dài-zǒu 带走 102

**take off, to** qǐ-fēi 起飞 65

**talcum powder** n shuǎng-shēn-fěn 爽身粉 110

**tangerine** n jú-zi 桔子 56

**Taoist temple** n dào-guàn 道观 81

**tap** (water) n shuǐ-lóng-tóu 水龙头 29

**tape recorder** n cí-dài lù-yīn-jī 磁带录音机 119

**tax** n shuì 税 133

**taxi** n chū-zū qì-chē 出租汽车 20, 21, 32, 67

**taxi booking-office** n chū-zū qì-chē-zhàn 出租汽车站 20

**tea** n chá 茶 39, 60, 64, 127

**tea cup** n chá-bēi 茶杯 127

**tea pot** n chá-hú 茶壶 127

**team** n duì 队 90

**teaspoon** n tāng-chí 汤匙 145

**telegram** n diàn-bào 电报 135

**telephone** n diàn-huà 电话 29, 136

**telephone, to** dǎ diàn-huà 打电话 136

**telephone directory** n diàn-huà-bù 电话簿 135

**telephone number** n diàn-huà hào-mǎ 电话号码 96, 136, 137

**telephoto lens** n wàng-yuǎn jìng-tóu 望远镜头 125

**television** (set) n diàn-shì-jī 电视机 29, 119

**telex** n diàn-chuán 电传 135

**telex, to** fā diàn-chuán 发电传 131

**tell, to** gào-su 告诉 14, 73, 77, 137

**temperature** n wēn (dù) 温(度) 90; (body) tǐ-wēn 体温 142, 144

**Temple of Heaven** n tiān-tán 天坛 81

**ten** shí 十 148

**tendon** n jī-jiàn 肌腱 140

**tennis** n wǎng-qiú 网球 89

**tennis court** n wǎng-qiú-chǎng 网球场 89

**tenth** dì-shí 第十 151

**term** (word) n shù-yǔ 术语 132

**terminus** n zhōng-diǎn-zhàn 终点站 72

**tetanus** n pò-shāng-fēng 破伤风 142

**textile** n fǎng-zhī 纺织 133

**Thailand** n tài-guó 泰国 148

**thank you** xiè-xie 谢谢 10, 11

**that** nà 那 12, 100

**theatre** n jù-chǎng 剧场 80, 87

**theft** n tōu-qiè (-àn) 偷窃(案) 157

**then** (before) rán-hòu 然后 16

**there** nàr 那儿 15

**thermometer** n tǐ-wēn-biǎo 体温表 108, 146

**they** tā-mén 他们 161

**thick** hòu (de) 厚(的) 113

**thief** n zéi 贼 157

**thigh** n dà-tuǐ 大腿 140
**thin** báo (de) 薄 (的) 113
**think, to** jué-de 觉得 93, 94
**third** dì-sān 第三 151
**third** n sān-fēn-zhī-yī 三分之一 151
**third class** n sān-děng 三等 74
**thirsty, to be** kě le 渴了 14, 36
**thirteen** shí-sān 十三 149
**thirty** sān-shí 三十 149
**this** zhè 这 12, 100
**thousand** yì-qiān 一千 150
**thread** n xiàn 线 28
**three** sān 三 149
**throat** n sǎng-zi 嗓子 140
**throat lozenge** n hóu-lóng hán-piàn 喉咙含片 108
**through** jīng-guò 经过 16
**through train** n zhí-dá liè-chē 直达列车 69
**thumb** n mǔ-zhǐ 拇指 140
**thumbtack** n tú-dīng 图钉 106
**thunder** n léi 雷 94
**thunderstorm** n bào-fēng-yǔ 暴风雨 94
**Thursday** n xīng-qī-sì 星期四 153
**ticket** n piào 票 87, 90; (plane) jī-piào 机票 65; (bus, train) chē-piào 车票 69
**ticket office** n shòu-piào-chù 售票处 20, 67
**tide** n cháo 潮 91
**tie** n lǐng-dài 领带 117
**tie clip** n lǐng-dài jiā-zi 领带夹子 122
**tie pin** n lǐng-dài bié-zhēn 领带别针 122
**tight** (clothes) jǐn 紧 116
**tights** n kù-wà 裤袜 117
**time** n shí-jiān 时间 68; (clock) diǎn 点 155; (occasion) cì 次 145
**timetable** (train) n liè-chē shí-kè-biǎo 列车时刻表 68
**tin** (can) n guàn-tou 罐头 120
**tin opener** n kāi-guàn-qì 开罐器 64, 120
**tinted** zhuó-sè (de) 着色 (的) 123
**tired** lèi le 累了 14
**tissue** (handkerchief) n zhǐ-shǒu-juànr 纸手绢 110
**to** xiàng 向 16
**toast** n kǎo miàn-bāo-piàn 烤面包片 39
**tobacco** n yān-cǎo 烟草 126
**today** jīn-tiān 今天 153
**toe** n jiǎo-zhǐ 脚趾 140

**toilet** (lavatory) n cè-suǒ 厕所 24, 28, 29, 38, 67
**toilet paper** n wèi-shēng-zhǐ 卫生纸 110
**toiletry** n guàn-xǐ wèi-shēng yòng-pǐn 盥洗卫生用品 109
**toilet water** n shuǎng-shēn xiāng-shuǐ 爽身香水 110
**tomato** n xī-hóng-shì 西红柿 51, 64, 120
**tomb** n líng-mù 陵墓 80
**tomorrow** míng-tiān 明天 30, 76, 94, 153
**tongue** n shé-tou 舌头 140
**tonic water** n kuí-níng-shuǐ 奎宁水 60
**tonight** jīn-wǎn 今晚 30, 87, 96
**tonsil** n biǎn-táo-xiàn 扁桃腺 140
**too** tài 太 15, 25, 101, 118; (also) yě 也 16
**tooth** n yá 牙 147
**toothache** n yá-téng 牙疼 147
**toothbrush** n yá-shuā 牙刷 110
**toothpaste** n yá-gāo 牙膏 110
**toothpick** n yá-qiān 牙签 38
**top** n dǐng (bù) 顶 (部) 32
**topaz** n huáng-yù 黄玉 122
**torch** (flashlight) n shǒu-diàn-tǒng 手电筒 120
**touch, to** chù-mō 触摸 156
**tour** n yóu-lǎn-lù-xiàn 游览路线 78
**towards** xiàng 向 16
**towel** n máo-jīn 毛巾 110
**towelling** n máo-jīn-bù 毛巾布 113
**tower** n tǎ 塔 80
**town** n chéng 城 20; shì 市 76
**town centre** n shì-zhōng-xīn 市中心 21
**toy** n wán-jù 玩具 127, 128
**toy shop** n wán-jù-diàn 玩具店 99
**tracksuit** n yí-tào yùn-dòng-shān 一套运动衫 117
**traffic light** n hóng-lǜ-dēng 红绿灯 77
**train** n liè-chē 列车 68, 69, 70, 73
**tram** (streetcar) n diàn-chē 电车 72
**tranquillizer** n zhèn-jìng-yào 镇静药 145
**transfer** (bank) n zhuǎn-zhàng 转账 132
**transformer** n biàn-yā-qì 变压器 119
**translate, to** fān-yì 翻译 13
**translator** n fān-yì 翻译 133
**transport** n jiāo-tōng 交通 76
**travel, to** lǚ-xíng 旅行 92

**travel agency** n lǚ-xíng-shè 旅行社 99

**travel guide** n lǚ-yóu zhǐ-nán 旅游指南 106

**traveller's cheque** n lǚ-xíng zhī-piào 旅行支票 20, 62, 102, 130

**travelling bag** n lǚ-xíng-dài 旅行袋 99

**travel sickness** n yūn-chē 晕车 107

**treatment** n zhì-liáo 治疗 145

**tree** n shù 树 84

**trim, to** xiū-jiǎn 修剪 32

**trip** n lǚ-xíng 旅行 154

**trolley** n shǒu-tuī-chē 手推车 19, 71

**trousers** n cháng-kù 长裤 117

**try, to** shì 试 115

**T-shirt** n zhēn-zhī chèn-shān 针织衬衫 117

**tube** n tǒng 筒 110

**Tuesday** n xīng-qī-èr 星期二 153

**turkey** n huǒ-jī 火鸡 49

**turn, to** (change direction) guǎi (wān) 拐(弯) 22, 77

**turquoise** qīng-lǜ-sè (de) 青绿色(的) 112

**turquoise** n lǜ-sōng-shí 绿松石 122

**turtle-neck** gāo-lǐng (de) 高领(的) 116

**tweezers** n niè-zi 镊子 110

**twelve** shí-èr 十二 149

**twenty** èr-shí 二十 149

**twice** liǎng cì 两次 151

**twin beds** n liǎng-zhāng dān-rén-chuáng 两张单人床 24

**two** èr 二 149

**typewriter** n dǎ-zì-jī 打字机 28

**typewriter ribbon** n dǎ-zì-jī sè-dài 打字机色带 106

**typing paper** n dǎ-zì-zhǐ 打字纸 106

## U

**ugly** nán-kàn 难看 15

**ulcer** n wèi-kuì-yáng 胃溃疡 143

**umbrella** n yǔ-sǎn 雨伞 117; (beach) zhē-yáng-sǎn 遮阳伞 91

**unconscious** hūn guo qu le 昏过去了 141

**under** zài...xià miàn 在…下面 16

**underdone** (meat) méi shóu 没熟 61

**underground** (rail) n dì-tiě 地铁 73

**underpants** n nán-nèi-kù 男内裤 117

**undershirt** n bèi-xīn 背心 117

**understand, to** dǒng 懂 13

**undress, to** tuō (yī) 脱 (衣) 144

**United States** n měi-guó 美国 148

**university** n dà-xué 大学 80

## V

**vacancy** n kōng fáng-jiān 空房间 24

**vacant** méi rén 没人 15

**vacation** n jià-qī 假期 153

**vaccinate, to** zhù-shè yù-fáng yì-miáo 注射预防疫苗 142

**vaccination** n yù-fáng zhù-shè 预防注射 17

**vacuum flask** n nuǎn-shuǐ-píng 暖水瓶 120

**valley** n shān-gǔ 山谷 84

**value** n jià-qí 价值 132

**vegetable** n shū-cài 蔬菜 51, 52

**vegetable store** n shū-cài-diàn 蔬菜店 99

**vegetarian** sù (de) 素(的) 38

**vein** n jìng-mài 静脉 140

**velvet** n tiān-é-róng 天鹅绒 113

**venereal disease** n xìng-bìng 性病 144

**vermouth** n wèi-měi-sī 味美思 58

**very** hěn 很 16

**vest** n bèi-xīn 背心 117; (Am.) xī-fú kǎn-jiān 西服坎肩 117

**veterinarian** n shòu-yī 兽医 99

**video camera** n shè-xiàng-jī 摄像机 124

**video cassette** n lù-xiàng-dài 录像带 119, 124

**video recorder** n lù-xiàng-jī 录像机 119

**Vietnam** n yuè-nán 越南 148

**view** n hǎo-kàn de fēng-jǐng 好看的风景 24, 26

**village** n cūn-zhuāng 村庄 84

**vinegar** n cù 醋 38

**vineyard** n pú-tao-yuán 葡萄园 84

**visa** n qiān-zhèng 签证 17

**visiting hours** n tàn-shì shí-jiān 探视时间 146

**V-neck** jī-xīn-lǐng (de) 鸡心领(的) 117

**vodka** n fú-tè-jiā 伏特加 58

**volleyball** n pái-qiú 排球 89

**voltage** n diàn-yā 电压 28

**vomit, to** ǒu-tù 呕吐 142

# W

**waist** n yāo 腰 114

**waistcoat** n xī-fú kǎn-jiān 西服坎肩 117

**wait, to** děng 等 22, 95, 108

**waiter** n fú-wù-yuán 服务员 37

**waiting room** (station) n hòu-chē-shì 候车室; (airport) hòu-jī-shì 候机室 65

**waitress** n fú-wù-yuán 服务员 37

**wake, to** jiào-xǐng 叫醒 27, 70

**Wales** n wēi-ěr-shì 威尔士 148

**wallet** n qián-bāo 钱包 157

**walnut** n hé-tao 核桃 56

**want, to** (xiǎng-) yào (想)要 20, 101, 112, 123

**warm** rè (de) 热(的) 94

**wash, to** xǐ 洗 30

**washbasin** n shuǐ-chí-zi 水池子 29

**watch** n biǎo 表 121, 122

**watchmaker's** n zhōng-biǎo-diàn 钟表店 99, 121

**watchstrap** n biǎo-dài 表带 122

**water** n shuǐ 水 24, 34, 90

**waterfall** n pù-bù 瀑布 84

**water flask** n shuǐ-hú 水壶 120

**watermelon** n xī-guā 西瓜 56

**water ski** n huá-shuǐ-bǎn 滑水板 91

**wave** n làng 浪 91

**way** (road) n lù 路 77

**weather** n tiān-qì 天气 94

**weather forecast** n tiān-qì yù-bào 天气预报 94

**wedding ring** n jié-hūn jiè-zhi 结婚戒指 122

**Wednesday** n xīng-qī-sān 星期三 153

**week** n xīng-qī 星期 17, 22, 25, 153

**weekend** n zhōu-mò 周末 153

**well** (healthy) hěn hǎo 很好 11

**west** n xī 西 77

**Western** xī (fāng de) 西(方的) 108

**Western-style** xī (shì de) 西(式的) 39

**what** shén-me 什么 12

**when** (date) jǐ hào 几号 12; (time) jǐ diǎn 几点 12

**where** nǎr 哪儿 12

**which** nǎ-ge 哪个 12

**whisky** n wēi-shì-jì 威士忌 18, 58

**white** bái-sè (de) 白色(的) 112

**who** shéi 谁 12

**why** wèi-shén-me 为什么 12

**wick** n dēng-xīn 灯芯 126

**wide** kuān (de) 宽(的) 101

**wide-angle lens** n guǎng-jiǎo jìng-tóu 广角镜头 125

**wife** n qī-zi 妻子 93

**wig** n jiǎ-fà 假发 110

**wild boar** n yě-zhū 野猪 49

**wind** n fēng 风 94

**window** n chuāng-hù 窗户 29, 37; (shop) chú-chuāng 橱窗 111

**wine** n pú-tao-jiǔ 葡萄酒 64

**winter** n dōng (tiān) 冬(天) 152

**with** (thing) yǒu 有 16; (person) gēn…yi-qǐ 跟…一起 16

**withdraw, to** (bank) qǔ 取 131

**without** méi-yǒu 没有 16

**woman** n fù-nǚ 妇女 143

**wood** (forest) n shù-lín 树林 84

**wool** n chún-máo 纯毛 113

**word** n cí 词 15

**work** n gōng-zuò 工作 93

**working day** n gōng-zuò-rì 工作日 153

**worse** gèng huài le 更坏了 15

**wound** n shāng-kǒu 伤口 141

**wrap, to** bāo 包 103

**wrapping paper** n bāo-zhuāng-zhǐ 包装纸 106

**wrist** n shǒu-wàn 手腕 140

**wristwatch** n shǒu-biǎo 手表 122

**write, to** xiě 写 13, 101, 132

**writing pad** n pāi-zhǐ-bù 拍纸簿 106

**writing paper** n xìn-zhǐ 信纸 28

**wrong** cuò (de) 错(的) 15

# X

**X-ray** (photo) n x guāng piān-zi X光片子 142

# Y

**year** n nián 年 151

**yellow** huáng-sè (de) 黄色(的) 112

**yes** duì 对, shì 是 11

**yesterday** zuó-tiān 昨天 153

**yoghurt** n suān-nǎi 酸奶 39, 64

**you** nǐ 你; (pl) nǐ-mén 你们 161

**young** nián-qīng (de) 年轻(的) 15

# Z

**zero** líng 零 149

**zip** (per) n lā-suǒ 拉锁 117

**zoo** n dòng-wù-yuán 动物园 73, 80

**zoology** n dòng-wù-xué 动物学 81

# 汉语索引